Sp[illegible]h

A ROUGH GUIDE PHRASEBOOK

Compiled by Lexus

Credits

Compiled by Lexus with Fernando León Solís

Lexus Series Editor:	Sally Davies
Rough Guides Phrase Book Editor:	Jonathan Buckley
Rough Guides Series Editor:	Mark Ellingham

This first edition published in 1995 by Rough Guides Ltd, 1 Mercer Street, London WC2H 9QJ.

Distributed by the Penguin Group.

Penguin Books Ltd, 27 Wrights Lane, London W8 5TZ
Penguin Books USA Inc., 375 Hudson Street, New York 10014, USA
Penguin Books Australia Ltd, 487 Maroondah Highway, PO Box 257, Ringwood, Victoria 3134, Australia
Penguin Books Canada Ltd, Alcorn Avenue, Toronto, Ontario, Canada M4V 1E4
Penguin Books (NZ) Ltd, 182–190 Wairau Road, Auckland 10, New Zealand

Typeset in Rough Serif and Rough Sans to an original design by Henry Iles.
Printed by Cox & Wyman Ltd, Reading.

240pp.

British Library Cataloguing in Publication Data
A catalogue for this book is available from the British Library.

ISBN 1-85828-147-4

CONTENTS

INTRODUCTION

The Rough Guide Spanish phrasebook is a highly practical introduction to the contemporary language. Laid out in clear A-Z style, it uses key-word referencing to lead you straight to the words and phrases you want – so if you need to book a room, just look up 'room'. The Rough Guide gets straight to the point in every situation, in bars and shops, on trains and buses, and in hotels and banks.

The main part of the Rough Guide is a double dictionary: English-Spanish then Spanish-English. Before that, there's a page explaining the pronunciation system we've used, then a section called **The Basics**, which sets out the fundamental rules of the language, with plenty of practical examples. You'll also find here other essentials like numbers, dates and telling the time.

Forming the heart of the guide, the **English-Spanish** section gives easy-to-use transliterations of the Spanish words wherever pronunciation might be a problem, and to get you involved quickly in two-way communication, the Rough Guide includes dialogues featuring typical responses on key topics – such as renting a car and asking directions. Feature boxes fill you in on cultural pitfalls as well as the simple mechanics of how to make a phone call, what to do in an emergency, where to change money, and more. Throughout this section, cross-references enable you to pinpoint key facts and phrases, while asterisked words indicate where further information can be found in the Basics.

In the **Spanish-English** dictionary, we've given not just the phrases you're likely to hear, but also all the signs, labels, instructions and other basic words you might come across in print or in public places.

Finally the Rough Guide rounds off with an extensive **Menu Reader**, giving a run-down of food and drink terms that you'll find indispensable whether you're eating out, stopping for a quick drink, or browsing through a local food market.

¡buen viaje!
have a good trip!

PRONUNCIATION

In this phrasebook, the Spanish has been written in a system of imitated pronunciation so that it can be read as though it were English, bearing in mind the notes on pronunciation given below:

air	as in h**air**
ay	as in m**ay**
e	as in g**e**t
g	always hard as in **g**oat
H	a harsh 'ch' as in the Scottish way of pronouncing lo**ch**
ī	as the 'i' sound in m**igh**t
ow	as in n**ow**
y	as in **y**es

Letters given in bold type indicate the part of the word to be stressed.

As i and u are always pronounced 'ee' and 'oo' in Spanish, pronunciation has not been given for all words containing these letters unless they present other problems for the learner. Thus María is pronounced 'mar**ee**-a' and fútbol is 'f**oo**tbol'.

ABBREVIATIONS

adj	adjective	pl	plural
f	feminine	pol	polite
fam	familiar	sing	singular
m	masculine		

NOTE

In the Spanish-English section and Menu Reader, the letter ñ is treated as a separate letter, as is customary in Spanish. Alphabetically, it comes after n.

An asterisk (*) next to a word in the English-Spanish section means that you should refer to the Basics section or conversion tables for further information.

The Basics

NOUNS

All nouns in Spanish have one of two genders: masculine or feminine. Generally speaking, those ending in -o are masculine:

el zapato
el thap**a**to
the shoe

Those ending in -a, -d, -z or -ión are usually feminine:

la cama
la k**a**ma
the bed

la pensión
la pens-y**o**n
the boarding house

A small number of nouns ending in -o and -a (usually professions) can be either masculine or feminine:

el/la guía
el/la g**ee**-a
the tourist guide

el/la médico
el/la m**ay**deeko
the doctor

Plural Nouns

If the noun ends in a vowel, the plural is formed by adding -s:

el camino	los caminos
el kam**ee**no	loss kam**ee**noss
the path	the paths
la camarera	las camareras
la kamar**ai**ra	lass kamar**ai**rass
the waitress	the waitresses

If the noun ends in a consonant, the plural is formed by adding -es:

el conductor
el kondookt**o**r
the driver

los conductores
loss kondookt**o**ress
the drivers

la recepción
la rethepth-y**o**n
the reception desk

las recepciones
lass rethepth-y**o**ness
the reception desks

If the noun ends in a -z, change the -z to -ces to form the plural:

el andaluz
el andal**oo**th
the Andalusian

los andaluces
loss andal**oo**thess
the Andalusians

ARTICLES

There are different words for articles ('the' and 'a') in Spanish depending on the number (singular or plural) and gender of the noun. The definite article 'the' is as follows:

	singular	plural
masculine	el	los
feminine	la	las

el cuchillo/los cuchillos
el koochee-yo/loss koochee-yoss
the knife/the knives

la piscina/las piscinas
la peestheena/lass peestheenass
the swimming pool/the swimming pools

When the article el is used in combination with a (to) or de (of) it changes as follows:

a + el = al
de + el = del

vamos al museo
bamoss al moosay-o
let's go to the museum

cerca del hotel
thairka del otel
near the hotel

Plural Articles

The indefinite article (a, an, some), also changes according to the gender and number of the accompanying noun:

	singular	plural
masculine	un	unos
	oon	oonoss
feminine	una	unas
	oona	oonass

un sello	unos sellos
oon say-yo	oonoss say-yoss
a stamp	some stamps
una chica	unas chicas
oona cheeka	oonass cheekass
a girl	some girls

ADJECTIVES AND ADVERBS

Adjectives must agree in gender and number with the noun they refer to. In the English-Spanish section of this book, all adjectives are given in the masculine singular. Adjectives ending in -o change as follows for the plural:

el precio alto
el preth-yo alto
the high price

los precios altos
loss preth-yoss altoss
the high prices

The feminine singular of the adjective is formed by changing the masculine endings as follows:

masculine	feminine
-o	-a
-or	-ora
-és	-esa

un cocinero estupendo oon kotheen**ai**ro estoop**e**ndo a wonderful cook	una cocinera estupenda **oo**na kotheen**ai**ra estoop**e**nda a wonderful cook
un señor encantador oon sen-y**o**r enkantad**o**r a nice man	una señora encantadora **oo**na sen-y**o**ra enkantad**o**ra a nice woman
un chico inglés oon ch**ee**ko eengl**ay**ss an English boy	una chica inglesa **oo**na ch**ee**ka eengl**ay**sa an English girl

For other types of adjective, the feminine forms are the same as the masculine:

un hombre agradable oon h**o**mbray agrad**a**blay a nice man	una mujer agradable **oo**na mooH**air** agrad**a**blay a nice woman

Unlike English, Spanish adjectives usually follow the noun.

The plurals of adjectives are formed in the same way as the plurals of nouns, by adding an -s:

una tumbona roja **oo**na toomb**o**na r**o**Ha a red deckchair	dos tumbonas rojas doss toomb**o**nass r**o**Hass two red deckchairs

Comparatives

The comparative is formed by placing más (more) or menos (less) before the adjective or adverb and que (than) after it:

bonito bon**ee**to beautiful	más bonito mass bon**ee**to more beautiful
tranquilo trank**ee**lo quiet	menos tranquilo m**ay**noss trank**ee**lo less quiet

este hotel es más/menos caro que el otro
estay ot**e**l es mass/m**ay**noss k**a**ro kay el **o**tro
this hotel is more/less expensive than the other one

¿tiene una habitación más soleada?
t-y**ay**nay **oo**na abeetath-y**o**n mass solay-**a**da
do you have a sunnier room?

¿podría conducir más deprisa, por favor?
podr**ee**-a kondooth**ee**r mass depr**ee**sa por fab**o**r
could you drive faster please?

Superlatives

Superlatives are formed by placing one of the following before the adjective: **el más, la más, los más** or **las más** (depending on the noun's gender and number):

¿cuál es el más divertido?
kwal ess el mass deebairt**ee**do
which is the most entertaining?

el día más caluroso
el d**ee**-a mass kaloor**o**so
the hottest day

el coche más rápido
el k**o**chay mass r**a**pido
the fastest car

The following adjectives have irregular comparatives and superlatives:

bueno	**mejor**	**el mejor**
bw**ay**no	meH**or**	el meH**or**
good	better	the best
grande	**mayor**	**el mayor**
gr**a**nday	mī-**or**	el mī-**or**
big	bigger	the biggest
	older	the oldest
malo	**peor**	**el peor**
m**a**lo	pay-**or**	el pay-**or**
bad	worse	the worst
pequeño	**menor**	**el menor**
pek**e**n-yo	men**or**	el men**or**
small	younger	the youngest

Note that **más pequeño** means 'smaller'.

As ... as ... is translated as follows:

Madrid está tan bonita como siempre!
madr**ee** est**a** tan bon**ee**ta k**o**mo s-**ye**mpray
Madrid is as beautiful as ever!

The superlative form ending in **-ísimo** indicates that something is 'very/ extremely ... ' without actually comparing it to something else:

guapo	**guapísimo**
gw**a**po	gwap**i**simo
attractive	very attractive

Adverbs

There are two ways to form an adverb. If the adjective ends in -o, take the feminine and add -mente to form the corresponding adverb:

exacto	exactamente
esakto	esaktamente
accurate	accurately

If the adjective ends in any other letter, add -mente to the basic form:

feliz	felizmente
feleeth	feleethmentay
happy	happily

Possessive Adjectives

Possessive adjectives, like other Spanish adjectives, agree with the noun in gender and number:

	singular		plural	
	masc	fem	masc	fem
my	mi	mi	mis	mis
	mee	mee	meess	meess
your (sing, fam)	tu	tu	tus	tus
	too	too	tooss	tooss
his/her/its/your (sing, pol)	su	su	sus	sus
	soo	soo	sooss	sooss
our	nuestro	nuestra	nuestros	nuestras
	nwestro	nwestra	nwestross	nwestrass
your (pl, fam)	vuestro	vuestra	vuestros	vuestras
	bwestro	bwestra	bwestross	bwestrass
their/your (pl, pol)	su	su	sus	sus
	soo	soo	sooss	sooss

tu bolsa	sus pastillas
too bolsa	sooss pastee-yass
your bag	his/her/your tablets
vuestra maleta	nuestros trajes de baño
bwestra malayta	nwestross traHess day ban-yo
your suitcase	our swimming costumes

If when using **su/sus**, it is unclear whether you mean 'his', 'her', 'your' or 'their', you can use the following after the noun instead:

de él day el	his
de ella day **ay**-ya	her
de Usted day oost**ay**	your (sing, pol)
de ellos day **ay**-yoss	their (masculine)
de ellas day **ay**-yass	their (feminine)
de Ustedes day oost**ay**dess	your (pl, pol)

el dinero de usted
el deen**ai**ro day oost**ay**
your money

el dinero de ella
el deen**ai**ro day **ay**-ya
her money

el dinero de él
el deen**ai**ro day el
his money

POSSESSIVE PRONOUNS

To translated 'mine', 'yours' 'theirs' etc, use one of the following forms. Like possessive adjectives, possessive pronouns must agree in gender and number with the object or objects referred to:

	singular		plural	
	masculine	feminine	masculine	feminine
mine	**el mío** el m**ee**-o	**la mía** la m**ee**-a	**los míos** los m**ee**-oss	**las mías** las m**ee**-ass
yours (sing, fam)	**el tuyo** el t**oo**-yo	**la tuya** la t**oo**-ya	**los tuyos** loss t**oo**-yoss	**las tuyas** lass t**oo**-yass
his/hers	**el suyo** el s**oo**-yo	**la suya** la s**oo**-ya	**los suyos** loss s**oo**-yoss	**las suyas** lass s**oo**-yass
yours (sing, pol)	**el suyo** el s**oo**-yo	**la suya** la s**oo**-ya	**los suyos** loss s**oo**-yoss	**las suyas** lass s**oo**-yass
ours	**el nuestro** el nw**e**stro	**la nuestra** la nw**e**stra	**los nuestros** loss nw**e**stross	**las nuestras** lass nw**e**strass
yours (pl, fam)	**el vuestro** el bw**e**stro	**la vuestra** la bw**e**stra	**los vuestros** loss bw**e**stross	**las vuestras** lass bw**e**strass
theirs	**el suyo** el s**oo**-yo	**la suya** la s**oo**-ya	**los suyos** loss s**oo**-yoss	**las suyas** lass s**oo**-yass
yours (pl, pol)	**el suyo** el s**oo**-yo	**la suya** la s**oo**-ya	**los suyos** loss s**oo**-yoss	**las suyas** lass s**oo**-yass

esta es su llave y ésta la mía
esta ess soo y**a**bay ee **e**sta la m**ee**-a
this is your key and this is mine

no es la suya, es de sus amigos
no ess la s**oo**-ya ess day sooss am**ee**goss
it's not his, it's his friends'

PERSONAL PRONOUNS

Subject Pronouns

yo yo	I
tú too	you (sing, fam)
él el	he/it
ella **ay**-ya	she/it
ello **ay**-yo	it
usted oost**ay**	you (sing, pol)
nosotros nos**o**tross	we (masculine)
nosotras nos**o**trass	we (feminine)
vosotros bos**o**tross	you (pl, fam, masculine)
vosotras bos**o**trass	you (pl, fam, feminine)
ellos **ay**-yoss	they (masculine)
ellas **ay**-yass	they (feminine)
ustedes [oost**ay**dess]	you (pl, pol)

Tú is used when speaking to one person and is the familiar form generally used when speaking to family, friends and children. Vosotros/vosotras is the plural form of tú.

Usted and Ustedes are the polite forms of address to be used when talking to someone you don't know. They take the third person forms of verbs: Usted takes the same form as 'he/she/it'; Ustedes takes the same form as 'they'.

In Spanish the subject pronoun is usually omitted:

no saben no s**a**ben they don't know	está cansado est**a** kans**a**do he is tired

although it may be retained for emphasis or to avoid confusion:

¡soy yo! soy yo it's me!	¡somos nosotros! s**o**moss nos**o**tross it's us!

yo pagaré los bocadillos, tú pagas las cervezas
yo pagar**ay** loss bokad**ee**-yoss too p**a**gass lass thairb**ay**thass
I'll pay for the sandwiches, you pay for the beers

él es inglés y ella es americana
el ess eengl**ay**ss ee **ay**-ya ess amaireek**a**na
he's English and she's American

The pronouns as listed above are also used after prepositions:

para usted
p**a**ra oost**ay**
for you

con él
kon el
with him

sin ella
seen **ay**-ya
without her

después de usted
despw**ay**ss day oost**ay**
after you

The exceptions are **yo**, which is replaced by **mí**, and **tú** which is replaced by **ti**:

eso es para mí/ti
eso es p**a**ra mee/tee
that's for me/you

After **con** (with) **mí** and **ti** change as follows:

conmigo/contigo
konm**ee**go/kont**ee**go
with me/you

Object Pronouns

me	[may]	me
te	[tay]	you (sing, fam)
le	[lay]	him, you (pl, pol)
lo	[lo]	it
la	[la]	her/it, you (sing, pol)
nos	[noss]	us
os	[oss]	you (pl, fam)
les/los	[less/loss]	them, you (pl, pol, masculine)
las	[lass]	them, you (pl, pol, feminine)

Object pronouns generally precede the verb:

me la dio ayer
may la d**ee**-o a-y**air**
she gave it to me yesterday

las compré para ella
lass k**o**mpray p**a**ra **ay**-ya
I bought them for her

When used with infinitives, pronouns are added to the end of the infinitive:

¿puede llevarme al aeropuerto?
pw**ay**day yeb**a**rmay al airopw**ai**rto
can you take me to the airport?

intentaré recordarlo
eententar**ay** rekord**a**rlo
I'll try and remember it

GRAMMAR

When used with commands, pronouns are added to the end of the imperative form. See **Imperative** page 21.

If you are using an indirect pronoun to mean 'to me', 'to you' etc (although 'to' might not always be necessarily said in English), you generally use the following:

me	[may]	to me
te	[tay]	to you (sing, fam)
le	[lay]	to him/to her, to you (sing, pol)
nos	[noss]	to us
os	[oss]	to you (pl, fam)
les	[less]	to them, to you (pl, pol)

le compré flores
lay kompray fl**o**ress
I bought flowers for her

le pedí su dirección
lay ped**ee** soo deerekth-y**o**n
I asked him for his address

Reflexive Pronouns

These are used with reflexive verbs like **lavarse** 'to wash (oneself)', that is where the subject and the object are one and the same person:

me	[may]	myself (used with I)
te	[tay]	yourself (used with singular, familiar 'you')
se	[say]	him/her/itself (used with singular, polite 'you')
nos	[noss]	ourselves (used with 'we')
os	[oss]	yourselves (used with plural, familiar 'you')
se	[say]	themselves (used with 'they' and plural, polite 'you')

presentarse to introduce oneself

me presento: me llamo Richard
may pres**e**nto: may y**a**mo Richard
may I introduce myself? my name's Richard

divertirse to enjoy oneself

nos divertimos mucho en la fiesta
noss deebairt**ee**moss m**oo**cho en la f-y**e**sta
we enjoyed ourselves a lot at the party

DEMONSTRATIVES

The English demonstrative adjective 'this' is translated by the Spanish **este**. 'That' is translated by **ese** and 'that (over there/ further away)' is translated by **aquel**.

Ese refers to something near to the person being spoken to. **Aquel** refers to something further away.

Like other adjectives, they agree with the noun they qualify in gender and number but they come in front of the noun. Their forms are:

masculine singular			feminine singular		
este	**ese**	**aquel**	**esta**	**esa**	**aquella**
estay	**ay**say	ak**e**l	**e**sta	**ay**sa	ak**ay**-ya

masculine plural			feminine plural		
estos	**esos**	**aquellos**	**estas**	**esas**	**aquellas**
estoss	**ay**soss	ak**ay**-yoss	**e**stass	**ay**sass	ak**ay**-yass

este restaurante	**ese camarero**	**aquella playa**
estay restowr**a**ntay	**ay**say kamar**ai**ro	ak**ay**-ya pl**a**-ya
this restaurant	that waiter	that beach (in the distance)

'This one', 'that one', 'those', 'these' etc (as pronouns) are translated by the same words as above only they are spelt with an é:

éste	**ése**	**aquél**
estay	**ay**say	ak**e**l
this one	that one	that one (over there)

quisiera éstos/ésos/aquéllos
kees-y**ai**ra **e**stoss/**ay**soss/ak**ay**-yoss
I'd like these/those/those (over there)

The neuter forms **esto/eso/aquello** are used when no particular noun is being referred to:

esto	**eso**	**aquello**
esto	**ay**so	ak**ay**-yo

eso no es justo
ayso no ess H**oo**sto
that's not fair

¿qué es esto?
kay ess **e**sto
what is this?

VERBS

The basic form of the verb given in the English-Spanish and Spanish-English sections is the infinitive (e.g. to drive, to go etc). There are three verb types in Spanish which can be recognized by their infinitive endings: -ar, -er, -ir. For example:

hablar	[abl**ar**]	to talk
comer	[kom**air**]	to eat
abrir	[abr**ir**]	to open

Present Tense

The present tense corresponds to 'I leave' and 'I am leaving' in English. To form the present tense for the three main types of verb in Spanish, remove the -ar, -er or -ir and add the following endings:

hablar to speak

habl-o	[**a**blo]	I speak
habl-as	[**a**blass]	you speak (sing, fam)
habl-a	[**a**bla]	he/she speaks, you speak (sing, pol)
habl-amos	[abl**a**moss]	we speak
habl-áis	[abl**a**-eess]	you speak (pl, fam)
habl-an	[**a**blan]	they speak, you speak (pl, pol)

comer to eat

com-o	[**ko**mo]	I eat
com-es	[**ko**mess]	you eat (sing, fam)
com-e	[**ko**may]	he/she eats, you eat (sing, pol)
com-emos	[kom**ay**moss]	we eat
com-éis	[kom**ay**-eess]	you eat (pl, fam)
com-en	[**ko**men]	they eat, you eat (pl, pol)

abrir to open

abr-o	[**a**bro]	I open
abr-es	[**a**bress]	you open (sing, fam)
abr-e	[**a**bray]	he/she opens, you open (sing, pol)
abr-imos	[abr**ee**moss]	we open
abr-ís	[abr**ee**ss]	you open (pl, fam)
abr-en	[**a**bren]	they open, you open (pl, pol)

Some common verbs are irregular:

haber to have

he	[ay]	I have
has	[ass]	you have (sing, fam)
ha	[a]	he/she/it has, you have (sing, pol)
hemos	[**ay**moss]	we have
habéis	[ab**ay**-eess]	you have (pl, fam)
han	[an]	they have, you have (pl, pol)

tener to have

tengo	[t**e**ngo]
tienes	[t-y**ay**ness]
tiene	[t-y**ay**nay]
tenemos	[ten**ay**moss]
tenéis	[ten**ay**-eess]
tienen	[t-y**ay**nen]

venir to come

vengo	[b**e**ngo]
vienes	[b-y**ay**ness]
viene	[b-y**ay**nay]
venimos	[ben**ee**moss]
venís	[ben**ee**ss]
vienen	[b-y**ay**nen]

ir to go

voy	[boy]
vas	[bass]
va	[ba]
vamos	[**ba**moss]
vais	[b**a**-eess]
van	[ban]

dar to give

doy	[doy]
das	[dass]
da	[da]
damos	[**da**moss]
dais	[d**a**-eess]
dan	[dan]

poder to be able

puedo	[pw**ay**do]
puedes	[pw**ay**dess]
puede	[pw**ay**day]
podemos	[pod**ay**mos]
podéis	[pod**ay**-eess]
pueden	[pw**ay**den]

querer to want

quiero	[k-y**ai**ro]
quieres	[k-y**ai**ress]
quiere	[k-y**ai**ray]
queremos	[kair**ay**moss]
queréis	[kair**ay**-eess]
quieren	[k-y**ai**ren]

The first person singular (the 'I' form) of the following verbs is irregular:

decir to say	**digo**	[d**ee**go]
hacer to do, to make	**hago**	[**a**-go]
poner to put	**pongo**	[p**o**ngo]
saber to know	**sé**	[say]
salir to go out	**salgo**	[s**a**lgo]

See page 19 for the present tense of the verbs **ser** and **estar** 'to be'.

Past Tense:

Perfect Tense

The perfect tense is used to express an action that has taken place in the past. It is formed with the present tense of **haber** (see page 14) and the past participle of the verb.

To form the past participles, make the following changes to the infinitive forms:

infinitive	past participle	
hablar	**hablado**	[abl**a**do]
comer	**comido**	[kom**ee**do]
abrir	**abrido**	[abr**ee**do]

hemos dado una propina
aymoss d**a**do **oo**na prop**ee**na
we have given a tip

hemos comido bien
aymoss kom**ee**do b-yen
we've eaten well, we've had a good meal

he encendido la luz
ay enthend**ee**do la looth
I (have) put the light on

Some verbs have irregular past participles:

hacer to do/make	**hecho** [**ay**cho]
abrir to open	**abierto** [ab-y**ai**rto]
decir to say	**dicho** [d**ee**cho]
volver to return	**vuelto** [bw**e**lto]
poner to put	**puesto** [pw**e**sto]
ver to see	**visto** [b**ee**sto]
satisfacer to satisfy	**satisfecho** [sateesf**e**cho]

Past Historic

The Past Historic is used to express what happened or what somebody did at a particular time in the past.

habl-é	[abl**ay**]	I spoke
habl-aste	[abl**a**stay]	you spoke (sing, fam)
habl-ó	[abl**o**]	he/she spoke, you spoke (sing, pol)
habl-amos	[abl**a**moss]	we spoke
habl-asteis	[abl**a**stay-eess]	you spoke (pl, fam)
habl-aron	[abl**a**ron]	they spoke, you spoke (pl, pol)

com-í	[kom**ee**]	I ate
com-iste	[kom**ee**stay]	you ate (sing, fam)
com-ió	[komi-**o**]	he/she ate, you ate (sing, pol)
com-imos	[kom**ee**moss]	we ate
com-isteis	[kom**ee**stay-eess]	you ate (pl, fam)
com-ieron	[kom-y**ai**ron]	they ate, you ate (pl, pol)

abr-í	[abr**ee**]	I opened
abr-iste	[abr**ee**stay]	you opened (sing, fam)
abr-ió	[abri-**o**]	he/she opened, you opened (sing, pol)
abr-imos	[abr**ee**moss]	we opened
abr-isteis	[abr**ee**stay-eess]	you opened (pl, fam)
abr-ieron	[abr-y**ai**ron]	they opened, you opened (pl, pol)

¿quién te dijo eso?
k-y**e**n tay d**ee**Ho **ay**so
who told you that?

nos conocimos en Málaga
noss konoth**ee**moss en m**a**laga
we met each other in Malaga

lo compramos el año pasado
lo kompr**a**moss el **a**n-yo pas**a**do
we bought it last year

Imperfect Tense

This tense is used to express what was going on regularly over an indefinite period of time and is sometimes translated by 'used to + infinitive'. It it is formed as follows:

hablar to talk

habl-aba	[abl**a**ba]	I was speaking
habl-abas	[abl**a**bass]	you were speaking (sing, fam)
habl-aba	[abl**a**ba]	he/she/it was speaking, you were speaking (sing, pol)
habl-ábamos	[abl**a**bamoss]	we were speaking
habl-abais	[abl**a**ba-eess]	you were speaking (pl, fam)
habl-aban	[abl**a**ban]	they were speaking, you were speaking (pl, polite)

comer to eat		
com-ía	[kom**ee**-a]	I was eating
com-ías	[kom**ee**-ass]	you were eating (sing, fam)
com-ía	[kom**ee**-a]	he/she/it was eating, you were eating (sing, pol)
com-íamos	[kom**ee**-amoss]	we were eating
com-íais	[kom**ee**-a-eess]	you were eating (pl, fam)
com-ían	[kom**ee**-an]	they were eating, you were eating (pl, pol)

abrir to open		
abr-ía	[abr**ee**-a]	I was opening
abr-ías	[abr**ee**-ass]	you were opening (sing, fam)
abr-ía	[abr**ee**-a]	he/she/it was opening, you were opening (sing, pol)
abr-íamos	[abr**ee**-amoss]	we were opening
abr-íais	[abr**ee**-a-eess]	you were opening (pl, fam)
abr-ían	[abr**ee**-an]	they were opening, you were opening (pl, pol)

Two other useful regular verbs in the imperfect tense are:

tener to have		
tenía	[ten**ee**-a]	I had
tenías	[ten**ee**-ass]	you had (sing, fam)
tenía	[ten**ee**-a]	he/she/it had, you had (sing, pol)
teníamos	[ten**ee**-amoss]	we had
teníais	[ten**ee**-a-eess]	you had (pl, fam)
tenían	[ten**ee**-an]	they had, you had (pl, pol)

estar to be		
estaba	[est**a**ba]	I was
estabas	[est**a**bass]	you were (sing, fam)
estaba	[est**a**ba]	he/she/it was, you were (sing, pol)
estábamos	[est**a**bamoss]	we were
estabais	[est**a**ba-eess]	you were (pl, fam)
estaban	[est**a**ban]	they were, you were (pl, pol)

The following are irregular in the imperfect tense:

ir to go

iba	[**ee**ba]	I was going
ibas	[**ee**bass]	you were going (sing, fam)
iba	[**ee**ba]	he/she/it was going, you were going (sing, pol)
íbamos	[**ee**bamoss]	we were going
ibais	[**ee**ba-eess]	you were going (pl, fam)
iban	[**ee**ban]	they were going, you were going (pl, pol)

ser to be (see opposite for more on this)

era	[**ai**ra]	I was
eras	[**ai**rass]	you were (sing, fam)
era	[**ai**ra]	he/she/it was, you were (sing, pol)
éramos	[**ai**ramoss]	we were
erais	[**ai**ra-eess]	you were (pl, fam)
eran	[**ai**ran]	they were, you were (pl, pol)

todos los viernes salíamos a dar un paseo
t**o**dos loss b-y**ai**rness sal**ee**-amoss a dar oon pass**ay**-o
every Friday we used to go for a walk, every Friday we went for a walk

Future Tense

To form the future tense in Spanish (I will do, you will do etc) add the following endings to the infinitive. The same endings are used whether verbs end in -ar, -er or -ir:

hablar-é	[ablar**ay**]	I will speak
hablar-ás	[ablar**a**ss]	you will speak
hablar-á	[ablar**a**]	he/she/you will speak
hablar-emos	[ablar**ay**moss]	we will speak
hablar-éis	[ablar**ay**-eess]	you will speak
hablar-án	[ablar**a**n]	they/you will speak

volveré más tarde
bolbair**ay** mass t**a**rday
I'll come back later

The immediate future can also be translated by ir + a + infinitive:

vamos a comprar una botella de vino tinto
b**a**moss a kompr**ar** **oo**na bot**ay**-ya day b**ee**no t**ee**nto
we're going to buy a bottle of red wine

iré a recogerle
[eer**ay** a raykoH**air**lay]
I'll fetch him, I'll go and fetch him

Sometimes the future tense in Spanish indicates probability:

será verdad
sair**a** baird**a**
it might be true

In Spanish, as in English, the future can sometimes be expressed by the present tense:

tu avión sale a la una
too aby-**o**n s**a**lay a la **oo**na
your plane takes off at one o'clock

However, Spanish often uses the present tense where the future would be used in English:

le doy ochocientas pesetas
lay doy ochoth-y**e**ntass pes**ay**tass
I'll give you 800 pesetas

The following verbs are irregular in the future tense:

decir	to say	**diré** I will say
hacer	to do	**haré**
poder	to be able	**podré**
poner	to put	**pondré**
querer	to want	**querré**
saber	to know	**sabré**
salir	to leave	**saldré**
tener	to have	**tendré**
venir	to come	**vendré**

The Verb 'To Be'

There are two verbs 'to be' in Spanish: **ser** and **estar**. The present tense is as follows:

ser

soy	[soy]	I am
eres	[**ai**ress]	you are (sing, fam)
es	[ess]	he/she/it is, you are (sing, pol)
somos	[s**o**moss]	we are
sois	[soyss]	you are (pl, fam)
son	[son]	they are, you are (pl, pol)

estar

estoy	[est**oy**]	I am
estás	[est**a**ss]	you are (sing, fam)
está	[est**a**]	he/she/it is, you are (sing, pol)
estamos	[est**a**moss]	we are
estáis	[est**a**-eess]	you are (pl, fam)
están	[est**a**n]	they are, you are (pl, pol)

Ser
Ser indicates an inherent quality, a permanent state or characteristic, something which is unlikely to change:

la nieve es blanca
la n-y**ay**bay ess bl**a**nka
snow is white

Ser is also used with occupations, nationalities, the time and to indicate possession:

somos escoceses
s**o**moss eskoth**ay**sess
we are Scottish

mi madre es profesora
mi m**a**dray ess profes**o**ra
my mum is a teacher

éste es nuestro coche
estay ess nw**e**stro k**o**chay
this is our car

son las cinco de la tarde
son lass th**ee**nko day la t**a**rday
it's five o'clock in the afternoon

Estar, on the other hand, is used for temporary qualities, for things which could change:

estoy enfadado contigo
est**oy** enfad**a**do kont**ee**go
I'm angry with you

estoy cansado
est**oy** kans**a**do
I'm tired

este filete está frío
estay feel**ay**tay est**a** fr**ee**-o
this steak is cold

Notice the difference between the following two phrases:

Isabel es muy guapa
Isabel ess mwee gw**a**pa
Isabel is very pretty

Isabel está muy guapa (esta noche)
Isabel est**a** mwee gw**a**pa **e**sta n**o**chay
Isabel looks pretty (tonight)

Estar is also used to indicate position and situation:

Barcelona está en Cataluña
barthel**o**na est**a** en katal**oo**n-ya
Barcelona is in Catalonia

Negatives

To express a negative in Spanish, to say 'I don't want', 'it's not here' etc, place the word **no** in front of the verb:

comprendo kompr**e**ndo I understand	**no comprendo** no kompr**e**ndo I don't understand

me gusta este helado
may g**oo**sta **ay**stay el**a**do
I like this ice cream

no me gusta este helado
no may g**oo**sta **ay**stay el**a**do
I don't like this ice cream

lo alquilé aquí
lo alkeel**ay** ak**ee**
I rented it here

no lo alquilé aquí
no lo alkeel**ay** ak**ee**
I didn't rent it here

van a cantar	no van a cantar
ban a kant**ar**	no ban a kant**ar**
they're going to sing	they're not going to sing

Unlike English, Spanish makes use of double negatives with words like nothing/anything or nobody/anybody:

no hay nadie ahí
no ī n**a**d-yay a-**ee**
there's nobody there

no compramos nada
no kompr**a**moss n**a**da
we didn't buy anything

no sabemos nada de ella
no sab**ay**moss n**a**da day **ay**-ya
we don't know anything about her

To say 'there's no ...', 'I've no ...' etc, make the accompanying verb negative:

no hay vino
no ī b**ee**no
there's no wine

no tengo cerillas
no t**e**ngo thair**ee**-yass
I've no matches

To say 'not him', 'not her' etc just use the personal pronoun followed by no:

nosotros, no	ella, no	yo, no
nos**o**tross no	**ay**-ya no	yo no
not us	not her	not me

Imperative

When speaking to people using the Usted or Ustedes forms, you make commands by removing the -ar, -er or -ir from the infinitive and adding these endings:

	singular	plural
hablar to speak	habl-e	habl-en
	ablay	**a**blen
comer to eat	com-a	com-an
	k**o**ma	k**o**man
abrir to open	abr-a	abr-an
	abra	**a**bran

coma despacio
k**o**ma desp**a**th-yo
eat slowly

When you are telling someone not to do something, use the forms above and place no in front of the verb:

no me moleste, por favor
no may mol**e**stay por fab**o**r
don't disturb me, please

¡no beba alcohol!
no b**ay**ba alkoh**o**l
don't drink alcohol!

¡no venga esta noche!
no b**e**nga **e**sta n**o**chay
don't come tonight

To form the imperative used to give commands to people you would normally address as tú and vosotros, remove the endings -ar, -er, and -ir from the verb and add these endings:

	tú		vosotros	
hablar (to speak)	habl-a	[**a**bla]	habl-ad	[abl**a**d]
comer (to eat)	com-e	[k**o**may]	com-ed	[kom**ay**d]
abrir (to open)	abr-e	[**a**bray]	abr-id	[abr**ee**d]

To form a negative imperative to people addressed as tú and vosotros, no is placed in front of the verb and the endings change:

	tú			vosotros	
habla	no habl-es	[no **a**bless]	hablad	no habl-éis	[no abl**ay**-eess]
come	no com-as	[no k**o**mass]	comed	no com-áis	[no kom**a**-eess]
abre	no abras	[no **a**brass]	abrid	no abr-áis	[no abr**a**-eess]

por favor, no hables tan rápido (to one person)
por fab**o**r no **a**bless tan r**a**peedo
please, do not speak so fast

por favor, no habléis tan rápido (to several people)
por fab**o**r no abl**ay**-eess tan r**a**peedo
please, don't speak so fast

Pronouns are added to the end of the imperative form:

despiérteme a las ocho, por favor
desp-y**air**temay a lass **o**cho por fab**o**r
wake me up at eight o'clock, please

bébelo
b**ay**belo
drink it

ciérralas
th-y**air**alass
close them

ayúdeme, por favor
a-y**oo**demay por fab**o**r
help me please

but when the imperative is negative, they are placed in front of it:

no lo bebas
no lo b**ay**bass
don't drink it

no las cierres
no lass th-y**air**ess
don't close them

QUESTIONS

Often the word order remains the same in a question, but the intonation changes, the voice rising at the end of the question:

quiero bailar
k-y**ai**ro ba-eel**ar**
I want to dance

¿no quieres bailar?
no k-y**ai**ress ba-eel**ar**
don't you want to dance?

DATES

Use the numbers on page 24 to express the date. In formal Spanish, the ordinal number may be used for 'the first', but not for other dates:

el uno/el primero de septiembre [**oo**no/el preem**ai**ro day sept-y**e**mbray] the first of September
el dos de diciembre [doss day deeth-y**e**mbray] the second of December
el treinta de mayo [tr**ay-ee**nta day m**a**-yo] the thirtieth of May
el treinta y uno de mayo [tr**ay-ee**ntī **oo**no day m**a**-yo] the thirty-first of May

TIME

what time is it? ¿qué hora es? [kay **o**ra ess]
one o'clock la una [la **oo**na]
two o'clock las dos [lass doss]
it's one o'clock es la una [ess la **oo**na]
it's two o'clock son las dos [son lass doss]
it's ten o'clock son las diez [son lass d-yeth]
five past one la una y cinco [la **oo**na ee th**ee**nko]
ten past two las dos y diez [lass doss ee d-yeth]
quarter past one la una y cuarto [la **oo**na ee kw**a**rto]
quarter past two las dos y cuarto [lass doss ee kw**a**rto]
half past ten las diez y media [lass d-yeth ee m**ay**d-ya]
twenty to ten las diez menos veinte [lass d-yeth m**ay**noss b**ay-ee**ntay]
quarter to ten las diez menos cuarto [lass d-yeth m**ay**noss kw**a**rto]
at eight o'clock a las ocho [a lass **o**cho]
at half past four a las cuatro y media [a lass kw**a**tro ee m**ay**d-ya]
2 a.m. las dos de la mañana [lass doss day la man-y**a**na]
2 p.m. las dos de la tarde [lass doss day la t**a**rday]
6 a.m. las seis de la mañana [lass say-eess day la man-y**a**na]

6 p.m. las seis de la tarde [lass say-eess day la t**a**rday]
noon mediodía [m**ay**d-yo d**ee**-a]
midnight medianoche [m**ay**d-ya n**o**chay]
an hour una hora [**oo**na **o**ra]
a minute un minuto [oon meen**oo**to]
two minutes dos minutos [doss meen**oo**toss]
a second un segundo [oon seg**oo**ndo]
a quarter of an hour un cuarto de hora [kw**a**rto day **o**ra]
half an hour media hora [m**ay**d-ya **o**ra]
three quarters of an hour tres cuartos de hora [tress kw**a**rtoss day **o**ra]

NUMBERS

0 cero [th**ai**ro]
1 uno, una [**oo**no, **oo**na]
2 dos [doss]
3 tres [tress]
4 cuatro [kw**a**tro]
5 cinco [th**ee**nko]
6 seis [say-eess]
7 siete [s-y**ay**tay]
8 ocho [**o**cho]
9 nueve [nw**ay**bay]
10 diez [d-yeth]
11 once [**o**nthay]
12 doce [d**o**thay]
13 trece [tr**ay**thay]
14 catorce [kat**o**rthay]
15 quince [k**ee**nthay]
16 dieciséis [d-yetheees**ay**-eess]
17 diecisiete [d-yethees-y**ay**tay]
18 dieciocho [d-yethee-**o**cho]
19 diecinueve [d-yetheenw**ay**bay]
20 veinte [b**ay**-**ee**ntay]
21 veintiuno [bay-eentee-**oo**no]
22 veintidós [bay-eenteed**o**ss]
23 veintitrés [bay-eenteetr**e**ss]
30 treinta [tr**ay**-**ee**nta]
31 treinta y uno [tr**ay**-**ee**ntī **oo**no]
40 cuarenta [kwar**e**nta]
50 cincuenta [theenkw**e**nta]
60 sesenta [ses**e**nta]
70 setenta [set**e**nta]
80 ochenta [och**e**nta]
90 noventa [nob**e**nta]
100 cien [th-yen]
120 ciento veinte [th-y**e**nto b**ay**-**ee**ntay]
200 doscientos, doscientas [dosth-y**e**ntoss, dosth-y**e**ntass]
300 trescientos, trescientas [tresth-y**e**ntoss, tresth-y**e**ntass]
400 cuatrocientos, cuatrocientas [kwatroth-y**e**ntoss, kwatroth-y**e**ntass]
500 quinientos, quinientas [keen-y**e**ntoss, keen-y**e**ntass]
600 seiscientos, seiscientas [say-eesth-y**e**ntoss, say-eesth-y**e**ntass]
700 setecientos, setecientas [seteth-y**e**ntoss, seteth-y**e**ntass]

800	ochocientos, ochocientas [ochoth-**ye**ntoss, ochoth-**ye**ntass]
900	novecientos, novecientas [nobeth-**ye**ntoss, nobeth-**ye**ntass]
1,000	mil [meel]
2,000	dos mil [doss meel]
5,000	cinco mil [th**ee**nko meel]
10,000	diez mil [d-yeth meel]
1,000,000	un millón [meel-y**o**n]

When uno is used with a masculine noun, the final -o is dropped:

un coche
oon k**o**chay
one car

una is used with feminine nouns:

una bicicleta
oona beetheekl**ay**ta
one bike

With multiples of a hundred, the -as ending is used with feminine nouns:

trescientos hombres
tresth-**ye**ntoss **o**mbress
300 men

quinientas mujeres
keen-**ye**ntass mooH**ai**ress
500 women

ORDINALS

1st	primero [preem**ai**ro]
2nd	segundo [seg**oo**ndo]
3rd	tercero [tairth**ai**ro]
4th	cuarto [kw**a**rto]
5th	quinto [k**ee**nto]
6th	sexto [s**e**sto]
7th	séptimo [s**e**pteemo]
8th	octavo [okt**a**bo]
9th	noveno [nob**ay**no]
10th	décimo [d**e**theemo]

CONVERSION TABLES

1 centimetre = 0.39 inches

1 metre = 39.37 inches = 1.09 yards

1 kilometre = 0.62 miles = 5/8 mile

1 inch = 2.54 cm

1 foot = 30.48 cm

1 yard = 0.91 m

1 mile = 1.61 km

km	1	2	3	4	5	10	20	30	40	50	100
miles	0.6	1.2	1.9	2.5	3.1	6.2	12.4	18.6	24.8	31.0	62.1

miles	1	2	3	4	5	10	20	30	40	50	100
km	1.6	3.2	4.8	6.4	8.0	16.1	32.2	48.3	64.4	80.5	161

1 gram = 0.035 ounces

g	100	250	500
oz	3.5	8.75	17.5

1 kilo = 1000 g = 2.2 pounds

1 oz = 28.35 g

1 lb = 0.45 kg

kg	0.5	1	2	3	4	5	6	7	8	9	10
lb	1.1	2.2	4.4	6.6	8.8	11.0	13.2	15.4	17.6	19.8	22.0

kg	20	30	40	50	60	70	80	90	100
lb	44	66	88	110	132	154	176	198	220

lb	0.5	1	2	3	4	5	6	7	8	9	10	20
kg	0.2	0.5	0.9	1.4	1.8	2.3	2.7	3.2	3.6	4.1	4.5	9.0

1 litre = 1.75 UK pints / 2.13 US pints

1 UK pint = 0.57 l

1 US pint = 0.47 l

1 UK gallon = 4.55 l

1 US gallon = 3.79 l

centigrade / Celsius

C = (F - 32) × 5/9

C	-5	0	5	10	15	18	20	25	30	36.8	38
F	23	32	41	50	59	64	68	77	86	98.4	100.4

Fahrenheit

F = (C × 9/5) + 32

F	23	32	40	50	60	65	70	80	85	98.4	101
C	-5	0	4	10	16	18	21	27	29	36.8	38.3

English-Spanish

A

a, an* un, una [oon, **oo**na]
about: about 20 unos v**e**inte
it's about 5 o'clock son aproximadamente las c**i**nco [aproxeem**a**damentay]
a film about Spain una película sobre España [s**o**bray]
above ... encima de ... [enth**ee**ma day]
abroad en el extranjero [estranH**airo**]
absolutely (I agree) ¡desde luego! [d**e**sday lw**ay**go]
accelerator el acelerador [athelairad**o**r]
accept aceptar [athept**a**r]
accident el accidente [aktheed**e**ntay]
there's been an accident ha habido un accidente [a ab**ee**do]
accommodation alojamiento [aloHam-y**e**nto]
see **room** and **hotel**
accurate exacto
ache el dolor
my back aches me duele la espalda [may dw**ay**lay]
across: across the road al otro lado de la calle [k**a**-yay]
adapter el adaptador
address la dirección [deerekth-y**o**n]
what's your address? ¿cuál es su dirección? [kwal]

> Addresses in Spain are written as follows:
>
> Don José García
> c/Picasso 2, 4 izda.
> 14600 Madrid
>
> – which means Picasso street (**calle**) no. 2, fourth floor, left-hand (**izquierda**) flat or office; **dcha**, (**derecha**) means right and **cto.** (**centro**) means centre. Other confusions in Spanish addresses result from the different spellings, and sometimes words, used in Catalan, Basque and Gallego – all of which are to some extent replacing their Castilian counterparts.

address book la libreta de direcciones [leebr**ay**ta day deerekth-y**o**ness]
admission charge la entrada
adult el adulto
advance: in advance por adelantado
aeroplane el avión [ab-y**o**n]
after después (de) [despw**e**ss day]
after you usted primero [oost**ay** preem**airo**]
after lunch después del almuerzo
afternoon la tarde [t**a**rday]
in the afternoon por la tarde
this afternoon esta tarde
aftershave el 'aftershave'
aftersun cream la crema para

después del sol [krayma para despwess]
afterwards después [despwess]
again otra vez [beth]
against contra
age la edad [aydath]
ago: a week ago hace una semana [athay]
an hour ago hace una hora
agree: I agree estoy de acuerdo [day akwairdo]
AIDS el SIDA [seeda]
air el aire [a-eeray]
by air en avión [ab-yon]
air-conditioning el aire acondicionado [a-eeray akondeeth-yonado]
airmail: by airmail por avión [ab-yon]
airmail envelope el sobre aéreo [sobray a-airay-o]
airport el aeropuerto [a-airopwairto]
to the airport, please al aeropuerto, por favor
airport bus el autobús del aeropuerto [owtobooss]
aisle seat asiento de pasillo [as-yento day pasee-yo]
alarm clock el despertador
alcohol el alcohol [alkol]
alcoholic alcohólico
Algeria Argelia [arHaylee-a]
all: all the boys todos los chicos
all the girls todas las chicas
all of it todo
all of them todos ellos [ay-yoss]
that's all, thanks eso es todo, gracias [ayso]
allergic: I'm allergic to ... soy alérgico/alérgica a ... [alairHeeko]
allowed: is it allowed? ¿está permitido?
all right ¡bien! [b-yen]
I'm all right estoy bien
are you all right? (fam) ¿estás bien?
(pol) ¿se encuentra bien? [say enkwayntra]
almond la almendra
almost casi
alone solo
alphabet el alfabeto

a a	j Hota	s aysay
b bay	k ka	t tay
c thay	l aylay	u oo
ch chay	m aymay	v oobay
d day	n aynay	w oobay doblay
e ay	ñ ayn-yay	x aykeess
f ayfay	o o	y ee gr-yayga
g Hay	p pay	z thayta
h achay	q koo	
i ee	r airray	

Alps los Alpes [alpess]
already ya
also también [tamb-yen]
although aunque [a-oonkay]
altogether del todo
always siempre [s-yempray]
am*: I am soy, estoy
a.m.: at seven a.m. a las 7 de la mañana [day la man-yana]
amazing (surprising) increíble [eenkray-eeblay]
(very good) estupendo

ambulance la ambulancia [amboolanth-ya]
call an ambulance! ¡llame a una ambulancia! [yamay]

> Dial 061 for the ambulance service (**emergencias sanitarias**).

America América
American (adj) americano
I'm American (man/woman) soy americano/americana
among entre [entray]
amount la cantidad [kanteeda] (money) la suma
amp: a 13-amp fuse el fusible de trece amperios [fooseeblay day – ampairee-oss]
amphitheatre el anfiteatro [anfeetay-atro]
and y [ee]
angry enfadado
animal el animal
ankle el tobillo [tobee-yo]
anniversary (wedding) el aniversario de boda [aneebairsar-yo day]
annoy: this man's annoying me este hombre me está molestando [estay ombray may]
annoying molesto
another otro
can we have another room? ¿puede darnos otra habitación? [pwayday – abeetath-yon]
another beer, please otra cerveza, por favor [thairbaytha]
antibiotics los antibióticos [anteeb-yoteekoss]
antifreeze el anticongelante [anteekonHelantay]
antihistamine el antihistamínico [antee-eestameeneeko]
antique: is it an antique? ¿es antiguo? [anteegwo]
antique shop la tienda de antigüedades [t-yenda day anteegway-dadess]
antiseptic el antiséptico
any: have you got any bread/tomatoes? ¿tiene pan/tomates? [t-yaynay]
do you have any change? ¿tiene cambio? [kamb-yo]
sorry, I don't have any lo siento, no tengo [s-yento]
anybody cualquiera [kwalk-yaira]
does anybody speak English? ¿habla alguien inglés? [abla alg-yen eenglayss]
there wasn't anybody there allí no había nadie [a-yee no abee-a nad-yay]
anything algo

•••••• DIALOGUES ••••••

anything else? ¿algo más?
nothing else, thanks nada más, gracias

would you like anything to drink? ¿le apetece beber algo? [lay apetethay bebair]

I don't want anything, thanks no quiero nada, gracias [no k-yairo nada]

apart from aparte de [apartay day]

apartment el apartamento, el piso

appendicitis la apendicitis [apendeetheeteess]

appetizer la entrada

aperitif el aperitivo [apereeteebo]

apology la disculpa

apple la manzana [manthana]

appointment la cita [theeta]

•••••• DIALOGUE ••••••

good afternoon, sir, how can I help you? buenas tardes, señor, ¿en qué puedo servirle? [bwenass tardess, sen-yor en kay pwaydo sairbeerlay]

I'd like to make an appointment quisiera pedir hora [kees-yaira pedeer ora]

what time would you like? ¿a qué hora le viene bien? [a kay ora lay b-yaynay b-yen]

three o'clock a las tres

I'm afraid that's not possible, is four o'clock all right? me temo que no será posible, está bien a las cuatro? [may taymo kay no saira poseeblay]

yes, that will be fine sí, está bien

the name was ...? ¿su nombre era ...? [nombray aira]

apricot el albaricoque [albarikokay]

April abril

Aranjuez Aranjuez [aranHweth]

are*: we are somos; estamos

you are (fam) eres [airess]; estás

(pol) es; está

they are son; están

area la zona [thona]

area code el prefijo [prefeeHo]

arm el brazo [bratho]

arrange: will you arrange it for us? ¿nos lo organiza usted? [organeetha oostay]

arrival la llegada [yegada]

arrive llegar [yegar]

when do we arrive? ¿cuándo llegamos? [kwando yegamoss]

has my fax arrived yet? ¿ha llegado ya mi fax? [a yegado]

we arrived today llegamos hoy [yegamoss oy]

art el arte [artay]

art gallery el museo de bellas artes [moosay-o day bay-yass artess]

artist (man/woman) el pintor/la pintora

as: as big as tan grande como [granday]

as soon as possible lo antes posible [antess poseeblay]

ashtray el cenicero [thayneethairo]

ask preguntar [pregoontar]

I didn't ask for this no había pedido eso [abee-a – ayso]

could you ask him to ...? ¿puede decirle que ...? [pwayday detheerlay kay]

asleep: she's asleep **está** dormida
aspirin la aspirina
asthma el asma
astonishing increíble [eenkray-**ee**blay]
at: at the hotel en el hotel
at the station en la estación
at six o'clock a las seis
at Pedro's en la casa de Pedro
athletics el atletismo
Atlantic Ocean el Océano Atlántico [oth**ay**-ano]
attractive guapo, atractivo [atrakt**ee**bo]
aubergine la berenjena [berenH**ay**na]
August agosto
aunt la tía [t**ee**-a]
Australia Australia [owstr**a**l-ya]
Australian (adj) australiano
I'm Australian (man/woman) soy australiano/australiana
automatic (car) automático [owtom**a**teeko]
automatic teller el cajero automático [kaH**ai**ro]
autumn el otoño [ot**o**n-yo]
in the autumn en otoño
avenue la avenida [aben**ee**da]
average (not good) regular [regool**a**r]
on average por término medio [t**ai**rmeeno m**ay**d-yo]
awake: is he awake? ¿**está** despierto? [desp-y**ai**rto]
away: go away! ¡lárguese! [l**a**rgaysay]
is it far away? ¿**está** lejos? [l**ay**Hoss]
awful terrible [terr**ee**blay]
axle el eje [**ay**Hay]

B

baby el bebé [bayb**ay**]
baby food la comida de bebé [day]
baby's bottle el biberón [beebair**o**n]
baby-sitter la niñera [neen-y**ai**ra]
back (of body) la espalda
(back part) la parte de atrás [p**a**rtay day]
at the back en la parte de atrás
can I have my money back? ¿puede devolverme el dinero? [pw**ay**day daybolb**ai**rmay el deen**ai**ro]
to come/go back volver [bolb**ai**r]
backache el dolor de espalda [day]
bacon el bacon [b**ay**kon], la panceta [panth**e**ta]
bad malo
a bad headache un fuerte dolor de cabeza [fw**ai**rtay – day kab**ay**tha]
badly mal
(injured) gravemente [grabem**ay**ntay]
bag la bolsa
(handbag) el bolso
(suitcase) la maleta [mal**ay**ta]

baggage el equipaje [ekeep**a**Hay]
baggage check la consigna [kons**ee**gna]
baggage claim la recogida de equipajes [rekoH**ee**da day ekeep**a**Hess]
bakery la panadería [panadair**ee**-a]
balcony el balcón
a room with a balcony una habitación con balcón [abeetath-y**o**n]
bald calvo [k**a**lbo]
Balearic Islands las Baleares [balay-**a**ress]
ball (large) la pelota
(small) la bola
ballet el ballet
banana el plátano
band (musical) la orquesta [ork**e**sta]
bandage la venda [b**e**nda]
Bandaid® la tirita
bank (money) el banco

> In winter, banking hours are 9 a.m. to 2 p.m. Monday to Friday and 9 a.m. to 1 p.m. on Saturdays. In summer, banks don't open on Saturdays.

bank account la cuenta bancaria [kw**e**nta]
bar el bar

> In many bars in Spain – especially the traditional ones – you do not have to pay when ordering. You can wait until just before you leave. In others, you may have to pay right after you have been served or pay first at the cash desk then show your receipt (**el ticket**) at the bar when ordering. It's usually cheaper if you stand at the bar to drink.

a bar of chocolate una barra de chocolate [day chokol**a**tay]
barber's el barbero [barb**ai**ro]
Barcelona Barcelona [barthayl**o**na]
basket el cesto [th**e**sto]
(in shop) la cesta
bath el baño [b**a**n-yo]
can I have a bath? ¿puedo bañarme? [pw**ay**do ban-y**a**rmay]
bathroom el cuarto de baño [kw**a**rto]
with a private bathroom con baño privado [preeb**a**do]
bath towel la toalla de baño [to-**a**-ya day]
battery la pila
(car) la batería [batair**ee**-a]
bay la bahía [ba-**ee**-a]
Bay of Biscay el Golfo de Vizcaya [day beethk**a**ya]
be* ser [sair]; estar [ayst**a**r]
beach la playa [pl**a**-ya]
beach mat la esterilla de playa [estair**ee**-ya]
beach umbrella la sombrilla [sombr**ee**-ya]

beans las judías [Hoo**dee**-ass]
runner beans las judías verdes [**bair**dess]
broad beans las habas [**a**bass]
beard la b**a**rba
beautiful bon**i**to
because porque [**po**rkay]
because of ... debido a ... [deb**ee**do]
bed la c**a**ma
I'm going to bed now me voy a acost**a**r ya [may boy]
bed and breakfast habitación y desayuno [abeetath-y**o**n ee desa-y**oo**no]
see **hotel**
bedroom el dormitorio [dormeet**o**r-yo]
beef la carne de vaca [k**a**rnay day b**a**ka]
beer la cerveza [thairb**ay**tha]
two beers, please dos cervezas, por fav**o**r

> In Spain if you order '**cerveza**' you will be served lager-type beer.
> Other terms are:
>
> **cerveza negra** [n**ay**gra] stout
> **clara** or **shandy** lager and lemonade
> **de grifo** [gr**ee**fo] on tap
> **de barril** [barr**ee**l] on draught
> **una caña** [k**a**n-ya] a small glass of draught lager
> **un tubo** [t**oo**bo] a long tumbler of draught lager
> **un botellín** [botay-y**ee**n] 1/5-litre bottle
> **un tercio** [t**ai**rth-yo] 1/3-litre bottle

before antes [**a**ntess]
begin empezar [empeth**a**r]
when does it begin? ¿cuándo empieza? [kw**a**ndo emp-y**e**tha]
beginner el/la principiante [preentheep-y**a**ntay]
beginning: at the beginning al principio [preenth**ee**p-yo]
behind detr**á**s
behind me detrás de mí
beige beige [bay-eess]
Belgium Bélgica [b**ay**lHeeka]
believe creer [kray-**air**]
below abajo [ab**a**Ho]
belt el cinturón [theentoor**o**n]
bend (in road) la curva [k**oo**rba]
berth (on ship) el camarote [kamar**o**tay]
beside: beside the ... al l**a**do de la ...
best el mejor [meH**o**r]
better mejor
are you feeling better? ¿se siente mejor? [say s-y**e**ntay]
between entre [**e**ntray]
beyond más allá [a-y**a**]
bicycle la bicicleta [beetheekl**ay**ta]
big grande [gr**a**nday]
too big demasiado grande [demass-y**a**do]
it's not big enough no es suficientemente grande [soofeeth-yentem**ay**ntay]

bike la bicicleta [beetheekl**ay**ta]
(motorbike) la motocicleta [mototheekl**ay**ta]
bikini el bikini [beek**ee**nee]
bill la cuenta [kw**e**nta]
(US: banknote) el billete [bee-y**ay**tay]
could I have the bill, please? la cuenta, por favor

If you go out informally with a group, it is usual to share the bill equally. When somebody invites other people out, say, for his/her birthday, he or she is expected to treat you.

bin el cubo de la basura [k**oo**bo day]
bin liners las bolsas de basura
binding (ski) la atadura
bird el pájaro [p**a**Haro]
biro® el bolígrafo
birthday el cumpleaños [koomplay**a**n-yoss]
happy birthday! ¡feliz cumpleaños! [fel**ee**th]
biscuit la galleta [ga-y**e**ta]
bit: a little bit un poquito [pok**ee**to]
a big bit un pedazo grande [ped**a**tho gr**a**nday]
a bit of ... un pedazo de ...
a bit expensive un poco caro
bite (by insect) la picadura
(by dog) la mordedura
bitter (taste etc) amargo
black negro [n**ay**gro]
blanket la manta
bleach (for toilet) la lejía [leH**ee**-a]
bless you! ¡Jesús! [Hays**oo**ss]
blind ciego [th-y**ay**go]
blinds las persianas [pers-y**a**nass]
blister la ampolla [amp**o**-ya]
blocked (road, pipe) obstruido [obstrw**ee**do]
(sink) atascado
block of flats el bloque de apartamentos [bl**o**kay day]
blond rubio [r**oo**b-yo]
blood la sangre [s**a**ngray]
high blood pressure la tensión alta [tenss-y**o**n]
blouse la blusa [bl**oo**sa]
blow-dry (verb) secar a mano
I'd like a cut and blow-dry quisiera un corte y un marcado [kees-y**ai**ra oon k**o**rtay ee]
blue azul [ath**oo**l]
blusher el colorete [kolor**ay**tay]
boarding house la casa de huéspedes [w**e**spaydess]
boarding pass la tarjeta de embarque [tarH**ay**ta day emb**a**rkay]
boat el barco
(for passengers) barco de pasajeros [pasaH**ai**ross]
body el cuerpo [kw**ai**rpo]
boil (water) hervir [airb**ee**r]
boiled egg el huevo pasado por agua [w**ay**bo – **a**gwa]
boiler la caldera [kald**ai**ra]
bone el hueso [w**ay**so]
bonnet (of car) el capó

book el libro [l**ee**bro]
(verb) reservar [resairb**a**r]
can I book a seat? ¿puedo reservar un asiento? [pw**ay**do – as-y**e**nto]

•••••• DIALOGUE ••••••

I'd like to book a table for two quisiera reservar una mesa para dos personas [kees-y**ai**ra resairb**a**r **oo**na m**ay**sa]
what time would you like it booked for? ¿para qué hora le gustaría reservarla? [kay **o**ra lay goostar**ee**-a resairb**a**rla]
half past seven las siete y media
that's fine de acuerdo [day akw**ai**rdo]
and your name? ¿y su nombre es ...? [ee soo n**o**mbray]

bookshop, bookstore la librería [leebrair**ee**-a]
boot (footwear) la bota
(of car) el maletero [malet**ai**ro]
border (of country) la frontera [front**ai**ra]
bored: I'm bored estoy aburrido
boring aburrido
born: I was born in Manchester nací en Manchester [nath**ee**]
I was born in 1960 nací en mil novecientos sesenta
borrow pedir prestado
may I borrow ...? ¿puede prestarme ...? [pw**ay**day prest**a**rmay]
both los dos
bother: sorry to bother you lamento tener que molestarle [ten**ai**r kay molest**a**rlay]
bottle la botella [bot**ay**-ya]
a bottle of house red una botella de tinto de la casa [day]
bottle-opener el abrebotellas [abraybot**ay**-yass]
bottom (of person) el trasero [trass**ai**ro]
at the bottom of the ... (hill/road) al pie del/de la ... [p-y**ay** del/day]
box la caja [k**a**Ha]
(wooden) la caja de madera [mad**ai**ra]
box office la taquilla [tak**ee**-ya]
boy el chico
boyfriend el amigo
bra el sujetador [sooHetad**o**r]
bracelet la pulsera [pools**ai**ra]
brake el freno [fr**ay**no]
brandy el coñac [kon-y**a**k]
bread el pan
white bread el pan blanco
brown bread el pan moreno [mor**ay**no]
wholemeal bread el pan integral
break (verb) romper [romp**ai**r]
I've broken the ... he roto el ... [ay]
I think I've broken my ... creo que me he roto el ... [kr**ay**-o kay may]
break down averiarse [abairee-**a**rsay]

I've broken down he tenido una avería [ay – abairee-a]
breakdown la avería

> If you break down phone the **Ayuda en Carretera** (National Road Assistance Organization) on 91-7421213 at the nearest phone. For peace of mind, it might be worth taking out an insurance policy like the AA Five-Star scheme or AA Europe cover, which will pay for any on-the-spot repairs, and in the case of emergencies, ship you and all your passengers back home free of charge.

breakdown service el servicio de grúa [serbeeth-yo day groo-a]
breakfast el desayuno [desa-yoono]
break-in: I've had a break-in han entrado los ladrones en mi casa [an – ladroness]
breast el pecho [paycho]
breathe respirar
breeze la brisa [breesa]
bridge (over river) el puente [pwentay]
brief breve [braybay]
briefcase el portafolios [portafol-yoss]
bright (light etc) brillante [bree-yantay]
bright red rojo vivo [roHo beebo]
brilliant (idea, person) brillante [bree-yantay]
bring traer [tra-air]
I'll bring it back later lo devolveré después [lo daybolbairay despwess]
Britain Gran Bretaña [bretan-ya]
British británico
I'm British (man/woman) soy británico/británica
brochure el folleto [fo-yeto]
broken roto
bronchitis la bronquitis [bronkeeteess]
brooch el broche [brochay]
broom la escoba
brother el hermano [airmano]
brother-in-law el cuñado [koon-yado]
brown marrón
brown hair el pelo castaño [castan-yo]
brown eyes los ojos castaños [oHoss]
bruise el cardenal
brush (for hair, cleaning) el cepillo [thepee-yo]
(artist's) el pincel [peenthel]
bucket el cubo [koobo]
buffet car el vagón restaurante [bagon restowrantay]
buggy (for child) el cochecito de niño [kochaytheeto day neen-yo]
building el edificio [edeefeeth-yo]
bulb (light bulb) la bombilla [bombee-ya]
bull el toro

bullfight la corrida de toros [day]
bullfighter el torero [tor**ai**ro]
bullring la plaza de toros [pl**a**tha day]
bumper el parachoques [parach**o**kess]
bunk la litera [leet**ai**ra]
bureau de change (oficina de) cambio [ofeeth**ee**na day k**a**mb-yo]
burglary el robo con allanamiento de morada [a-yanam-y**e**nto]
burn la quemadura [kemad**oo**ra]
(verb) quemar [kem**a**r]
burnt: this is burnt está quemado [kem**a**do]
burst: a burst pipe la cañería rota [kan-yair**ee**-a]
bus el autobús [owtob**oo**ss]
what number bus is it to ...? ¿qué número es para ...? [kay n**oo**mairo]
when is the next bus to ...? ¿cuándo sale el próximo autobús para ...? [kw**a**ndo s**a**lay]
what time is the last bus? ¿a qué hora es el último autobús? [kay **o**ra – **oo**lteemo]
could you let me know when we get there? ¿puede avisarme cuando lleguemos allí? [pw**ay**day abees**a**rmay kw**a**ndo yeg**ay**moss a-y**ee**]

City bus tickets in Spain are purchased on the bus from the driver or in books of ten from kiosks. Drivers cannot usually change large notes and in many cities from 9 a.m. onwards it is compulsory to have the exact change for your ticket. A **bono-bus** is a ten-ticket card that has to be validated in a ticket stamping machine inside the bus. It's always cheaper than buying individual tickets. In some cities a **bono-bus** ticket can be used for an hour from the time it was first validated, even if you change buses.

•••••• DIALOGUE ••••••

does this bus go to ...? ¿este autobús va a ...? [**e**stay owtob**oo**ss ba]
no, you need a number ... no, tiene que coger el ... [t-y**ay**nay kay koH**air**]

business el negocio [neg**o**th-yo]
bus station la estación de autobuses [estath-y**o**n day owtob**oo**sess]
bus stop la parada de autobús
bust el pecho [p**ay**cho]
busy (restaurant etc) concurrido
I'm busy tomorrow estoy ocupado mañana [man-y**a**na]
but pero [p**ai**ro]
butcher's la carnicería [karneethair**ee**-a]
butter la mantequilla

[mantekee-ya]
button el botón
buy (verb) comprar
where can I buy ...? ¿dónde puedo comprar ...? [donday pwaydo]
by: by bus/car en autobús/coche
written by ... escrito por ...
by the window junto a la ventana [Hoonto]
by the sea a orillas del mar [oree-yass]
by Thursday para el jueves
bye ¡adiós! [ad-yoss]

C

cabbage el repollo [repo-yo]
cabin (on ship) el camarote [kamarotay]
cable car el teleférico [telefaireeko]
Cadiz Cádiz [kadeeth]
café la cafetería [kafetairee-a]

> Apart from coffee, tea and cakes, you can have alcoholic drinks in Spanish cafés. In many of them you can also get inexpensive light snacks and meals, normally called **platos combinados**, which usually include fish or meat and fries and salad.
> see **bar**

cagoule el chubasquero [choobaskairo]
cake el pastel [pastayl]
cake shop la pastelería [pastelairee-a]
call (verb) llamar [yamar]
(to phone) llamar (por teléfono)
what's it called? cómo se llama esto? [say yama]
he/she is called ... se llama ...
please call the doctor llame al médico, por favor [yamay]
please give me a call at 7.30 am tomorrow por favor, llámeme mañana a las siete y media de la mañana [yamamay man-yana]
please ask him to call me por favor, dígale que me llame [deegalay kay may yamay]
call back: I'll call back later volveré más tarde [bolbairay mass tarday]
(phone back) volveré a llamar [yamar]
call round: I'll call round tomorrow me paso mañana [may]
camcorder la videocámara [beeday-o kamaira]
camera la máquina de fotos [makeena]
camera shop la tienda de cámaras fotográficas [t-yenda day]
camp (verb) acampar
can we camp here? ¿se puede acampar aquí? [say pwayday – akee]
camping gas canister la bombona de butano

[bootano]

> Camping gas canisters can be bought either from a ferretería (hardware store) or from campsite shops.

campsite el camping

> In Spain it is legal to camp almost anywhere unless there is a sign prohibiting camping. The limitations include urban areas, military premises and the surroundings of campsites and touristic zones.

can la lata
a can of beer una lata de cerveza [thairbaytha]
can*: can you ...? ¿puede ...? [pwayday]
can I have ...? ¿me da ...? [may]
I can't ... no puedo ...
Canada el Canadá
Canadian canadiense [kanad-yensay]
I'm Canadian soy canadiense
canal el canal
Canaries las Islas Canarias [eeslass kanar-yass]
cancel anular [anoolar]
candies los caramelos [karamayloss]
candle la vela [bayla]
canoe la piragua [peeragwa]
canoeing el piragüismo [peeragweesmo]
can-opener el abrelatas
cap (hat) la gorra
(of bottle) el tapón
car el coche [kochay]
by car en coche
carafe la garrafa
a carafe of house white, please una garrafa de vino blanco de la casa, por favor [day beeno]
caravan la caravana [karabana]
caravan site el camping
carburettor el carburador
card (birthday etc) la tarjeta [tarHayta]
here's my (business) card aquí tiene mi tarjeta (de visita) [akee t-yaynay – day beeseeta]
cardigan la rebeca [rebayka]
cardphone el teléfono de tarjeta [telayfono day tarHeta]
careful prudente [proodentay]
be careful! ¡tenga cuidado! [kweedado]
caretaker el encargado
car ferry el ferry, el transbordador de coches [kochess]
car hire el alquiler de coches [alkeelair day]
car park el aparcamiento [aparkam-yento]
carpet la moqueta [mokayta]
carriage (of train) el vagón [bagon]
carrier bag la bolsa de plástico [day plasteeko]
carrot la zanahoria [thana-or-ya]
carry llevar [yebar]
carry-cot el capazo [kapatho]

carton el cartón
carwash el lavacoches [labak**o**chess]
case (suitcase) la maleta [mal**ay**ta]
cash el dinero [deen**air**o]
(verb) cobrar
will you cash this for me? ¿podría hacerme efectivo un cheque? [podr**ee**-a ath**air**may efekt**ee**bo oon ch**ay**kay]
cash desk la caja [k**a**Ha]
cash dispenser el cajero automático [kaH**air**o owtom**a**teeko]
cashier (man/woman) el cajero/la cajera
cassette la cassette [kas**e**t]
cassette recorder el cassette
castanets las castañuelas [kastan-yw**ay**lass]
Castile Castilla [kast**ee**-ya]
Castilian castellano [kastay-y**a**no]
castle el castillo [kast**ee**-yo]
casualty department las urgencias [oorH**e**nth-yass]
cat el gato
Catalonia Cataluña [kata-l**oo**n-ya]
catch (verb) coger [koH**air**]
where do we catch the bus to ...? ¿dónde se coge el autobús a ...? [d**o**nday say k**o**Hay]
cathedral la catedral
Catholic (adj) católico
cauliflower la coliflor
cave la cueva [kw**ay**ba]
ceiling el techo [t**ay**cho]
celery el apio [**a**p-yo]
cellar (for wine) la bodega [bod**ay**ga]
cemetery el cementerio [thement**air**-yo]
Centigrade* centígrado [thent**ee**grado]
centimetre* el centímetro [thent**ee**metro]
central central [thentr**a**l]
central heating la calefacción central [kalayfakth-y**o**n]
centre el centro [th**e**ntro]
how do we get to the city centre? ¿cómo se llega al centro? [say y**ay**ga]
cereal los cereales [theray-**a**less]
certainly desde luego [d**e**sday lw**ay**go]
certainly not desde luego que no [kay]
chair la silla [s**ee**-ya]
champagne el champán
change (money) el cambio [k**a**mb-yo]
(verb) cambiar [kamb-y**ar**]
can I change this for ...? ¿puedo cambiar esto por ...? [pw**ay**do]
I don't have any change no tengo nada suelto [sw**e**lto]
can you give me change for a 1,000 peseta note? ¿puede cambiarme un billete de mil pesetas? [pw**ay**day kamb-y**ar**may oon bee-y**ay**tay day meel pes**ay**tass]

•••••• DIALOGUE ••••••

do we have to change (trains)? ¿tenemos que cambiar de tren? [ten**ay**moss kay kamb-yar]

yes, change at Córdoba/no it's a direct train sí, cambie en Córdoba/no, es un tren directo [k**a**mb-yay]

changed: to get changed cambiarse [kamb-y**a**rsay]
chapel la capilla [kap**ee**-ya]
charge (verb) cobrar
charge card see **credit card**
cheap barato
do you have anything cheaper? tiene algo más barato? [t-y**ay**nay]
check (US) el cheque [ch**ay**kay] see **cheque**
(US: bill) la cuenta [kw**ay**nta] see **bill**
(verb) revisar [rebees**a**r]
could you check the ..., please? ¿puede revisar el ..., por favor? [pw**ay**day]
check book el talonario de cheques [ch**ay**kess]
check-in la facturación [faktoorath-y**o**n]
check in facturar
where do we have to check in? ¿dónde se factura? [d**o**nday say]
cheek la mejilla [meH**ee**-ya]
cheerio! hasta luego [**a**sta lw**ay**go]
cheers! (toast) ¡salud! [sal**oo**]
cheese el queso [k**ay**so]
chemist's la farmacia [farm**a**th-ya]

Spanish pharmacies are well-qualified to give you advice on minor ailments. There's generally one or more all-night pharmacies in bigger towns and cities. They work on a rota system and you generally find the address of the one on duty (**farmacia de guardia**) on the door of any pharmacist and in local newspapers.

cheque el cheque [ch**ay**kay]
do you take cheques? ¿aceptan cheques? [ath**e**ptan]

With most Eurocheque cards and cashline/cheque cards you can get cash from the majority of banks in Spain, including many cash dispensers (with instructions in four languages). You may have to pay a service charge of a few pounds. Eurocheques are widely accepted by shops and hotels. Also Mastercard and Visa cards can be used in cash dispensers in Spain - but you'd better find out before you go about your bank's arrangements with Spanish banks.

cheque book el talonario de

cheques [day]
cheque card la tarjeta de banco [tarHayta]
cherry la cereza [thairaytha]
chess el ajedrez [aHedreth]
chest el pecho [paycho]
chewing gum el chicle [cheeklay]
chicken el pollo [po-yo]
chickenpox la varicela [bareethela]
child (male/female) el niño [neen-yo]/la niña
children los niños
child minder la niñera [neen-yaira]
children's pool la piscina infantil [peestheena eenfanteel]
children's portion la ración pequeña (para niños) [rath-yon pekayn-ya – neen-yoss]
chin la barbilla [barbee-ya]
china la porcelana [porthelana]
Chinese (adj) chino [cheeno]
chips las patatas fritas
chocolate el chocolate [chokolatay]
milk chocolate el chocolate con leche [lechay]
plain chocolate el chocolate negro [naygro]
a hot chocolate la taza de chocolate [tatha]
choose elegir [eleHeer]
Christian name el nombre de pila [nombray day peela]
Christmas Navidad [nabeeda]
Christmas Eve Nochebuena [nochay-bwayna]
merry Christmas! ¡Feliz Navidad! [feleeth]
church la iglesia [eeglays-ya]
cider la sidra [seedra]
cigar el puro [pooro]
cigarette el cigarro [theegarro], el cigarrillo [theegarree-yo]
cigarette lighter el encendedor [enthendedor]
cinema el cine [theenay]
circle el círculo [theerkoolo] (in theatre) anfiteatro [anfeetay-atro]
city la ciudad [thee-oo-da]
city centre el centro de la ciudad [thentro day]
clean (adj) limpio [leemp-yo]
can you clean these for me? ¿puede limpiarme estos? [pwayday leemp-yarmay]
cleaning solution (for contact lenses) líquido limpiador para las lentillas [leekeedo leemp-yador – lentee-yass]
cleansing lotion la crema limpiadora [krayma leemp-yadora]
clear claro
clever listo
cliff el acantilado
climbing el alpinismo
cling film el plástico de envolver [day embolbair]
clinic la clínica
cloakroom el guardarropa [gwardarropa]
clock el reloj [reloH]
close (verb) cerrar [therrar]

•••••• DIALOGUE ••••••

what time do you close? **¿a qué hora se cierra?** [kay **o**ra say th-y**ai**rra]

we close at 8 p.m. on weekdays and 1:30 p.m. on Saturdays **cerramos a las ocho de la tarde entre semana y a la una y media los sábados** [therr**a**moss – day la t**a**rday **e**ntray]

do you close for lunch? **¿cierra al mediodía?** [th-y**ai**rra – med-yod**ee**-a]

yes, between 1 and 3.30 p.m. **sí, entre una y tres y media de la tarde** [**e**ntray – day la t**a**rday]

closed cerrado [thairr**a**do]

cloth (fabric) **la tela** [t**ay**la]

(for cleaning etc) **el trapo**

clothes la ropa

clothes line la cuerda para tender [kw**ai**rda p**a**ra tend**air**]

clothes peg la pinza de la ropa [p**ee**ntha day]

cloud la nube [n**oo**bay]

cloudy nublado

clutch el embrague [embr**a**gay]

coach (bus) **el autocar** [owtok**ar**]

(on train) **el vagón** [bag**o**n]

coach station la estación de autobuses [estath-y**o**n day owtob**oo**sess]

coach trip la excursión (en autobús) [eskoorss-y**o**n]

coast la costa

on the coast **en la costa**

coat (long coat) **el abrigo**

(jacket) **la chaqueta** [chak**ay**ta]

coathanger la percha [p**ai**rcha]

cockroach la cucaracha [kookar**a**cha]

cocoa el cacao [kak**a**-o]

coconut el coco

code (for phoning) **el prefijo** [pref**ee**Ho]

what's the (dialling) code for Málaga? **¿cuál es el prefijo de Málaga** [kwal]

coffee el café [kaf**ay**]

two coffees, please **dos cafés, por favor**

> If you ask for '**un café**' you will be given a **café sólo** which is strong black espresso-style coffee. If you want a large cup ask for a '**un café doble**' [d**o**blay]. Other types of coffee are:
>
> **un café con leche** [l**e**chay] very milky coffee
> **un cortado** with a dash of milk
> **un carajillo** [karaH**ee**-yo] with a liqueur (brandy, cognac or whisky)
> **un café descafeinado** [des-kafay-een**a**do] decaffeinated coffee (made with hot milk rather than with hot water)
> **una leche manchada** milk with a dash of coffee

coin la moneda [mon**ay**da]

Coke® la Coca-Cola

cold frío [fr**ee**-o]

I'm cold **tengo frío**

I have a cold **tengo catarro**

collapse: he's collapsed se ha desmayado [say a desma-y**a**do]
collar el cuello [kw**ay**-yo]
collect recoger [rekoH**air**]
I've come to collect ... he venido a recoger ... [ay ben**ee**do]
collect call la llamada a cobro revertido [yam**a**da – rebairt**ee**do]
college la Universidad [ooneebairseed**a**]
colour el color
do you have this in other colours? ¿tiene otros colores? [t-y**ay**nay]
colour film la película en color
comb el peine [p**ay-ee**nay]
come venir [bayn**ee**r]

•••••• DIALOGUE ••••••

where do you come from? ¿de dónde es? [day d**o**nday]
I come from Edinburgh soy de Edimburgo

come back volver [bolb**air**]
I'll come back tomorrow volveré mañana [bolbair**ay**]
come in entrar
comfortable cómodo
compact disc el compact disc
company (business) la compañía [kompan-y**ee**-a]
compartment (on train) el compartimento
compass la brújula [br**oo**-Hoola]
complain quejarse [kayH**a**rsay]
complaint la queja [k**ay**Ha]
I have a complaint tengo una queja
completely completamente [kompl**ay**tamentay]
computer el ordenador
concert el concierto [konth-y**air**to]
concussion la conmoción cerebral [kommoth-y**o**n thairebr**a**l]
conditioner (for hair) el acondicionador de pelo [akondeeth-yonad**o**r day p**ay**lo]
condom el condón
conference el congreso
confirm confirmar
congratulations! ¡enhorabuena! [enorabw**ay**na]
connecting flight el vuelo de conexión [bw**ay**lo day koneks-y**o**n]
connection el enlace [enl**a**thay]
conscious consciente [konth-y**e**ntay]
constipation el estreñimiento [estren-yeem-y**e**nto]
consulate el consulado [konsool**a**do]
contact (verb) ponerse en contacto con [pon**air**say]
contact lenses las lentes de contacto, las lentillas [l**e**ntess – lent**ee**-yass]
contraceptive el anticonceptivo [anteekonthept**ee**bo]
convenient a mano
that's not convenient eso no viene bien [b-y**ay**nay b-y**e**n]
cook (verb) cocinar [kotheen**a**r]

not cooked poco hecho [**e**cho]
cooker la cocina [koth**ee**na]
cookie la galleta [ga-y**ay**ta]
cooking utensils los utensilios de cocina [ootens**ee**l-yoss day koth**ee**na]
cool fresco [fr**ay**sko]
cork el corcho
corkscrew el sacacorchos
corner: on the corner en la esquina [esk**ee**na]
in the corner en el rincón
cornflakes los cornflakes
correct (right) correcto
corridor el pasillo [pas**ee**-yo]
cosmetics los cosméticos
cost (verb) costar
how much does it cost? ¿cuánto cuesta? [kw**a**nto kw**e**sta]
cot la cuna
cotton el algodón
cotton wool el algodón
couch (sofa) el sofá
couchette la litera [leet**ai**ra]
cough la tos
cough medicine la medicina para la tos [medeeth**ee**na]
could: could you ...? ¿podría ...?
could I have ...? quisiera ... [kees-y**ai**ra...]
I couldn't ... no podría ...
country (nation) el país [pa-**ee**ss]
(countryside) el campo
countryside el campo
couple (two people) la pareja [par**ay**Ha]
a couple of ... un par de ... [day]
courgette el calabacín [kalabath**ee**n]
courier el/la guía turístico [g**ee**-a]
course (main course etc) el plato
of course por supuesto [soopw**e**sto]
of course not ¡claro que no! [kay]
cousin (male/female) el primo [pr**ee**mo]/la prima
cow la vaca [b**a**ka]
crab el cangrejo [kangr**ay**Ho]
cracker la galleta salada [ga-y**ay**ta]
craft shop la tienda de artesanía [t-y**e**nda day artesan**ee**-a]
crash el accidente [akthee**de**ntay]
I've had a crash he tenido un accidente [ay ten**ee**do]
crazy loco
cream (on milk, in cake) la nata
(lotion) la crema [kr**ay**ma]
(colour) color crema
creche la guardería infantil [gwardair**ee**-a]
credit card la tarjeta de crédito [tarH**ay**ta day]

> Major credit cards and charge cards are accepted in many shops and also for cash advances at many banks and automatic tellers. They're not usually accepted in small shops, or inexpensive restaurants and hotels.

•••••• DIALOGUE ••••••

can I pay by credit card? ¿puedo pagar con tarjeta? [pw**ay**do]

which card do you want to use? ¿qué tarjeta quiere usar? [kay – k-y**ai**ray oos**ar**]

yes, sir sí, señor [sen-y**or**]

what's the number? ¿qué número es? [n**oo**mairo]

and the expiry date? ¿y la fecha de caducidad? [f**e**cha day kadootheed**a**]

crisps las patatas fritas (de bolsa)

crockery la loza [l**o**tha]

crossing (by sea) la travesía [trabes**ee**-a]

crossroads el cruce [kr**oo**thay]

crowd la muchedumbre [moochay-d**oo**mbray]

crowded lleno [y**ay**no]

crown (on tooth) la funda [f**oo**nda]

cruise el crucero [krooth**ai**ro]

crutches la muleta [mool**ay**ta]

cry (verb) llorar [yor**ar**]

cucumber el pepino

cup la taza [t**a**tha]

a cup of ..., please una taza de ..., por favor

cupboard el armario [arm**ar**-yo]

cure la cura [k**oo**ra]

curly rizado [reeth**a**do]

current la corriente [korr-y**e**ntay]

curtains las cortinas

cushion el cojín [koH**ee**n]

custom la costumbre [kost**oo**mbray]

Customs la aduana [adw**a**na]

cut el corte [k**o**rtay]

(verb) cortar

I've cut myself me he cortado [may ay]

cutlery los cubiertos [koob-y**ai**rtoss]

cycling el ciclismo [theekl**ee**smo]

cyclist el/la ciclista [theekl**ee**sta]

D

dad el papá

daily el periódico [pair-y**o**deeko]

damage: damaged estropeado [estropay-**a**do]

I'm sorry, I've damaged this lo siento, he estropeado esto [s-y**e**nto – ay]

damn! ¡maldita sea! [s**ay**-a]

damp (adj) húmedo [**oo**maydo]

dance el baile [b**a-ee**lay]

(verb) bailar [b**a-ee**lar]

would you like to dance? ¿quiere bailar? [k-y**ai**ray]

dangerous peligroso

Danish el danés [dan**ay**ss]

dark (adj: colour) oscuro [osk**oo**ro]

(hair) moreno [mor**ay**no]

it's getting dark está oscureciendo [oskooreth-y**e**ndo]

date*: what's the date today? ¿qué día es hoy? [kay – oy]

let's make a date for next Monday vamos a quedar para el lunes que viene

[**ba**moss a ked**ar** – kay b-**yay**nay]
dates (fruit) los dátiles [**da**teeless]
daughter la hija [**ee**Ha]
daughter-in-law la nuera [nw**ai**ra]
dawn el amanecer [amaneth**air**]
at dawn al amanecer
day el día
the day after el día siguiente [seeg-**ye**ntay]
the day after tomorrow pasado mañana [man-**ya**na]
the day before el día anterior [antair-**yo**r]
the day before yesterday anteayer [antay-a-**yair**]
every day todos los días
all day todo el día
in two days' time dentro de dos días
have a nice day! ¡que pase un buen día! [kay **pa**say oon bwen]
day trip la excursión [exkoors-**yo**n]
dead muerto [mw**ai**rto]
deaf sordo
deal (business) la transacción [transakth-**yo**n]
it's a deal trato hecho [**ay**cho]
death la muerte [mw**ai**rtay]
decaffeinated coffee el café descafeinado [kaf**ay** deskafay-een**a**do]
December diciembre [deeth-**ye**mbray]
decide decidir [detheed**ee**r]
we haven't decided yet todavía no hemos decidido [todab**ee**-a no **ay**moss detheed**ee**do]
decision la decisión [detheess-**yo**n]
deck (on ship) la cubierta [koob-**yai**rta]
deckchair la tumbona
deduct descontar
deep profundo
definitely claramente, ¡desde luego! [klara**me**ntay **de**sday lw**ay**go]
definitely not desde luego que no [kay]
degree (qualification) la carrera [karr**ai**ra]
delay el retraso
deliberately a propósito
delicatessen la charcutería [charkootair**ee**-a]
delicious delicioso [deleeth-**yo**so]
deliver repartir
delivery (of mail) el reparto
Denmark Dinamarca
dental floss el hilo dental [**ee**lo]
dentist el/la dentista

•••••• DIALOGUE ••••••

it's this one here es ésta de aquí [day ak**ee**]
this one? ¿ésta?
no, that one no, esa [**ay**sa]
here? ¿aquí?
yes sí

dentures la dentadura postiza [post**ee**tha]
deodorant el desodorante

[desodor**a**ntay]
department el departam**e**nto
department store los grandes almacenes [gr**a**ndess almath**ay**ness]
departure la sal**i**da
departure lounge la s**a**la de embarque [day emb**a**rkay]
depend: it depends depende [dep**e**nday]
it depends on ... depende de ... [day]
deposit (as security) la fianza [fee-**a**ntha]
(as part payment) el depósito
description la descripción [deskreepth-y**o**n]
dessert el postre [p**o**stray]
destination el dest**i**no
develop (photos) revelar [rebel**a**r]

•••••• DIALOGUE ••••••

could you develop these films?
¿puede revelar estos carretes? [pw**ay**day – karr**ay**tess]
when will they be ready? ¿cuándo estarán listos? [kw**a**ndo]
tomorrow afternoon mañana por la tarde [man-y**a**na por la t**a**rday]
how much is the four-hour service? ¿cuánto es el servicio de cuatro horas? [kw**a**nto ess el sairb**ee**th-yo day kw**a**tro **o**rass]

diabetic (man/woman) el diabético [dee-ab**ay**teeko]/la diabética
diabetic foods la com**i**da para diabéticos
dial marc**a**r
dialling code el prefijo [pref**ee**Ho]

The dialling code for international calls is 07. When you hear a high-pitched tone dial the country codes as follows:

UK	44
US/Canada	1
New Zealand	64
Australia	61
Ireland	353

then dial the area code and number, omitting the inital zero.

diamond el diamante [d-yam**a**ntay]
diaper el pañal [pan-y**a**l]
diarrhoea la diarrea [d-yarr**ay**-a]
diary (business etc) la agenda [aH**e**nda]
(for personal experiences) el diario [d-y**a**r-yo]
dictionary el diccionario [deekth-yon**a**r-yo]
didn't
see not
die mor**i**r
diesel el gas**o**il
diet la dieta [d-y**ay**ta]
I'm on a diet estoy a dieta
I have to follow a special diet tengo que seguir una dieta especial [kay seg**ee**r – espeth-y**a**l]
difference la diferencia [deefair**e**nth-ya]

what's the difference? ¿cuál es la diferencia? [kwal]
different diferente [deefairentay]
this one is different éste es diferente [estay]
a different table otra mesa [maysa]
difficult difícil [deefeetheel]
difficulty la dificultad [deefeekoolta]
dinghy el bote [botay]
dining room el comedor [komaydor]
dinner (evening meal) la cena [thayna]
to have dinner cenar
direct (adj) directo
is there a direct train? ¿hay un tren directo? [ī]
direction la dirección [deerekth-yon]
which direction is it? ¿en qué dirección está? [kay]
is it in this direction? ¿es por aquí? [akee]
directory enquiries información [eenformath-yon]

The number for directory enquiries is 003 for Spain; 008 for Europe, and 005 for the rest of the world.

dirt la suciedad [sooth-yayda]
dirty sucio [sooth-yo]
disabled minusválido [meenoosbaleedo]
is there access for the disabled? ¿hay acceso para minusválidos? [ī akthayso]
disappear desaparecer [dessaparethair]
it's disappeared ha desaparecido [a dessaparetheedo]
disappointed desilusionado [deseelooss-yonado]
disappointing decepcionante [dethepth-yonantay]
disaster el desastre [desastray]
disco la discoteca
discount el descuento [deskwento]
is there a discount? ¿hacen descuento? [athen]
disease la enfermedad [enfairmeda]
disgusting repugnante [repoognantay]
dish (meal) el plato
dishcloth el paño de cocina [pan-yo day kotheena]
disinfectant el desinfectante [deseenfektantay]
disk (for computer) diskette [deeskaytay]
disposable diapers los pañales (braguita) [pan-yaless brageeta]
disposable nappies los pañales (braguita)
distance la distancia [deestanth-ya]
in the distance a lo lejos [layHoss]
distilled water el agua destilada [agwa]
district el distrito

disturb molestar
diversion (detour) el desvío [desbee-o]
diving board el trampolín
divorced divorciado [deeborth-yado]
dizzy: I feel dizzy estoy mareado [maray-ado]
do hacer [athair]
  what shall we do? ¿qué hacemos? [kay athaymoss]
  how do you do it? ¿cómo se hace? [say athay]
  will you do it for me? ¿me lo puede hacer usted? [pwayday athair oostay]

•••••• DIALOGUES ••••••

how do you do? ¿qué tal? [kay]
nice to meet you encantado de conocerle [day konothairlay]
what do you do? (work) ¿a qué se dedica? [say]
I'm a teacher, and you? soy profesor, ¿y usted? [ee oostay]
I'm a student soy estudiante [estood-yantay]
what are you doing this evening? ¿qué hace esta tarde? [athay]
we're going out for a drink; do you want to join us? vamos a salir a tomar una copa; ¿nos acompaña? [bamoss – akompan-ya]

do you want cream? ¿quiere crema? [k-yairay krayma]
I do, but she doesn't yo sí, pero ella no [pairo ay-ya]

doctor el/la médico
  we need a doctor necesitamos un médico [naytheseetamoss]
  please call a doctor por favor, llame a un médico [yamay]

> British citizens should take form E111 with them. This is obtainable from post offices before you leave and should enable you to get free treatment and pay for prescriptions at the local rate.

•••••• DIALOGUE ••••••

where does it hurt? ¿dónde le duele? [donday lay dwaylay]
right here justo aquí [Hoosto akee]
does that hurt now? ¿le duele ahora? [lay dwaylay a-ora]
yes sí
take this to the chemist's lleve esto a la farmacia [yaybay – farmath-ya]

document el documento [dokoomento]
dog el perro [pairro]
doll la muñeca [moon-yayka]
domestic flight el vuelo nacional [bwaylo nath-yonal]
donkey el burro [boorro]
don't! ¡no lo haga! [aga]
  don't do that! ¡no haga eso! [ayso]
  see not
door la puerta [pwairta]
doorman el portero [portairo]
double doble [doblay]

double bed la cama de matrimonio [matreemon-yo]
double room la habitación doble [abeetath-yon doblay]
doughnut el dónut [donoot]
down: down here aquí abajo [akee abaHo]
put it down over there póngalo ahí [a-ee]
it's down there on the right está ahí a la derecha [dairecha]
it's further down the road está bajando la calle [baHando la ka-yay]
downhill skiing el esquí alpino [ayskee alpeeno]
downmarket (restaurant etc) barato
downstairs abajo [abaHo]
dozen la docena [dothayna]
half a dozen media docena [mayd-ya]
drain el desagüe [desagway]
draught beer la cerveza de grifo [thairbaytha day]
draughty: it's draughty hay corriente [ī korr-yentay]
drawer el cajón [kaHon]
drawing el dibujo [deebooHo]
dreadful horrible [orreeblay]
dream el sueño [swayn-yo]
dress el vestido [besteedo]
dressed: to get dressed vestirse [besteersay]
dressing (for cut) el vendaje [bendaHay]
salad dressing el aliño [aleen-yo]
dressing gown la bata
drink (alcoholic) la copa
(non-alcoholic) la bebida
(verb) beber [bebair]
a cold drink una bebida fría
can I get you a drink? ¿quiere beber algo? [k-yairay]
what would you like (to drink)? ¿qué le apetece beber? [kay lay apetaythay]
no thanks, I don't drink no gracias, no bebo [grath-yass no baybo]
I'll just have a drink of water voy a beber sólo agua [boy – agwa]

> In Spain it is usual to have water and table wine (very often with **gaseosa** [gasay-osa] (lemonade) with your meal. It is also customary to have a drink (**aperitivo**) and a snack (**tapa**) just before the lunchtime meal either at home or in a bar.
> see **bar**

drinking water agua potable [agwa potablay]
is this drinking water? ¿esto es agua potable?
drive (verb) conducir [kondootheer]
we drove here vinimos en coche [beenemoss en kochay]
I'll drive you home te llevaré a casa en el coche [tay yebaray – kochay]

Most foreign driver's licences are honoured in Spain – including all EC, US and Canadian ones – but an international Driver's Licence is an easy way to set your mind at rest. If you're bringing your own car, you must have a green card from your insurers, and a bail bond or extra coverage for legal costs is also worth having, since if you do have an accident, it'll be your fault, as a foreigner, regardless of the circumstances. Without a bail bond, both you and the car could be locked up pending investigation. Away from main roads, you yield to vehicles approaching from the right. Speed limits are posted – maximum on urban roads is 60kph, other roads 90kph, motorways 120kph – and (on the main highways at least) speed traps are common. If you're stopped for any violation, the Spanish police can and usually will levy a stiff on-the-spot fine before letting you go on your way, especially since as a foreigner you're unlikely to want, or be able to appear in court. The legal alcohol limit when driving is .08% but do not drink and drive.

driver (man/woman) el conductor [kondookt**o**r]/la conduct**o**ra
driving licence el permiso de conducir [pairm**ee**so day kondooth**ee**r]
drop: just a drop, please (of drink) un poquito [pok**ee**to]
drug la medicina [maydeeth**ee**na]
drugs (narcotics) la dr**o**ga
drunk (adj) borr**a**cho
drunken driving conducir en est**a**do de embriaguez [kondooth**ee**r – embr-yag**e**th]
dry (adj) seco [s**ay**ko]
(sherry) fino
dry-cleaner la tintorería [teentorair**ee**-a]
duck el p**a**to
due: he was due to arrive yesterday tenía que llegar ayer [ten**ee**-a kay yeg**a**r a-y**air**]
when is the train due? ¿cuándo tiene el tren la llegada? [kw**a**ndo t-y**ay**nay – yeg**a**da]
dull (pain) sordo
(weather) gris [greess]
dummy (baby's) el chupete [choop**ay**tay]
during durante [door**a**ntay]
dust el polvo [p**o**lbo]
dusty polvoriento [polbor-y**e**nto]
dustbin el cubo de la bas**u**ra [k**oo**bo day]
duty-free (goods) (los prod**u**ctos) duty free
duty-free shop la tienda de

duty free [t-yenda day]
duvet el edredón

E

each cada
how much are they each? ¿cuánto es cada uno? [kwanto]
ear la oreja [orayHa]
earache: I have earache tengo dolor de oídos [o-eedoss]
early temprano
early in the morning por la mañana temprano [man-yana]
I called by earlier vine antes [beenay antess]
earring el pendiente [pend-yentay]
east este [estay]
in the east en el este
Easter la Semana Santa
easy fácil [fatheel]
eat comer [komair]
we've already eaten, thanks ya hemos comido, gracias [aymoss]

eating habits
Eating times in Spain are different from the rest of the Continent. Spaniards usually have a very light breakfast **desayuno** [desa-yoono] consisting of coffee and biscuits or a cake or bread and butter and jam. The main meal, **la** → **comida** or **el almuerzo** [al-mwairtho], is taken sometime in between 1.30 and 3.30. It usually consists of three courses: a hot soup or stew; a second course of fish or meat, followed by fruit and coffee. **La cena** [thayna] (dinner), sometime between 8 and 10.30 p.m. or even later, is not as substantial and very often it's just an informal snack. Some people have a mid-morning snack, an afternoon snack (around 6 p.m.) called a **merienda** and an **aperitivo** just before the afternoon meal.

eau de toilette el agua de baño [agwa day ban-yo]
EC la CE [thay-ay]
economy class la clase turista [klassay]
Edinburgh Edimburgo [edeemboorgo]
egg el huevo [waybo]
eggplant la berenjena [berenHayna]
either: either ... or ... o ... o ...
either of them cualquiera de ellos [kwalk-yaira day ay-yoss]
elastic el elástico
elastic band la goma elástica
elbow el codo
electric eléctrico
electrical appliances los electrodomésticos
electric fire la estufa eléctrica

electrician el electricista [elektreetheesta]
electricity la electricidad [elektreetheeda]
see voltage
elevator el ascensor [asthensor]
else: something else algo más
somewhere else en otra parte [partay]

•••••• DIALOGUE ••••••

would you like anything else? ¿quiere algo más? [k-yairay]
no, nothing else, thanks nada más, gracias

embassy la embajada [embaHada]
emergency la emergencia [emairHenth-ya]
this is an emergency! ¡es una emergencia!
emergency exit la salida de emergencia
empty vacío [bathee-o]
end el final [feenal]
(verb) terminar [tairmeenar]
at the end of the street al final de la calle [day la ka-yay]
when does it end? ¿cuándo termina? [kwando tairmeena]
engaged (toilet) ocupado
(telephone) comunicando
(to be married) prometido
engine (car) el motor
England Inglaterra [eenglatairra]
English inglés [eenglayss]
I'm English (man/woman) soy inglés/inglesa
do you speak English? ¿habla inglés? [abla]
enjoy: to enjoy oneself divertirse [deebairteersay]

•••••• DIALOGUE ••••••

how did you like the film? ¿le gustó la película? [lay goosto]
I enjoyed it very much, did you enjoy it? me gustó mucho, ¿le gustó a usted? [may – moocho – lay – oostay]

enjoyable entretenido
enlargement (of photo) la ampliación [ampl-yath-yon]
enormous enorme [enormay]
enough suficiente [soofeeth-yentay]
there's not enough no hay bastante [ī bastantay]
it's not big enough no es suficientemente grande [soofeeth-yentementay]
that's enough es suficiente
entrance la entrada
envelope el sobre [sobray]
epileptic epiléptico
equipment el equipo [ekeepo]
error el error
especially especialmente [espeth-yalmentay]
essential imprescindible [eemprestheendeeblay]
it is essential that ... es imprescindible que ... [kay]
EU UE [oo-ay]
Eurocheque el eurocheque [ay-oorochekay]
Eurocheque card la tarjeta

eurocheque [tarHayta]
Europe Europa [ay-ooropa]
European europeo [ay-ooropay-o]
European Union la Unión Europea [oon-yon]
even (including) incluso [eenklooso]
even if ... incluso si ...
evening (early evening) la tarde [tarday]
(after nightfall) la noche [nochay]
this evening esta tarde/noche
in the evening por la tarde/noche
evening meal la cena [thayna]
eventually finalmente [feenalmentay]
ever alguna vez [beth]

•••••• DIALOGUE ••••••

have you ever been to Barcelona?
¿ha estado alguna vez en Barcelona? [a]
yes, I was there two years ago sí, estuve allí hace dos años
[estoobay a-yee athay – an-yoss]

every cada
every day todos los días
everyone todos
everything todo
everywhere en todas partes [partess]
exactly! ¡exactamente! [exactamentay]
exam el examen
example el ejemplo [eHaymplo]
for example por ejemplo
excellent excelente [esthelentay]
excellent! ¡estupendo!
except excepto [esthepto]
excess baggage el exceso de equipaje [esthayso day ekeepaHay]
exchange rate el cambio [kamb-yo]
exciting emocionante [emoth-yonantay]
excuse me (to get past) con permiso
(to get attention) ¡por favor! [fabor]
(to say sorry) perdone [pairdonay]
exhaust (pipe) el tubo de escape [toobo day eskapay]
exhausted (tired) agotado
exhibition la exposición [exposeeth-yon]
exit la salida
where's the nearest exit? ¿cuál es la salida más próxima? [kwal]
expect esperar [espairar]
expensive caro
experienced con experiencia [espair-yenth-ya]
explain explicar [espleekar]
can you explain that? ¿puede explicármelo? [pwayday]
express (mail) urgente [oorHentay]
(train) expreso [esprayso]
extension (phone) extensión [estens-yon]
extension 221, please

extensión doscientos veintiuno, por favor
extension lead el alargador
extra: can we have an extra one? ¿nos puede dar otro? [pwayday]
do you charge extra for that? ¿esto tiene recargo? [t-yaynay]
extraordinary extraordinario [estra-ordeenar-yo]
extremely extremadamente [estremadamentay]
eye el ojo [oHo]
will you keep an eye on my suitcase for me? ¿puede cuidarme la maleta? [pwayday kweedarmay la malayta]
eyebrow pencil el lápiz de cejas [lapeeth day thayHass]
eye drops el colirio [koleer-yo]
eyeglasses las gafas
eyeliner el lápiz de ojos [lapeeth day oHoss]
eye make-up remover el desmaquillador de ojos [desmakee-yador]
eye shadow la sombra de ojos

F

face la cara
factory la fábrica
Fahrenheit* Fahrenheit
faint (verb) desmayarse [desma-yarsay]
she's fainted se ha desmayado [say a desma-yado]
I feel faint estoy mareado [maray-ado]
fair la feria [fair-ya]
(adj) justo [Hoosto]
fairly bastante [bastantay]
fake la falsificación [falseefeekath-yon]
Fall el otoño [oton-yo]
see **autumn**
fall caerse [ka-airsay]
she's had a fall se ha caído [say a ka-eedo]
false falso [fal-so]
family la familia [fameel-ya]
famous famoso
fan (electrical) el ventilador [benteelador]
(hand held) el abanico
(sports) el/la hincha [eencha]
fan belt la correa del ventilador [korray-a del benteelador]
fantastic fantástico
far lejos [layHoss]

DIALOGUE

is it far from here? ¿está lejos de aquí? [day akee]
no, not very far no, no muy lejos [mwee]
well how far? bueno, ¿cuánto? [bwayno kwanto]
it's about 20 kilometres unos veinte kilómetros

fare el precio [prayth-yo]
farm la granja [granHa]
fashionable de moda
fast rápido
fat (person) gordo

(on meat) la **grasa**
father el padre [padray]
father-in-law el suegro [swaygro]
faucet el grifo [greefo]
fault el defecto
sorry, it was my fault lo siento, fue culpa mía [s-yento fway koolpa mee-a]
it's not my fault no es culpa mía
faulty defectuoso [dayfektwoso]
favourite favorito [faboreeto]
fax el fax
(verb: person) mandar un fax a
(document) mandar por fax
February febrero [febrairo]
feel sentir
I feel hot tengo calor
I feel unwell no me siento bien [may s-yento b-yen]
I feel like going for a walk me apetece dar un paseo [apetaythay – pasay-o]
how are you feeling today? ¿qué tal se encuentra hoy? [kay tal say enkwentra oy]
I'm feeling better me siento mejor [mayHor]
felt-tip (pen) el rotulador
fence la valla [ba-ya]
fender el parachoques [parachokess]
ferry el ferry
festival el festival [festeebal]
fetch: I'll fetch him yo iré a recogerle [eeray a raykoHairlay]
will you come and fetch me later? ¿quiere venir a buscarme más tarde? [k-yairay beneer a booskarmay mass tarday]
feverish con fiebre [f-yaybray]
few: a few unos pocos
a few days unos pocos días
fiancé el novio [nob-yo]
fiancée la novia
field el campo
fight la pelea [pelay-a]
figs los higos [eegoss]
fill (verb) llenar [yenar]
fill in rellenar [ray-yenar]
do I have to fill this in? ¿tengo que rellenar esto? [kay]
fill up llenar [yenar]
fill it up, please lleno, por favor [yayno]
filling (in cake, sandwich) el relleno [ray-yeno]
(in tooth) el empaste [empastay]
film (movie, for camera) la película

•••••• DIALOGUE ••••••

do you have this kind of film? ¿tiene películas de este tipo? [t-yaynay – day estay]
yes, how many exposures? sí, ¿de cuántas fotos? [kwantass]
36 treinta y seis

film processing el revelado [rebelado]
filter coffee el café de filtro [kafay day feeltro]
filter papers los filtros
filthy sucísimo [sootheeseemo]
find (verb) encontrar

I can't find it no lo encuentro [enkw**e**ntro]
I've found it lo he encontr**a**do [ay]
find out enterarse [enter**a**rsay]
could you find out for me? ¿me lo puede preguntar? [may lo pw**ay**day pregoont**a**r]
fine (weather) bueno [bw**ay**no]
(noun) la multa [m**oo**lta]

•••••• DIALOGUES ••••••

how are you? ¿cómo estás?
I'm fine, thanks bien, gracias [b-yen gr**a**th-yass]

is that OK? ¿va bien así? [ba]
that's fine, thanks está bien, gracias

finger el dedo [d**ay**do]
finish (verb) terminar [tairmeen**a**r], acabar
I haven't finished yet no he terminado todavía [ay tairmeen**a**do todab**ee**-a]
when does it finish? ¿cuándo termina? [kw**a**ndo term**ee**na]
fire: fire! ¡fuego! [fw**ay**go]
can we light a fire here? ¿se puede encender fuego aquí? [say pw**ay**day enthend**air** – ak**ee**]
it's on fire está ardiendo [ard-y**e**ndo]
fire alarm la alarma de incendios [day eenth**e**nd-yoss]
fire brigade los bomberos [bomb**air**oss]

> In the event of a fire, the number to ring is 080.

fire escape la salida de incendios [day eenth**e**nd-yoss]
fire extinguisher el extintor [esteent**o**r]
first primero [preem**air**o]
I was first fui el primero [fwoo-ee]
at first al principio [preenth**ee**p-yo]
the first time la primera vez [beth]
first on the left la primera a la izquierda [eethk-y**air**da]
first aid primeros auxilios [owks**ee**l-yoss]
first aid kit el botiquín [boteek**ee**n]
first class (travel etc) de primera (clase) [preem**air**a kl**a**say]
first floor la primera planta
(US) la planta baja [b**a**Ha]
first name el nombre de pila [n**o**mbray day]
fish el pez [peth]
(food) el pescado
fishing village el pueblo de pescadores [pw**e**blo day peskad**o**ress]
fishmonger's la pescadería [peskadair**ee**-a]
fit (attack) el ataque [at**a**kay]
fit: it doesn't fit me no me viene bien [b-y**ay**nay b-yen]
fitting room el probador
fix (verb) arreglar

(arrange) fijar [feeHar]
can you fix this? ¿puede arreglar esto? [pwayday]
fizzy con gas
flag la bandera [bandaira]
flannel la manopla
flash (for camera) el flash
flat (noun: apartment) el piso
(adj) llano [yano]
I've got a flat tyre tengo un pinchazo [peenchatho]
flavour el sabor
flea la pulga
flight el vuelo [bwaylo]
flight number el número de vuelo [noomairo day]
flippers las aletas [alaytass]
flood la inundación [eenoondath-yon]
floor (of room) el suelo [swaylo]
(of building) el piso
on the floor en el suelo
florist la floristería [floreestairee-a]
flour la harina [areena]
flower la flor
flu la gripe [greepay]
fluent: he speaks fluent Spanish domina el castellano [kastay-yano]
fly la mosca
(verb) volar [bolar]
can we fly there? ¿podemos ir en avión allí? [podaymoss eer en ab-yon a-yee]
fly in llegar en avión [yegar]
fly out irse en avión [eersay]
fog la niebla [n-yebla]
foggy: it's foggy hay niebla [ī]
folk dancing el baile tradicional [ba-eelay tradeeth-yonal]
folk music la música popular [mooseeka popoolar]
follow seguir [segeer]
follow me sígame [seegamay]
food la comida
food poisoning la intoxicación alimenticia [eentoxeekath-yon aleementeeth-ya]
food shop/store la tienda de comestibles [t-yenda day komesteebless]
foot* el pie [p-yay]
on foot a pie
football (game) el fútbol
(ball) el balón
football match el partido de fútbol
for para, por
do you have something for ...? (headache/diarrhoea etc) ¿tiene algo para ...? [t-yaynay]

•••••• DIALOGUES ••••••

who's the chicken paella for?
¿para quién es la paella con pollo?
[k-yen ess la pa-ay-ya con po-yo]
that's for me es para mí
and this one? ¿y ésta? [ee]
that's for her ésa es para ella
[aysa – ay-ya]

where do I get the bus for Granada? ¿dónde se coge el autobús para Granada? [donday say koHay]
the bus for Granada leaves from Plaza de España el autobús para

Granada sale de la Plaza de España [salay day]

how long have you been here for? ¿cuánto tiempo lleva aquí? [kwanto t-yempo yayba akee]
I've been here for two days, how about you? llevo aquí dos días, ¿y usted? [yaybo – ee oostay]
I've been here for a week llevo aquí una semana

forehead la frente [frentay]
foreign extranjero [estranHairo]
foreigner (man/woman) el extranjero/la extranjera
forest el bosque [boskay]
forget olvidar [olbeedar]
I forget no me acuerdo [no may akwairdo]
I've forgotten me he olvidado [ay olbeedado]
fork el tenedor
(in road) la bifurcación [beefoorkath-yon]
form (document) el impreso [eemprayso]
formal (dress) de etiqueta [day eteekayta]
fortnight quince días [keenthay]
fortunately afortunadamente [afortoonadamentay]
forward: could you forward my mail? ¿puede enviarme el correo? [pwayday emb-yarmay el korray-o]
forwarding address la nueva dirección [nwayba deerekth-yon]

foundation (make-up) la crema base [krayma basay]
fountain la fuente [fwentay]
foyer (of hotel, theatre) el hall [Hol]
fracture la fractura [fraktoora]
France Francia [franth-ya]
free libre [leebray]
(no charge) gratuito [gratweeto]
is it free (of charge)? ¿es gratis?
freeway la autopista [owtopeesta]
freezer el congelador [konHaylador]
French francés [franthess]
French fries las patatas fritas
frequent frecuente [frekwentay]
how frequent is the bus to Seville? ¿cada cuánto tiempo hay autobús a Sevilla? [kwanto t-yempo ī]
fresh fresco
fresh orange el zumo de naranja natural [thoomo de naranHa natooral]
Friday viernes [b-yairness]
fridge el frigorífico
fried frito
fried egg el huevo frito [waybo]
friend (male/female) el amigo/la amiga
friendly simpático
from de, desde [day, desday]
when does the next train from Tarragona arrive? ¿cuándo llega el próximo tren de Tarragona? [kwando yayga]
from Monday to Friday de

lunes a viernes [day]
from next Thursday desde el próximo jueves

• • • • • • DIALOGUE • • • • • •

where are you from? ¿de dónde es usted? [day donday ess oostay]
I'm from Slough soy de Slough [soy day]

front la parte delantera [partay delantaira]
in front delante [delantay]
in front of the hotel delante del hotel
at the front delante
frost la escarcha
frozen congelado [konHaylado]
frozen food los congelados
fruit la fruta
fruit juice el zumo de frutas [thoomo]
fry freír [fray-eer]
frying pan la sartén
full lleno [yayno]
it's full of ... está lleno de ... [day]
I'm full estoy lleno/llena
full board pensión completa [pens-yon komplayta]
fun: it was fun fue muy divertido [fway mwee deebairteedo]
funeral el funeral [foonairal]
funny (strange) raro
(amusing) gracioso [grath-yoso]
furniture los muebles [mwaybless]
further más allá [a-ya]
it's further down the road está más adelante [adelantay]

• • • • • • DIALOGUE • • • • • •

how much further is it to Cáceres? ¿cuánto queda para Cáceres? [kwanto kayda]
about 5 kilometres unos cinco kilómetros

fuse el fusible [fooseeblay]
the lights have fused se han fundido los plomos [say an]
fuse box la caja de fusibles [kaHa day fooseebless]
fuse wire el plomo
future el futuro [footooro]
in the future en lo sucesivo [sootheseebo]

G

gallon* el galón
game (cards etc) el juego [Hwaygo]
(match) el partido
(meat) la caza [catha]
garage (for fuel) la gasolinera [gasoleenaira]
(for repairs) el taller (de reparaciones) [ta-yair day reparath-yoness]
(for parking) el garaje [garaHay]
garden el jardín [Hardeen]
garlic el ajo [aHo]
gas el gas
(US) la gasolina
see petrol
gas cylinder (camping gas) la bombona de gas

gasoline la gasolina
see **petrol**
gas permeable lenses las lentillas porosas [lent**ee**-yass]
gas station la gasolinera [gasoleen**ai**ra]
gate la puerta [pw**ai**rta]
(at airport) la puerta de embarque [emb**a**rkay]
gay el gay
gay bar el bar gay
gears la marcha
gearbox la caja de cambios [k**a**Ha day k**a**mb-yoss]
gear lever la palanca de velocidades [belotheed**a**dess]
general general [Hener**a**l]
gents (toilet) el aseo de caballeros [as**ay**-o day kaba-y**ai**ross]
genuine (antique etc) genuino [Henw**ee**no]
German alemán
German measles la rubéola [roobay-**o**la]
Germany Alemania [alem**a**n-ya]
Gerona Gerona [Her**o**na]
get (fetch) traer [tr**a**-air]
will you get me another one, please? me quiere traer otro, por favor [may kee**ai**ray]
how do I get to ...? ¿cómo se va a ...? [say ba]
do you know where I can get them? ¿sabe dónde las puedo comprar? [s**a**bay d**o**nday lass pw**ay**do]

DIALOGUE

can I get you a drink? ¿puedo ofrecerle algo de beber? [pw**ay**do ofreth**air**-lay – day beb**air**]
no, I'll get this one; what would you like? no, ésta la pago yo; ¿qué le apetece? [kay lay apayt**ay**thay]
a glass of red wine un vaso de vino tinto [b**a**so day b**ee**no t**ee**nto]

get back (return) volver [bolb**air**]
get in (arrive) llegar [yeg**a**r]
get off bajarse [baH**a**rsay]
where do I get off? ¿dónde tengo que bajarme? [d**o**nday – kay baH**a**rmay]
get on (to train etc) subirse [soob**ee**rsay]
get out (of car etc) bajarse [baH**a**rsay]
get up (in the morning) levantarse [lebant**a**rsay]
gift el regalo

> Some Spaniards give presents at Christmas, but they all exchange presents on the sixth of January on **la noche de los Reyes Magos** (Night of The Three Wise Men – Twelfth Night).

gift shop la tienda de regalos [t-y**e**nda]
gin la ginebra [Heen**ay**bra]
a gin and tonic, please un gintónic, por favor [Heent**o**neek]
girl la chica [ch**ee**ka]

girlfriend la novia [nob-ya]
give dar
can you give me some change? ¿me puede dar cambio? [may pwayday – kamb-yo]
I gave it to him se lo dí a él [say]
will you give this to ...? ¿podría entregarle esto a ...? [entregarlay]

•••••• DIALOGUE ••••••

how much do you want for this? ¿cuánto quiere por esto? [kwanto k-yairay]
1,000 pesetas mil pesetas [pesaytass]
I'll give you 800 pesetas le doy ochocientas pesetas [lay]

give back devolver [debolbair]
glad alegre [alegray]
glass (material) el cristal [kreestal]
(tumbler) el vaso [baso]
(wine glass) la copa
a glass of wine un vaso de vino [day beeno]
glasses las gafas
gloves los guantes [gwantess]
glue el pegamento
go (verb) ir [eer]
we'd like to go to the swimming-pool nos gustaría ir a la piscina [peestheena]
where are you going? ¿adónde va? [adonday ba]
where does this bus go? ¿adónde va este autobús? [estay]
let's go! ¡vamos! [bamoss]
she's gone (left) se ha marchado [say a]
where has he gone? ¿dónde se ha ido? [donday – eedo]
I went there last week fui allí la semana pasada [fwee a-yee]
go away irse [eersay]
go away! ¡váyase! [bayasay]
go back (return) volver [bolbair]
go down (the stairs etc) bajar [baHar]
go in entrar
go out (in the evening) salir
do you want to go out tonight? ¿quiere salir esta noche? [k-yairay – nochay]
go through pasar por
go up (the stairs etc) subir
goat la cabra
God Dios [d-yoss]
goggles las gafas protectoras
gold el oro
golf el golf
golf course el campo de golf
good bueno [bwayno]
good! ¡muy bien! [mwee b-yen]
it's no good es inútil [eenooteel]
goodbye adiós [ad-yoss]
good evening buenas tardes [bwenass tardess]
Good Friday el Viernes Santo [b-yairness]

> Good Friday is a public holiday in Spain. All over the country, but especially in the south, there are religious processions that will make it almost impossible to drive in large towns and cities.

good morning buenos **dí**as [bw**ay**noss]
good night b**ue**nas noches [n**o**chess]
goose el g**a**nso
got: we've got to ... tenemos que ... [tayn**ay**moss kay]
have you got any apples? ¿tiene manz**a**nas? [t-y**ay**nay]
government el gobierno [gob-y**ai**rno]
gradually gradualmente [gradwalm**e**ntay]
grammar la gram**á**tica
gram(me) el gr**a**mo
granddaughter la nieta [n-y**ay**ta]
grandfather el abuelo [abw**ay**lo]
grandmother la ab**ue**la
grandson el nieto [n-y**ay**to]
grapefruit el pomelo [pom**ay**lo]
grapefruit juice el zumo de pomelo [th**oo**mo]
grapes las uvas [**oo**bass]
grass la hierba [y**ai**rba]
grateful agradecido [agradeth**ee**do]
gravy la s**a**lsa
great (excellent) muy bueno [mwee bw**ay**no]
that's great! ¡estupendo! [estoop**e**ndo]
a great success un gran **é**xito
Great Britain Gran Bretaña [bret**a**nya]
Greece Grecia [gr**ay**th-ya]
greedy comil**ó**n
Greek (adj) griego [gr-y**ay**go]
green verde [b**ai**rday]
green card (car insurance) la c**a**rta verde
greengrocer's la frutería [frootair**ee**-a]
grey gris
grill la parrilla [parr**ee**-ya]
grilled a la parrilla
grocer's (la tienda de) comestibles [t-y**e**nda day komest**ee**bless]
ground el suelo [sw**ay**lo]
on the ground en el suelo
ground floor la pl**a**nta baja [b**a**Ha]
group el gr**u**po
guarantee la garantía
is it guaranteed? ¿est**á** garantizado? [garanteeth**a**do]
guest (man/woman) el invitado [eembeet**a**do]/la invit**a**da
guesthouse la c**a**sa de huéspedes [day w**e**spedess] see hotel
guide el/la guía [g**ee**-a]
guidebook la guía
guided tour la visita con guía [bees**ee**ta]
guitar la guitarra [geet**a**rra]
gum (in mouth) la encía [enth**ee**-a]
gun la pist**o**la
gym el gimnasio [Heemn**a**s-yo]

H

hair el pelo [p**ay**lo]
hairbrush el cepillo p**a**ra el pelo [thep**ee**-yo]
haircut el corte de pelo [k**o**rtay]
hairdresser's (men's) la barbería (women's) la peluquería [pelookair**ee**-a]
hairdryer el secad**o**r de pelo [day p**ay**lo]
hair gel el fijador (p**a**ra el pelo) [feehad**o**r]
hairgrips la horquilla [ork**ee**-ya]
hair spray la l**a**ca
half* la mitad [la meet**a**]
half an hour media hora [m**ay**d-ya **o**ra]
half a litre medio l**i**tro
about half that aproximadamente la mitad de eso [aproximadam**e**ntay – day **ay**so]
half board la media pensión [pens-y**o**n]
half-bottle la botella pequeña [bot**ay**-ya pek**ay**n-ya]
half fare el medio billete [m**ay**d-yo bee-y**ay**tay]
half price la mitad del precio [meet**a** del pr**e**th-yo]
ham el jamón [Ham**o**n]

> **Jamón serrano** is cured ham, similar to Parma ham. **Jamón de York** or **jamón cocido** is similar to British ham. Both kinds of **jamón** are sold in **charcuterías** in thin slices and are used in sandwiches, starters and a variety of dishes. **Jamón serrano** is also sold as a whole leg and is often seen hanging in **charcuterías** and bars. The best kind of **jamón serrano** is called **pata negra**.

hamburger la hamburguesa [amboorg**ay**sa]
hammer el martillo [mart**ee**-yo]
hand la m**a**no
handbag el b**o**lso
handbrake el freno de m**a**no [fr**ay**no day]
handkerchief el pañuelo [pan-yw**ay**lo]
handle (on door) la manilla [man**ee**-ya]
(on suitcase etc) el **a**sa
hand luggage el equipaje de mano [ekeep**a**hay]
hang-gliding el **a**la delta
hangover la res**a**ca
I've got a hangover tengo resaca
happen suceder [soothed**ai**r]
what's happening? ¿qué pasa? [kay]
what has happened? ¿qué ha pas**a**do? [a]
happy contento
I'm not happy about this **e**sto no me agr**a**da [may]
harbour el puerto [pw**ai**rto]
hard duro [d**oo**ro]

(difficult) difícil [deef**ee**theel]
hard-boiled egg el huevo duro [w**ay**bo]
hard lenses las lentillas duras [lent**ee**-yass]
hardly apenas [ap**ay**nass]
hardly ever casi nunca
hardware shop la ferretería [fairretair**ee**-a]
hat el sombrero
hate (verb) odiar
have* tener [ten**air**]
can I have a ...? ¿me da ...? [may]
do you have ...? ¿tiene ...? [t-y**ay**nay]
what'll you have? ¿qué va a tomar? [kay ba]
I have to leave now tengo que dejarle ahora [dayH**a**rlay a-**o**ra]
do I have to ...? ¿tengo que ...?
can we have some ...? ¿nos pone ...? [p**o**nay]
hayfever la fiebre del heno [f-y**ay**bray del **ay**no]
hazelnut la avellana [abay-y**a**na]
he* él
head la cabeza [kab**ay**tha]
headache el dolor de cabeza
headlights el faro
headphones los auriculares [owreekool**a**ress]
health food shop la tienda naturista [t-y**e**nda natoor**ee**sta]
healthy sano
hear oir [o-**ee**r]

•••••• DIALOGUE ••••••
can you hear me? ¿me oye? [may **oy**-ay]
I can't hear you, could you repeat that? no le oigo, podría repetirlo [lay **oy**go podr**ee**-a]

hearing aid el aparato del oído [o-**ee**do]
heart el corazón [korath**o**n]
heart attack el infarto
heat el calor
heater (in room) el calefactor
(in car) la calefacción [kalayfakth-y**o**n]
heating la calefacción
heavy pesado
heel (of foot) el talón
(of shoe) el tacón
could you heel these? ¿podría cambiarles los tacones? [kamb-y**a**rless – tak**o**ness]
heelbar el zapatero [thapat**ai**ro]
height la altura
helicopter el helicóptero
hello ¡hola! [**o**la]
(answer on phone) ¡dígame! [d**ee**gamay]
helmet el casco
help la ayuda [a-y**oo**da]
(verb) ayudar [a-yood**a**r]
help! ¡socorro!
can you help me? ¿puede ayudarme? [pw**ay**day a-yood**a**rmay]
thank you very much for your help gracias por su ayuda
helpful amable [am**a**blay]
hepatitis la hepatitis

[epat**ee**teess]
her*: I haven't seen her no la he visto [ay]
to her a ella [**ay**-ya]
with her con ella
for her para ella
that's her ésa es (ella) [**ay**sa]
that's her towel ésa es su toalla
herbal tea el té de hierbas [t**ay** day y**ai**rbass]
herbs las hierbas
here aquí [ak**ee**]
here is/are ... aquí está/están ...
here you are (offering) tenga
hers* (el) suyo [s**oo**-yo], (la) suya
that's hers es de ella [day **ay**-ya], es suyo/suya
hey! ¡oiga!
hi! (hello) ¡hola! [**o**la]
hide (verb) esconder [eskond**air**]
high alto
highchair la silla alta para bebés [s**ee**-ya – bayb**ay**ss]
highway (US) la autopista [owtop**ee**sta]
hill la colina
him*: I haven't seen him no le he visto [lay ay]
to him a él
with him con él
for him para él
that's him ése es (él) [**ay**say]
hip la cadera [kad**ai**ra]
hire: (verb) alquilar [alkeel**a**r]
for hire de alquiler [alkeel**air**]
where can I hire a bike? ¿dónde puedo alquilar una bicicleta? [d**o**nday pw**ay**do]
see rent
his*: it's his car es su coche
that's his eso de él [**ay**so day], eso es suyo [s**oo**-yo]
hit (verb) golpear [golpay-**a**r]
hitch-hike hacer autostop [ath**air** owtost**o**p]
hobby el pasatiempo [pasat-y**e**mpo]
hold (verb) sostener [sostayn**air**]
hole el agujero [agooH**ai**ro]
holiday las vacaciones [bakath-y**o**ness]
on holiday de vacaciones
home la casa
at home (in my house) en casa (in my country) en mi país [pa-**ee**ss]
we go home tomorrow volvemos a casa mañana [bolb**ay**moss]
honest honrado [onr**a**do]
honey la miel [m-yel]
honeymoon la luna de miel [l**oo**na day]
hood (US) el capó
hope la esperanza [espair**a**ntha]
I hope so espero que sí [esp**ai**ro kay]
I hope not espero que no
hopefully it won't rain no lloverá, eso espero [no yobair**a** **ay**so]
horn (of car) la bocina [both**ee**na]
horrible horrible [orr**ee**blay]

horse el caballo [kab**a**-yo]
horse riding la equitación [ekeetath-y**o**n]
hospital el hospital [ospeet**a**l]
hospitality la hospitalidad [ospeetaleed**a**]
thank you for your hospitality gracias por su hospitalidad [soo]
hot caliente [kal-y**e**ntay]
(spicy) picante [peek**a**ntay]
I'm hot tengo calor
it's hot today hoy hace calor [oy **a**thay]
hotel el hotel [ot**e**l]

> The one thing all travellers need to master is the elaborate variety of accommodation. Least expensive of all are **fondas** (identifiable by a square blue sign with a white **F** on it, and often positioned above a bar), closely followed by **casas de huéspedes** (**CH** on a similar sign), **pensiones** (**P**) and, less commonly, **hospedajes**. Distinctions between all of these are rather blurred, but in general you'll find food served at both **fondas** and **pensiones** (some of which may offer rooms only on a meals-inclusive basis). **Casas de huéspedes** – literally 'guest houses' – were traditionally for longer stays, and to some extent, particularly in the older family seaside resorts, they still are. Slightly more expensive but far more common are **hostales** (marked **Hs**) and **hostal-residencias** (**H&R**). These are categorized from one star to three stars, but even so prices vary enormously according to location – in general the more remote, the less expensive. Most **hostales** offer good functional rooms, usually with private shower, and, for doubles at least, they can be excellent value. The **residencia** designation means that no meals other than perhaps breakfast are served. Moving up the scale you finally reach fully-fledged **hoteles** (**H**), again star-graded by the authorities (from one to five). Near the top end of this scale there are also state-run **paradores**: beautiful places, often converted from castles, monasteries and other minor Spanish monuments.

hotel room: in my hotel room en mi habitación del hotel [abeetath-y**o**n]
hour la hora [**o**ra]
house la casa
house wine el vino de la casa [b**ee**no day]
hovercraft el aerodeslizador [a-airodesleethad**o**r]

how como
how many? ¿cuántos? [kw**a**ntoss]
how do you do? ¡mucho gusto! [m**oo**cho]

•••••• DIALOGUES ••••••

how are you? ¿cómo está?
fine, thanks, and you? bien gracias, y usted [b-yen – ee oost**ay**]

how much is it? ¿cuánto es? [kw**a**nto]
1,000 pesetas mil pesetas [pes**ay**tass]
I'll take it me lo quedo [may lo k**ay**do]

humid húmedo [**oo**medo]
humour el humor [oom**o**r]
hungry hambriento [ambr-y**e**nto]
I'm hungry tengo hambre [**a**mbray]
are you hungry? ¿tiene hambre? [t-y**ay**nay]
hurry (verb) darse prisa [d**a**rsay pr**ee**sa]
I'm in a hurry tengo prisa
there's no hurry no hay prisa [ī]
hurry up! ¡dese prisa! [d**ay**say]
hurt doler [dol**air**]
it really hurts me duele mucho [may dw**ay**lay m**oo**cho]
husband mi marido
hydrofoil la hidroala [eedro-**a**la]
hypermarket el hipermercado [eepairmairk**a**do]

I

I yo
ice el hielo [y**ay**lo]
with ice con hielo
no ice, thanks sin hielo, gracias [seen]
ice cream el helado [el**a**do]
ice-cream cone el cucurucho de helado [kookoor**oo**choo]
iced coffee el café helado
ice lolly el polo
idea la idea [eed**ay**-a]
idiot el/la idiota [eed-y**o**ta]
if si
ignition el encendido [enthend**ee**do]
ill enfermo [enf**ai**rmo]
I feel ill me encuentro mal [may enkw**e**ntro]
illness la enfermedad [enfairmayd**a**]
imitation (leather etc) de imitación [day eemeetath-y**o**n]
immediately ahora mismo [a-**o**ra m**ee**smo]
important importante [eemport**a**ntay]
it's very important es muy importante [mwee]
it's not important no tiene importancia [t-y**ay**nay eemport**a**nth-ya]
impossible imposible [eempos**ee**blay]
impressive impresionante

[eempres-yon**a**ntay]
improve mejorar [mayHor**a**r]
I want to improve my Spanish quiero mejorar mi español [k-y**ai**ro – espan-y**o**l]
in: it's in the centre está en el centro
in my car en mi coche
in Córdoba en Córdoba
in two days from now dentro de dos días [day]
in five minutes dentro de cinco minutos
in May en mayo
in English en inglés
in Spanish en español?
is he in? ¿está?
inch* la pulgada [poolg**a**da]
include incluir [eenklw**ee**r]
does that include meals? ¿eso incluye las comidas? [**ay**so eenkl**oo**-yay]
is that included? ¿está eso incluido en el precio? [eenklw**ee**do en el pr**ay**th-yo]
inconvenient inoportuno [eenoport**oo**no]
incredible increíble [eenkray-**ee**blay]
Indian (adj) indio [**ee**nd-yo]
indicator el intermitente [eentairmeet**e**ntay]
indigestion la indigestión [eendeeHest-y**o**n]
indoor pool la piscina cubierta [peesth**ee**na koob-y**ai**rta]
indoors dentro
inexpensive barato
see **cheap**
infection la infección [eenfekth-y**o**n]
infectious infeccioso [eenfekth-y**o**so]
inflammation la inflamación [eenflamath-y**o**n]
informal (occasion, meeting) informal [eenform**a**l]
(dress) de sport [day]
information la información [eenformath-y**o**n]
do you have any information about ...? ¿tiene información sobre ... ? [t-y**ay**nay – s**o**bray]
information desk la información
injection la inyección [een-yekth-y**o**n]
injured herido [er**ee**do]
she's been injured está herida
in-laws mi familia política [fam**ee**l-ya]
inner tube (for tyre) la cámara de aire [**a-ee**ray]
innocent inocente [eenoth**e**ntay]
insect el insecto
insect bite la picadura de insecto [day]
do you have anything for insect bites? ¿tiene algo para la picadura de insectos? [t-y**ay**nay]
insect repellent el repelente de insectos [repel**e**ntay day]
inside dentro de [day]
inside the hotel dentro del hotel
let's sit inside vamos a

sent**a**rnos adentro [b**a**moss]
insist insistir [eenseest**ee**r]
I insist ins**i**sto
insomnia el insomnio [eens**o**mn-yo]
instant coffee el café instantáneo [kaf**ay** eenstant**a**nay-o]
instead: give me that one instead deme ese **o**tro [d**ay**may **ay**say]
instead of ... en lug**a**r de ... [day]
intersection el cruce [kr**oo**thay]
insulin la insulina [eensool**ee**na]
insurance el seguro [seg**oo**ro]
intelligent inteligente [eenteleeH**e**ntay]
interested: I'm interested in ... est**oy** interes**a**do en ...
interesting interesante [eenteres**a**ntay]
that's very interesting eso es muy interesante [**ay**so ess mwee]
international internacional [internath-yon**a**l]
interpret actuar de intérprete [actoo-**a**r day eent**air**pretay]
interpreter el/la intérprete
interval (at theatre) el desc**a**nso
into en
I'm not into ... no me gusta ... [may g**oo**sta]
introduce present**a**r
may I introduce ...? le presento a ...
invitation la invitación [eembeetath-y**o**n]
invite invitar [eembeet**a**r]
Ireland Irlanda [eerl**a**nda]
Irish irlandés [eerland**ay**ss]
I'm Irish (man/woman) soy irlandés/irland**e**sa
iron (for ironing) la pl**a**ncha
can you iron these for me? ¿puede planchármelos? [pw**ay**day]
is* es, está
island la isla [**ee**ssla]
it ello, lo [**ay**-yo]
it is ... es ...; está ...
is it ...? ¿es ...?; ¿está ... ?
where is it? ¿dónde está? [d**o**nday]
it's him es él
it was ... era ...; est**a**ba ... [**ai**ra]
Italian (adj) italiano [eetal-y**a**no]
Italy It**a**lia
itch: it itches me p**i**ca [may]

J

jack (for car) el g**a**to
jacket la chaqueta [chak**ay**ta]
jar el t**a**rro
jam la mermelada [mairmayl**a**da]
jammed: it's jammed está atasc**a**do
January enero [en**ai**ro]
jaw la mandíbula [mand**ee**boola]
jazz el jazz
jealous celoso [thel**o**so]
jeans los vaqueros [bak**ai**ross]
jellyfish la medusa [med**oo**sa]
jersey el jersey [Hairs**ay**]

jetty el muelle [mw**ay**-yay]
Jewish judío [Hood**ee**-o]
jeweller's la joyería [Ho-yer**ee**-a]
jewellery las joyas [H**oy**ass]
job el trabajo [trab**a**Ho]
jogging el footing
  to go jogging hacer footing [ath**air**]
joke el chiste [ch**ee**sstay]
journey el viaje [b-y**a**Hay]
  have a good journey! ¡buen viaje! [bwen b-y**a**Hay]
jug la jarra [H**a**rra]
  a jug of water una jarra de agua [**a**gwa]
juice el zumo [th**oo**mo]
July julio [H**oo**l-yo]
jump (verb) saltar
jumper el jersey [Hairs**ay**]
jump leads las pinzas (para la batería) [p**ee**nthass – batair**ee**-a]
junction el cruce [kr**oo**thay]
June junio [H**oo**n-yo]
just (only) solamente [solam**e**ntay]
  just two sólo dos
  just for me sólo para mí
  just here aquí mismo [ak**ee** m**ee**smo]
  not just now ahora no [a-**o**ra]
  we've just arrived acabamos de llegar [yeg**a**r]

K

keep quedarse [ked**a**rsay]
  keep the change quédese con el cambio [k**ay**-daysay – k**a**mb-yo]
  can I keep it? ¿puedo quedármelo? [pw**ay**do ked**a**rmelo]
  please keep it por favor, quédeselo [k**ay**dayselo]
ketchup el ketchup
kettle el hervidor [airbeed**o**r]
key la llave [y**a**bay]
  the key for room 201, please la llave de la habitacion doscientos uno, por favor [day la abeetath-y**o**n]
key ring el llavero [yab**ai**ro]
kidneys los riñones [reen-y**o**ness]
kill matar
kilo* el kilo
kilometre* el kilómetro
  how many kilometres is it to ...? ¿cuántos kilómetros hay a ...? [kw**a**ntoss – ī]
kind (nice) amable [am**a**blay]
  that's very kind es muy amable [mwee]

•••••• DIALOGUE ••••••

which kind do you want? ¿qué tipo quiere? [kay t**ee**po k-y**ai**ray]
I want this/that kind quiero este/aquel tipo [k-y**ai**ro **e**stay/ak**e**l]

king el rey [ray]
kiosk el quiosco [kee-**o**sko]
kiss el beso [b**ay**so]
  (verb) besarse [bays**a**rsay]

kissing
It is customary to greet friends and relatives by kissing them on both cheeks, apart from men who shake hands with each other on meeting – except if they are close relatives. Foreign visitors are expected to do the same.

kitchen la cocina [kotheena]
kitchenette la cocina pequeña [pekwayn-ya]
Kleenex® el kleenex®
knee la rodilla [rodee-ya]
knickers las bragas
knife el cuchillo [koochee-yo]
knitwear los géneros de punto [Henaiross]
knock (verb: on door) llamar [yamar]
knock down atropellar [atropay-yar]
  he's been knocked down le han atropellado [lay an atropay-yado]
knock over (object) volcar [bolkar]
  (pedestrian) atropellar [atropay-yar]
know (somebody, a place) conocer [konothair]
  (something) saber [sabair]
  I don't know no sé [say]
  I didn't know that no lo sabía
  do you know where I can find ...? ¿sabe dónde puedo encontrar ...? [sabay donday pwaydo]

•••••• DIALOGUE ••••••

do you know how this works?
¿sabe cómo funciona esto? [foonth-yona]
sorry, I don't know lo siento, no sé [s-yento – say]

L

label la etiqueta [eteekayta]
ladies' (toilets) el aseo de señoras [asay-o day sen-yorass]
ladies' wear la ropa de señoras
lady la señora [sen-yora]
lager la cerveza [thairbaytha]
  see **beer**
lake el lago
lamb (meat) el cordero [kordairo]
lamp la lámpara
lane (motorway) el carril [karreel]
  (small road) la callejuela [ka-yay-Hwayla]
language el idioma [eed-yoma]
language course el curso de idioma [koorso day]
large grande [granday]
last último [oolteemo]
  last week la semana pasada
  last Friday el viernes pasado
  last night anoche [anochay]
  what time is the last train to Toledo? ¿a qué hora es el último tren a Toledo? [kay ora]

late tarde [t**a**rday]
sorry I'm late siento llegar tarde [s-y**ay**nto yeg**a**r]
the train was late el tren llegó con retraso [yayg**o**]
we must go – we'll be late debemos irnos – llegaremos tarde [deb**ay**moss **ee**rnoss – yegar**ay**moss]
it's getting late se hace tarde [say **a**thay]
later más tarde
I'll come back later volveré más tarde [bolbair**ay**]
see you later hasta luego [**a**sta lw**ay**go]
later on más tarde
latest lo último [**oo**lteemo]
by Wednesday at the latest para el miércoles lo más tarde
laugh (verb) reirse [r**ay**-**ee**rsay]
launderette/laundromat la lavandería [labandair**ee**-a]
laundry (clothes) la ropa sucia [s**oo**th-ya]
(place) la lavandería
lavatory el lavabo [lab**a**bo]
law la ley [lay]
lawn el césped [th**e**sped]
lawyer (man/woman) el abogado/la abogada
laxative el laxante [lax**a**ntay]
lazy perezoso [paireth**o**so]
lead (electrical) el cable [k**a**blay]
lead (verb) conducir [kondooth**ee**r]
where does this lead to? ¿adónde va esta carretera? [ad**o**nday ba – karrayt**ai**ra]
leaf la hoja [**o**Ha]
leaflet el folleto [fo-y**ay**to]
leak (in roof) la gotera [got**ai**ra]
(gas, water) el escape [esk**a**pay]
(verb) filtrar [feeltr**a**r]
the roof leaks el tejado tiene goteras [teH**a**do t-y**ay**nay got**ai**rass]
learn aprender [aprend**air**]
least: not in the least de ninguna manera [day neeng**oo**na man**ai**ra]
at least por lo menos [m**ay**noss]
leather (fine) la piel [p-yel]
(heavy) el cuero [kw**ai**ro]
leave (verb) irse [**ee**rsay]
I am leaving tomorrow me marcho mañana [may]
he left yesterday se marchó ayer [say]
may I leave this here? ¿puedo dejar esto aquí? [pw**ay**do dayH**a**r – ak**ee**]
I left my coat in the bar me he dejado el abrigo en el bar [ay dayH**a**do]

•••••• DIALOGUE ••••••

when does the bus for Montoro leave? ¿cuándo sale el autobús para Montoro? [kw**a**ndo s**a**lay]
it leaves at 9 o'clock sale a las nueve

leek el puerro [pw**ai**rro]
left izquierda [eethk-y**ai**rda]
on the left a la izquierda
to the left a la izquierda

turn left gire a la izquierda [Heeray]
there's none left no queda ninguno [kayda]
left-handed zurdo [thoordo]
left luggage (office) la consigna [konseegna]
leg la pierna [p-yairna]
lemon el limón [leemon]
lemonade la limonada
lemon tea el té con limón [tay]
lend prestar
will you lend me your ... ? ¿podría prestarme su ...? [prestarmay]
lens (of camera) el objetivo [obHeteebo]
lesbian la lesbiana
less menos [maynoss]
less expensive menos caro
less than 10 menos de diez
less than you menos que tú [kay too]
lesson la lección [lekth-yon]
let (allow) dejar [dayHar]
will you let me know? ¿me lo dirá? [may]
I'll let you know se lo diré [say lo deeray]
let's go for something to eat vamos a comer algo [bamoss a komair]
let off: will you let me off at ...? ¿me para en ...? [may]
letter la carta
do you have any letters for me? ¿tiene cartas para mí? [t-yaynay]
letterbox el buzón [boothon]

Letterboxes in Spain are yellow.

lettuce la lechuga [lechooga]
lever la palanca
library la biblioteca [beebl-yotayka]
licence el permiso
lid la tapa
lie (verb: tell untruth) mentir
lie down acostarse [akostarsay], echarse [aycharsay]
life la vida [beeda]
lifebelt el salvavidas [salbabeedass]
lifeguard el/la socorrista
life jacket el chaleco salvavidas [chalayko salbabeedass]
lift (in building) el ascensor [asthensor]
could you give me a lift? ¿podría llevarme en su coche? [yebarmay – kochay]
would you like a lift? ¿quiere que le lleve? [k-yairay kay lay yaybay]
lift pass el forfait [forfa-ee]
a daily/weekly lift pass un forfait de un día/una semana
light la luz [looth]
(not heavy) ligero [leeHairo]
do you have a light? (for cigarette) ¿tiene fuego? [t-yaynay fwaygo]
light green verde claro [bairday]
light bulb la bombilla [bombee-ya]

I need a new light bulb necesito una bombilla nueva [netheseeto – nwayba]
lighter (cigarette) el encendedor [enthendedor]
lightning el relámpago
like (verb) gustar [goostar]
I like it me gusta [may]
I like going for walks me gusta pasear [pasay-ar]
I like you me gustas
I don't like it no me gusta
do you like ...? ¿le gusta ...? [lay]
I'd like a beer quisiera una cerveza [kees-yaira oona thairbaytha]
I'd like to go swimming me gustaría ir a nadar
would you like a drink? ¿le apetece beber algo? [apaytaythay bebair]
would you like to go for a walk? ¿le apetece dar un paseo? [lay – pasay-o]
what's it like? ¿cómo es?
I want one like this quiero uno como éste [k-yairo – estay]
lime la lima [leema]
lime cordial el zumo de lima [thoomo day]
line la línea [leenay-a]
could you give me an outside line? ¿puede darme línea? [pwayday darmay]
lips el labio [lab-yo]
lip salve la crema de labios [krayma]
lipstick el lápiz de labios [lapeeth]
liqueur el licor
listen escuchar [eskoochar]
litre* el litro
a litre of white wine un litro de vino blanco [day beeno]
little pequeño [paykayn-yo]
just a little, thanks sólo un poco, gracias
a little milk un poco de leche [lechay]
a little bit more un poquito más [pokeeto]
live (verb) vivir [beebeer]
we live together vivimos juntos [beebeemoss Hoontoss]

•••••• DIALOGUE ••••••

where do you live? ¿dónde vive? [donday beebay]
I live in London vivo en Londres [beebo]

lively alegre [alaygray]
liver el hígado [eegado]
loaf el pan
lobby (in hotel) el vestíbulo [besteeboolo]
lobster la langosta
local local
can you recommend a local wine/restaurant? puede recomendarme un vino/un restaurante local [pwayday rekomendarmay oon beeno/oon restowrantay]

Every region in Spain has its own distinctive wines. If you want to try the local wine ask for **vino del país** or **vino de la casa**. It is usually quite cheap although the quality varies.

lock la cerradura [thairradoora]
(verb) cerrar [thairrar]
it's locked está cerrado con llave [thairrado kon yabay]
lock in dejar encerrado [day-Har enthairrado]
lock out: I've locked myself out he cerrado la puerta con las llaves dentro [ay – la pwairta – yabayss]
locker (for luggage etc) la consigna automática [konseegna owtomateeka]
lollipop el chupa-chups® [choopa-choopss]
London Londres [londress]
long largo
how long will it take to fix it? ¿cuánto tiempo llevará arreglarlo? [kwanto t-yempo yaybara]
how long does it take? ¿cuánto tiempo se tarda? [say]
a long time mucho tiempo [moocho]
one day/two days longer un día/dos días más
long distance call la conferencia [konfairenth-ya]
look: I'm just looking, thanks sólo estoy mirando, gracias
you don't look well no tienes buen aspecto [t-yayness bwen]
look out! ¡cuidado! [kweedado]
can I have a look? ¿puedo mirar? [pwaydo]
look after cuidar [kweedar]
look at mirar
look for buscar
I'm looking for ... estoy buscando ...
look forward to: I'm looking forward to it: tengo muchas ganas [moochass]
loose (handle etc) suelto [swelto]
lorry el camión [kam-yon]
lose perder [pairdair]
I've lost my way me he perdido [may ay pairdeedo]
I'm lost, I want to get to ... estoy perdido/perdida, quiero ir a ... [k-yairo]
I've lost my bag he perdido el bolso [ay]
lost property (office) (la oficina de) objetos perdidos [ofeetheena day obHaytoss pairdeedoss]
lot: a lot, lots mucho, muchos [moocho]
not a lot no mucho
a lot of people mucha gente [Hentay]
a lot bigger mucho mayor
I like it a lot me gusta mucho [may goosta]

lotion la loción [loth-**yon**]
loud fuerte [fw**air**tay]
lounge (in house, hotel) el sal**ó**n
(in airport) la s**a**la de espera
[day esp**air**a]
love el am**o**r
(verb) querer [kair**air**]
I love Spain me enc**a**nta
Esp**a**ña [may]
lovely encantad**o**r
low bajo [b**a**Ho]
luck la suerte [sw**air**tay]
good luck! ¡buena suerte!
[bw**ay**na]
luggage el equipaje
[ekeep**a**Hay]
luggage trolley el carr**i**to
portaequipaje [porta-ekeep**a**Hay]
lump (on body) la hinchaz**ó**n
[eenchath**on**]
lunch el almuerzo [almw**air**tho]
lungs los pulmones
[poolm**o**ness]
luxurious (hotel, furnishings) de
lujo [l**oo**Ho]
luxury el l**u**jo

M

machine la máquina [m**a**keena]
mad (insane) l**o**co
(angry) furioso [foor-y**o**so]
Madrid Madrid [madr**ee**]
magazine la revista [reb**ee**sta]
maid (in hotel) la camarera
[kamar**air**a]
maiden name el nombre de
soltera [n**o**mbray day solt**air**a]
mail el correo [korr**ay**-o]
is there any mail for me? ¿hay
correspondencia p**a**ra mí?
[ī korrespond**e**nth-ya]
see **post**
mailbox el buzón [booth**on**]
see **letterbox**
main principal [preentheep**a**l]
main course el pl**a**to principal
main post office la oficina
central de correos
[ofeeth**ee**na thentr**a**l day
korr**ay**-oss]
main road (in town) la calle
principal [k**a**-yay preentheep**a**l]
(in country) la carretera
principal [karret**air**a]
mains (for water) la llave de
p**a**so [y**a**bay day]
mains switch (for electricity) el
interruptor de la red
el**é**ctrica [eentairroopt**o**r day]
Majorca Mallorca [ma-y**o**rka]
make (brand name) la m**a**rca
(verb) hacer [ath**air**]
I make it 500 pesetas creo
que son quini**e**ntas pesetas
[kr**ay**o kay – pes**ay**tass]
what is it made of? ¿de qué
est**á** hecho? [day kay –
aycho]
make-up el maquillaje [makee-y**a**Hay]
man el hombre [**o**mbray]
manager el gerente [Hair**e**ntay]
can I see the manager?
¿puedo ver al gerente?
[pw**ay**do bair]
manageress la gerente

manual (car with manual gears) el coche de marchas [kochay]
many muchos [moochoss]
  not many no muchos
map (city plan) el plano
  (road map, geographical) el mapa
March marzo [martho]
margarine la margarina
market el mercado [mairkado]
marmalade la mermelada de naranja [mairmelada day naranHa]
married: I'm married (said by a man/woman) estoy casado/casada
  are you married? (said to a man/woman) ¿está casado/casada?
mascara el rímel
match (football etc) el partido
matches las cerillas [thaireeyass]
material (fabric) el tejido [teHeedo]
matter: it doesn't matter no importa
  what's the matter? ¿qué pasa? [kay]
mattress el colchón
May mayo [ma-yo]
may: may I have another one? ¿me da otro? [may]
  may I come in? ¿se puede entrar? [say pwayday]
  may I see it? ¿puedo verlo? [pwaydo bairlo]
  may I sit here? ¿puedo sentarme aquí? [sentarmay akee]
maybe tal vez [beth]
mayonnaise la mayonesa [ma-yonaysa]
me*: that's for me eso es para mí [ayso]
  send it to me envíemelo [embee-aymelo]
  me too yo también [tamb-yen]
meal la comida

•••••• DIALOGUE ••••••

did you enjoy your meal? ¿te ha gustado la comida? [tay a goostado]
it was excellent, thank you estaba riquísima, gracias [reekeeseema]

mean (verb) querer decir [kairair detheer]
  what do you mean? ¿qué quiere decir? [kay k-yairay]

•••••• DIALOGUE ••••••

what does this word mean? ¿qué significa esta palabra? [kay]
it means ... in English significa ... en inglés [eenglayss]

measles el sarampión [saramp-yon]
meat la carne [karnay]
mechanic el mecánico
medicine la medicina [medeetheena]
Mediterranean el Mediterráneo [medeetairranay-o]
medium (adj: size) medio [mayd-yo]
medium-dry semi-seco [sayko]
  (sherry) amontillado [amontee-yado]

medium-rare poco hecho [**ay**cho]
medium-sized de tamaño medio [tam**a**n-yo m**ay**d-yo]
meet encontrar
(for the first time) conocer [konoth**air**]
nice to meet you encantado de conocerle [day konoth**air**lay]
where shall I meet you? ¿dónde nos vemos? [d**o**nday noss b**ay**moss]
meeting la reunión [ray-oon-y**o**n]
meeting place el lugar de reunión [loog**a**r]
melon el melón
men los hombres [**o**mbress]
mend arreglar
could you mend this for me? ¿puede arreglarme esto? [pw**ay**day arregl**a**rmay]
men's toilet el servicio de caballeros [sairb**ee**th-yo day kaba-y**ai**ross]
menswear la ropa de caballero
mention (verb) mencionar [menth-yon**a**r]
don't mention it de nada [day]
menu el menú [men**oo**]
may I see the menu, please? ¿puede traerme el menú? [pw**ay**day tra-**ai**rmay]
see menu reader page 207
message: are there any messages for me? ¿hay algún recado para mí? [ī]
I want to leave a message for ... quisiera dejar un recado para ... [kees-y**ai**ra day-H**a**r]
metal el metal
metre* el metro
microwave (oven) el (horno) microondas [**o**rno meekro-**o**ndass]
midday el mediodía [m**ay**d-yod**ee**-a]
at midday al mediodía
middle: in the middle en el medio [m**ay**d-yo]
in the middle of the night a mitad de la noche [meet**a** day la n**o**chay]
the middle one el del medio
midnight la medianoche [m**ay**d-ya-n**o**chay]
at midnight a medianoche
might: I might es posible [pos**ee**blay]
I might not puede que no [pw**ay**day kay]
I might want to stay another day quizás decida quedarme otro día [keeth**a**ss deth**ee**da ked**a**rmay]
migraine la jaqueca [Hak**ay**ka]
mild (taste) suave [sw**a**bay]
(weather) templado
mile* la milla [m**ee**-ya]
milk la leche [l**e**chay]
milkshake el batido
millimetre* el milímetro
minced meat la carne picada [k**a**rnay]
mind: never mind ¡qué más da! [kay]

I've changed my mind he cambiado de idea [ay kamb-yado day eed**ay**-a]

•••••• DIALOGUE ••••••

do you mind if I open the window? ¿le importa si **a**bro la ventana? [lay eemp**o**rta – bent**a**na]

no, I don't mind no, no me importa [may]

mine*: it's mine es mío
mineral water el agua mineral [**a**gwa meenair**a**l]
mint-flavoured con sab**o**r a m**e**nta
mints los caramelos de m**e**nta [karam**ay**loss day]
minute el minuto [meen**oo**to]
in a minute en seguida [seg**ee**da]
just a minute un momento
mirror el espejo [esp**ay**Ho]
Miss Señorita [sen-yor**ee**ta]
miss: I missed the bus he perdido el autob**ú**s [ay paird**ee**do]
missing: one of my ... is missing me f**a**lta uno de mis ... [may — day]
there's a suitcase missing falta una mal**e**ta
mist la niebla [n-y**ay**bla]
mistake el err**o**r
I think there's a mistake me parece que hay una equivocación [may par**e**thay kay ī **oo**na ekeebokath-y**o**n]
sorry, I've made a mistake perd**ó**n, me he equivocado [may ay ekeebok**a**do]
misunderstanding el malentendido
mix-up: sorry, there's been a mix-up perd**ó**n ha habido una confusión [a ab**ee**do **oo**na konfoos-y**o**n]
modern moderno [mod**ai**rno]
modern art gallery la galería de arte moderno [galair**ee**-a day **a**rtay]
moisturizer la crema hidratante [kr**ay**ma eedrat**a**ntay]
moment: I won't be a moment vuelvo enseguida [bw**e**lbo enseg**ee**da]
monastery el monasterio [monast**air**-yo]
Monday lunes [l**oo**ness]
money el dinero [deen**ai**ro]
month el mes
monument el monumento [monoom**e**nto]
(statue) la estatua [est**a**twa]
moon la l**u**na
moped el ciclomotor [theeklomot**o**r]
more* más
can I have some more water, please? más **a**gua, por fav**o**r
more expensive/interesting más c**a**ro/interes**a**nte
more than 50 más de cincuenta
more than that más que eso [kay **ay**so]
a lot more mucho más [m**oo**cho]

•••••• DIALOGUE ••••••

would you like some more? ¿quiere más? [k-y**ai**ray]
no, no more for me, thanks no, para mí no, gracias
how about you? ¿y usted? [ee oost**ay**]
I don't want any more, thanks no quiero más, gracias [k-y**ai**ro]

morning la mañana [man-y**a**na]
this morning esta mañana
in the morning por la mañana
Morocco Marruecos [marrw**ay**koss]
mosquito el mosquito
mosquito repellent el repelente de mosquitos [repel**e**ntay]
most: I like this one most of all éste es el que más me gusta [**e**stay – kay mass may g**oo**sta]
most of the time la mayor parte del tiempo [ma-y**o**r p**a**rtay del t-y**e**mpo]
most tourists la mayoría de los turistas [ma-yor**ee**-a day]
mostly generalmente [Haynairalm**e**ntay]
mother la madre [m**a**dray]
motorbike la moto
motorboat la (lancha) motora
motorway la autopista [owtop**ee**sta]
mountain la montaña [mont**a**n-ya]
in the mountains en las montañas
mountaineering el montañismo [montan-y**ee**smo]
mouse el ratón
moustache el bigote [beeg**o**tay]
mouth la boca
mouth ulcer la llaga [y**a**ga]
move: he's moved to another room se ha cambiado a otra habitación [say a kamb-y**a**do – abeetath-y**o**n]
could you move your car? ¿podría cambiar de sitio su coche? [podr**ee**-a kamb-y**a**r day s**ee**t-yo]
could you move up a little? ¿puede correrse un poco? [pw**ay**day corr**ai**rsay]
where has it moved to? ¿adónde se ha trasladado? [ad**o**nday say a]
movie la película [pel**ee**koola]
movie theater el cine [th**ee**nay]
Mr Señor [sen-y**o**r]
Mrs Señora [sen-y**o**ra]
Ms Señorita [sen-yor**ee**ta]
much mucho [m**oo**cho]
much better/worse mucho mejor/peor [ma-y**o**r/pay-**o**r]
much hotter mucho más caliente [kal-y**e**ntay]
not (very) much no mucho
I don't want very much no quiero mucho [k-y**ai**ro]
mud el barro
mug (for drinking) la taza [t**a**tha]
I've been mugged me han asaltado [may an]
mum la mamá
mumps las paperas [pap**ai**rass]
museum el museo [moos**ay**-o]
mushrooms los champiñones

[champeen-y**o**ness]
music la música [m**oo**seeka]
musician el/la músico
Muslim (adj) musulmán [moosoolm**a**n]
mussels los mejillones [meHeey**o**ness]
must*: **I must** tengo que [kay]
I mustn't drink alcohol no debo beber alcohol [d**ay**bo beb**air** alko-**ol**]
mustard la mostaza [most**a**tha]
my* mi; (pl) mis
myself: **I'll do it myself** lo haré yo mismo [ar**ay** yo m**ee**smo]
by myself yo solo

N

nail (finger) la uña [**oo**n-ya]
(metal) el clavo [kl**a**bo]
nailbrush el cepillo para las uñas [thep**ee**-yo –**oo**n-yass]
nail varnish el esmalte para uñas [esm**a**ltay]
name el nombre [n**o**mbray]

> Spaniards have two surnames (the father's first surname + the mother's first surname) Women don't change their maiden name when they get married. First names are used in informal relationships, for example, between friends and relatives. In formal situations **don** or **doña** (Mr or Mrs/Ms) + first name are used.

my name's John me llamo John [may y**a**mo]
what's your name? ¿cómo se llama usted? [say – oost**ay**]
what is the name of this street? ¿cómo se llama esta calle?
napkin la servilleta [sairbee-y**ay**ta]
nappy el pañal [pan-y**a**l]
narrow (street) estrecho [estr**ay**cho]
nasty (person) desagradable [desagrad**a**blay]
(weather, accident) malo
national nacional [nath-yon**a**l]
nationality la nacionalidad [nath-yonaleed**a**]
natural natural [natoor**a**l]
nausea la nausea [n**ow**say-a]
navy (blue) azul marino [ath**oo**l mar**ee**no]
near cerca [th**air**ka]
is it near the city centre? ¿está cerca del centro? [th**e**ntro]
do you go near Las Ramblas? ¿pasa usted cerca de Las Ramblas? [oost**ay** – day]
where is the nearest ...? ¿dónde está el ... más cercano? [d**o**nday – thairk**a**no]
nearby por aquí cerca [ak**ee**]
nearly casi
necessary necesario [nethes**a**r-yo]
neck el cuello [kw**ay**-yo]
necklace el collar [ko-y**a**r]
necktie la corbata

need: I need ... necesito un ... [netheseeto]
do I need to pay? ¿necesito pagar?
needle la aguja [agooHa]
negative (film) el negativo [negateebo]
neither: neither (one) of them ninguno (de ellos) [neengoono day ay-yoss]
neither ... nor ... ni ... ni ...
nephew el sobrino
Nerja Nerja [nairHa]
net (in sport) la red
Netherlands Los Países Bajos [pa-eesess baHoss]
network map el mapa
never nunca [noonka]

•••••• DIALOGUE ••••••

have you ever been to Seville? ¿ha estado alguna vez en Sevilla? [a – beth]
no, never, I've never been there no, nunca, nunca he estado allí [ay – a-yee]

new nuevo [nwaybo]
news (radio, TV etc) las noticias [noteeth-yass]
newsagent's el kiosko de prensa [day]
newspaper el periódico [pair-yodeeko]
newspaper kiosk el kiosko de prensa [day]
New Year el Año Nuevo [an-yo nwaybo]

Spaniards celebrate New Year's Eve (La Noche Vieja) either in the streets or at parties. In many parts of Spain it is usual to have a special supper with relatives or friends. At twelve o'clock it is the custom to eat 12 grapes, one at each stroke of the clock. If you manage to eat them all in time you'll have a successful year.

Happy New Year! ¡Feliz Año Nuevo [feleeth]
New Year's Eve Nochevieja [nochay-b-yayHa]
New Zealand Nueva Zelanda [nwayba thelanda]
New Zealander: I'm a New Zealander (man/woman) soy neozelandés/neozelandesa [nayo-thelandayss]
next próximo
the next turning/street on the left la siguiente calle a la izquierda [seeg-yentay ka-yay a la eethk-yairda]
at the next stop en la siguiente parada
next week la próxima semana
next to al lado de [day]
nice (food) bueno [bwayno]
(looks, view etc) bonito
(person) simpático
niece la sobrina
night la noche [nochay]
at night por la noche

good night buenas noches [bw**ay**nass]

•••••• DIALOGUE ••••••

do you have a single room for one night? ¿tiene una habitación individual para una noche? [t-y**ay**nay **oo**na abeetath-y**o**n eendeebeedw**a**l]
yes, madam sí, señora [sen-y**o**ra]
how much is it per night? ¿cuánto es la noche? [kw**a**nto]
it's 3,000 pesetas for one night son tres mil pesetas la noche [pes**ay**tass]
thank you, I'll take it gracias, me la quedo [may la k**ay**do]

nightclub la discoteca [deeskot**ay**ka]
nightdress el camisón
night porter el portero [port**ai**ro]
no no
I've no change no tengo cambio [k**a**mb-yo]
there's no ... left no queda ... [k**ay**da]
no way! ¡ni hablar! [abl**a**r]
oh no! (upset, annoyed) ¡Dios mío!
nobody nadie [n**a**d-yay]
there's nobody there no hay nadie ahí [ī – a-**ee**]
noise el ruido [rw**ee**do]
noisy: it's too noisy hay demasiado ruido [ī daymas-y**a**do]
non-alcoholic sin alcohol [alko-**o**l]
none ninguno
non-smoking compartment no fumadores [foomad**o**ress]
noon el mediodía [m**ay**d-yo-d**ee**-a]
no-one nadie [n**a**d-yay]
nor: nor do I yo tampoco
normal normal
north norte [n**o**rtay]
in the north en el norte
north of Girona al norte de Girona
northeast nordeste [nord**e**stay]
northern del norte [n**o**rtay]
northwest noroeste [noro-**e**stay]
Northern Ireland Irlanda del Norte [eerl**a**nda del n**o**rtay]
Norway Noruega [norw**ay**ga]
Norwegian (adj) noruego
nose la nariz [nar**ee**th]
nosebleed la hemorragia nasal [emorr**a**H-ya]
not* no
no, I'm not hungry no, no tengo hambre [**a**mbray]
I don't want any, thank you no quiero ninguno, gracias [k-y**ai**ro]
it's not necessary no es necesario [naythes**a**r-yo]
I didn't know that no lo sabía
not that one – this one ése no – éste [**ay**say – **e**stay]
note (banknote) el billete [bee-y**ay**tay]
notebook el cuaderno [kwad**ai**rno]
notepaper (for letters) el papel de carta

nothing nada
nothing for me, thanks para mí nada, gracias
nothing else nada más
novel la novela [nobayla]
November noviembre [nob-yembray]
now ahora [a-ora]
number el número [noomairo]
I've got the wrong number me he equivocado de número [may ay ekeebokado day]
what is your phone number? ¿cuál es su número de teléfono? [kwal – telayfono]
number plate la matrícula
nurse (man/woman) el enfermero [enfairmairo]/la enfermera
nursery slope la pista de principiantes [day preentheep-yantess]
nut (for bolt) la tuerca [twairka]
nuts los frutos secos

O

o'clock* en punto [poonto]
occupied (toilet) ocupado [okoopado]
October octubre [oktoobray]
odd (strange) raro
of* de [day]
off (lights) apagado
it's just off calle Corredera está cerca de calle Corredera [thairka day ka-yay]
we're off tomorrow nos vamos mañana [bamoss]
offensive (language, behaviour) insultante [eensooltantay]
office (place of work) la oficina [ofeetheena]
officer (said to policeman) señor [sen-yor]
often a menudo
not often pocas veces [baythess]
how often are the buses? ¿cada cuánto son los autobuses? [kwanto]
oil el aceite [athay-eetay]
ointment la pomada
OK vale [balay]
are you OK? ¿está bien? [b-yen]
is that OK with you? ¿le parece bien? [lay paraythay]
is it OK to ...? ¿se puede ...? [say pwayday]
that's OK thanks (it doesn't matter) está bien, gracias
I'm OK (nothing for me) yo no quiero [k-yairo]
(I feel OK) me siento bien [may s-yento]
is this train OK for ...? ¿este tren va a...? [estay – ba]
I said I'm sorry, OK? he dicho que lo siento, ¿vale? [ay – kay – balay]
old viejo [b-yayHo]

•••••• DIALOGUE ••••••

how old are you? ¿cuántos años tiene? [kwantoss an-yoss t-yaynay]
I'm twenty-five tengo veinticinco
and you? ¿y usted? [ee oostay]

old-fashioned pasado de moda [day]
old town (old part of town) el casco antiguo [anteegwo]
in the old town en el casco antiguo
olive la aceituna [athay-eetoona], la oliva
black/green olives las aceitunas negras/verdes [bairdess]
olive oil el aceite de oliva [athay-eetay day oleeba]
omelette la tortilla [tortee-ya]
on* en
on the street/beach en la calle/la playa
is it on this road? ¿está en esta calle?
on the plane en el avión [ab-yon]
on Saturday el sábado
on television en la tele [taylay]
I haven't got it on me no lo llevo encima [yaybo entheema]
this one's on me (drink) ésta va de mi cuenta [ba day mee kwenta]
the light wasn't on la luz no estaba encendida [looth – enthendeeda]
what's on tonight? ¿qué ponen esta noche? [kay]
once (one time) una vez [oona beth]
at once (immediately) en seguida [segeeda]
one* uno [oono], una
the white one el blanco, la blanca
one-way: a one-way ticket to ... un billete de ida para ... [bee-yaytay day eeda]
onion la cebolla [thebo-ya]
only sólo
only one sólo uno
it's only 6 o'clock son sólo las seis
I've only just got here acabo de llegar [yegar]
on/off switch el interruptor [eentairrooptor]
open (adjective) abierto [ab-yairto]
(verb) abrir [abreer]
when do you open? ¿a qué hora abre? [kay ora abray]
I can't get it open no puedo abrirlo [pwaydo]
in the open air al aire libre [a-eeray leebray]
opening times el horario [orar-yo]
open ticket el billete abierto [bee-yaytay ab-yairto]
opera la ópera
operation (medical) la operación [opairath-yon]
operator (telephone: man/woman) el operador/la operadora
opposite: the opposite direction la dirección contraria [deerekth-yon kontrar-ya]
the bar opposite el bar de enfrente [day enfrentay]
opposite my hotel enfrente de

mi hotel
optician el óptico
or o
orange (fruit) la naranja [naranHa]
(colour) (color) naranja
orange juice (fresh) el zumo de naranja [thoomo day]
(fizzy, diluted) la naranjada [naranHada]
orchestra la orquesta [orkesta]
order: can we order now? (in restaurant) ¿podemos pedir ya? [podaymoss]
I've already ordered, thanks ya he pedido, gracias [ay]
I didn't order this no he pedido eso [ayso]
out of order averiado, fuera de servicio [abair-yado, fwaira day sairbeeth-yo]
ordinary corriente [korr-yentay]
other otro
the other one el otro
the other day el otro día
I'm waiting for the others estoy esperando a los demás
do you have any others? ¿tiene usted otros? [t-yaynay oostay]
otherwise de otra manera [manaira]
our* nuestro [nwestro], nuestra; (pl) nuestros, nuestras
ours* (el) nuestro, (la) nuestra
out: he's out no está
three kilometres out of town a tres kilómetros de la ciudad
outdoors fuera de casa [fwaira day]
outside ... fuera de ...
can we sit outside? ¿podemos sentarnos fuera? [podaymoss]
oven el horno [orno]
over: over here por aquí [akee]
over there por allí [a-yee]
over 500 más de quinientos
it's over se acabó [say]
overcharge: you've overcharged me me ha cobrado de más [may a – day]
overcoat el abrigo
overlook: I'd like a room overlooking the courtyard querría una habitación que dé al patio [kairree-a oona abeetath-yon kay day]
overnight (travel) de noche [day nochay]
overtake adelantar
owe: how much do I owe you? ¿cuánto le debo? [kwanto lay daybo]
own: my own ... mi propio ... [prop-yo]
are you on your own? (to a man/woman) ¿está solo/sola?
I'm on my own (man/woman) estoy solo/sola
owner (man/woman) el propietario [prop-yetar-yo]/la propietaria

P

pack: a pack of ... un paquete de ... [pak**ay**tay day]
(verb) hacer las maletas [mal**ay**tass]
package (eg at post office) el paquete [pak**ay**tay]
package holiday el viaje organizado [b-y**a**Hay organeeth**a**do]
packed lunch la bolsa con la comida
packet: a packet of cigarettes un paquete de cigarrillos [pak**ay**tay day theegar**ee**-yoss]
padlock el candado
page (of book) la página [p**a**Heena]
could you page Mr ...? ¿podría llamar al Señor (por altavoz) ...? [yam**a**r]
pain el dolor
I have a pain here me duele aquí [may dw**ay**lay ak**ee**]
painful doloroso
painkillers los analgésicos [analH**ay**seekoss]
paint la pintura
painting el cuadro [kw**a**dro]
pair: a pair of ... un par de ... [day]
Pakistani (adj) paquistaní [pakeestan**ee**]
palace el palacio [pal**a**th-yo]
pale pálido
pale blue azul claro [ath**oo**l]
pan la cazuela [kathw**ay**la]
panties (underwear: women's) las bragas
pants (underwear: men's) los calzoncillos [kalthonth**ee**-yoss]
(women's) las bragas
(US: trousers) los pantalones [pantal**o**ness]
pantyhose los panties
paper el papel
(newspaper) el periódico [pair-y**o**deeko]
a piece of paper un trozo de papel [thr**o**tho day]
paper handkerchiefs los kleenex®
parcel el paquete [pak**ay**tay]
pardon (me)? (didn't understand/hear) ¿cómo?
parents: my parents mis padres [p**a**dress]
parents-in-law los suegros [sw**e**gross]
park el parque [p**a**rkay]
(verb) aparcar
can I park here? ¿puedo aparcar aquí? [pw**ay**do – ak**ee**]
parking lot el aparcamiento [aparcam-y**e**nto]
part la parte [p**a**rtay]
partner (boyfriend, girlfriend etc) el compañero [kompan-y**ai**ro]
party (group) el grupo
(celebration) la fiesta
pass (in mountains) el puerto [pw**ai**rto]
passenger (man/woman) el pasajero [pasaH**ai**ro]/la pasajera

passport el pasaporte [pasap**o**rtay]
past*: in the past antiguamente [anteegwam**e**ntay]
just past the information office justo después de la oficina de información [H**oo**sto despw**ay**ss day]
path el camino
pattern el dibujo [deeb**oo**Ho]
pavement la acera [ath**ai**ra]
on the pavement en la acera
pavement café el café terraza [terr**a**tha]
pay (verb) pagar
can I pay, please? la cuenta, por favor [kwenta]
it's already paid for ya está pagado

•••••• DIALOGUE ••••••

who's paying? ¿quién paga? [k-yen]
I'll pay pago yo
no, you paid last time, I'll pay no, usted pagó la última vez, yo pago [oost**ay** – **oo**lteema beth]

pay phone el teléfono público [tel**ay**fono p**oo**bleeko]
peaceful tranquilo [trank**ee**lo]
peach el melocotón
peanuts los cacahuetes [kakaw**ay**tess]
pear la pera [p**ai**ra]
peas los guisantes [gees**a**ntess]
peculiar (taste, custom) raro
pedestrian crossing el paso de peatones [pay-at**o**ness]
pedestrian precinct la calle peatonal [k**a**-yay pay-aton**a**l]
peg (for washing) la pinza [p**ee**ntha]
(for tent) la estaca
pen la pluma [pl**oo**ma]
pencil el lápiz [l**a**peeth]
penfriend (male/female) el amigo/la amiga por correspondencia [korrespond**e**nth-ya]
penicillin la penicilina [peneetheel**ee**na]
penknife la navaja [nab**a**Ha]
pensioner el/la pensionista [pens-yon**ee**sta]
people la gente [H**e**ntay]
the other people in the hotel los otros huéspedes del hotel [w**e**spedess]
too many people demasiada gente [daymas-y**a**da]
pepper (spice) la pimienta [peem-y**e**nta]
(vegetable) el pimiento
peppermint (sweet) el caramelo de menta [karam**ay**lo day]
per: per night por noche [n**o**chay]
how much per day? ¿cuánto es por noche? [kw**a**nto]
per cent por ciento [th-y**e**nto]
perfect perfecto [pairf**e**kto]
perfume el perfume [pairf**oo**may]
perhaps quizás [keeth**a**ss]
perhaps not quizás no
period (of time, menstruation) el período [pair**ee**-odo]
perm la permanente

[pairmanentay]
permit el permiso [pairmeeso]
person la persona [pairsona]
personal stereo el walkman® [wolman]
petrol la gasolina

> The following types of petrol are available in Spain: **super** (4-star), **normal** (lower grade), **sin plomo** (unleaded).

petrol can la lata de gasolina [day]
petrol station la gasolinera [gasoleenaira]
pharmacy la farmacia [far-math-ya]
see **chemist's**
phone el teléfono [telayfono]
(verb) llamar por teléfono [yamar]

> Most payphones in Spain take both coins (all except one-peseta coins can be used) and phonecards (**tarjetas telefónicas**) which you can buy in tobacconists (**estanco**). The more modern payphones enable you to select the instructions in English. Phoning abroad costs less from 10 p.m. onwards and calls within Spain cost less after 8 p.m.
> see **speak**

phone book la guía telefónica [gee-a]
phone box la cabina telefónica [kabeena]
phonecard la tarjeta de teléfono [tarHayta day taylayfono]
phone number el número de teléfono [noomairo]
photo la foto
excuse me, could you take a photo of us? ¿le importaría hacernos una foto? [lay – athairnoss]
phrasebook el libro de frases [day frasess]
piano el piano [p-yano]
pickpocket el/la carterista
pick up: will you be there to pick me up? ¿va a ir a recogerme? [ba – rekoHairmay]
picnic el picnic
picture el cuadro [kwadro]
pie (meat) la empanada
(fruit) la tarta
piece el pedazo [pedatho]
a piece of ... un pedazo de ... [day]
pill la píldora
I'm on the pill estoy tomando la píldora
pillow la almohada [almo-ada]
pillow case la funda (de almohada) [foonda]
pin el alfiler [alfeelair]
pineapple la piña [peen-ya]
pineapple juice el zumo de piña [thoomo]
pink rosa
pipe (for smoking) la pipa [peepa]
(for water) el tubo [toobo]

pipe cleaners los limpiapipas [leemp-yap**ee**pass]
pity: it's a pity es una **lá**stima
pizza la pizza
place el sitio [s**ee**t-yo]
is this place taken? ¿est**á** ocup**a**do este sitio? [**e**stay]
at your place en tu c**a**sa
at his place en su c**a**sa
plain (not patterned) l**i**so
plane el avión [ab-y**o**n]
by plane en avión
plant la pl**a**nta
plaster cast la escayola [eska-y**o**la]
plasters las tir**i**tas
plastic pl**á**stico
(credit cards) las tarjetas de crédito [tarH**ay**tass day kr**ay**deeto]
plastic bag la b**o**lsa de plástico
plate el pl**a**to
platform el and**é**n
which platform is it for Saragossa, please? ¿qué andén p**a**ra Zarag**o**za, por fav**o**r? [kay]
play (in theatre) la **o**bra
(verb) jug**a**r [Hoog**a**r]
playground el patio de recreo [p**a**t-yo day rekr**ay**-o]
pleasant agradable [agrad**a**blay]
please por favor [fab**o**r]
yes please sí, por favor
could you please ...? ¿podría hacer el favor de ...? [ath**air** – day]
please don't no, por favor
pleased to meet you encant**a**do de conocerle [day konoth**air**lay]
pleasure: my pleasure es un placer [plath**air**]
plenty: plenty of ... mucho ... [m**oo**cho]
there's plenty of time tenemos mucho tiempo [tayn**ay**moss – t-y**e**mpo]
that's plenty, thanks es suficiente, gr**a**cias [soofeeth-y**e**ntay]
pliers los alicates [aleek**a**tess]
plug (electrical) el enchufe [ench**oo**fay]
(for car) la bujía [booH**ee**-a]
(in sink) el tap**ó**n
plumber el fontanero [fontan**air**o]
p.m.* de la tarde [day la t**a**rday]
poached egg el huevo escalf**a**do [w**ay**bo]
pocket el bolsillo [bols**ee**-yo]
point: two point five dos c**o**ma c**i**nco
there's no point no merece la pena [mair**ay**thay la p**ay**na]
points (in car) los plat**i**nos
poisonous venenoso [benen**o**so]
police la policía [poleeth**ee**-a]
call the police! ¡llame a la policía! [y**a**may]

> There are two basic types of police that operate all over the country: the **Guardia Civil** (dressed in green) and **Policía Nacional** (dressed in blue). Each town has its own body of local police (**Policía Municipal**). Some regions have their own independent police force. In The Basque Country they are called **Ertzantza**, in Catalonia **Mossos d'Esquadra** and in Andalucía **Policía Autonómica**. Dial 091 for the **Policía Nacional** or 062 for the **Guardia Civil**.

policeman el (agente de) policía [aHentay day]
police station la comisaría de policía
policewoman la policía
polish el betún [betoon]
polite educado [edookado]
polluted contaminado
pony el poney
pool (for swimming) la piscina [peestheena]
poor (not rich) pobre [pobray]
(quality) de baja calidad [day baHa kaleeda]
pop music la música pop [mooseeka]
pop singer el/la cantante de música pop [kantantay]
population la población [poblath-yon]
pork la carne de cerdo [karnay day thairdo]
port (for boats) el puerto [pwairto]
(drink) el Oporto
porter (in hotel) el conserje [konsairHay]
portrait el retrato
Portugal Portugal
Portuguese (adj) portugués [portoogayss]
posh (restaurant) de lujo [looHo]
(people) pijo [peeHo]
possible posible [poseeblay]
is it possible to ...? ¿es posible ...?
as ... as possible tan ... como sea posible [say-a]
post (mail) el correo [korray-o]
(verb) echar al correo
could you post this for me? ¿podría enviarme esto por correo? [emb-yarmay]

> **postal service**
> Post Offices (**Correos**) open Monday to Friday from 8.30 a.m. to 2 p.m. and in large towns and cities they open again from 4.30 p.m. to 8 p.m. although these times may vary depending on the season. It takes about two or three days for a letter to get to another area within Spain. If you want a quicker service tell the clerk you need **un sello urgente**. If you need to send a registered parcel or letter ask for **correo certificado**. If you need →

ordinary stamps you can buy them in an **estanco**. You should tell the assistant the destination of your letter.

postbox el buzón [boothon]
postcard la postal
poster el poster [postair], el cartel
post office Correos [korray-oss]
poste restante la lista de Correos [leesta]
potato la patata
potato chips las patatas fritas (de bolsa)
pots and pans (ie cooking implements) los cacharros de cocina [day kotheena]
pottery (objects) la cerámica [thairameeka]
pound* (money, weight) la libra
power cut el apagón
power point la toma de corriente [day korr-yentay]
practise: I want to practise my Spanish quiero practicar el español [k-yairo – espan-yol]
prawns las gambas
prefer: I prefer ... prefiero ... [pref-yairo]
pregnant embarazada [embarathada]
prescription (for chemist) la receta [rethayta]
present (gift) el regalo
president (of country) el/la presidente [preseedentay]
pretty mono
it's pretty expensive es bastante caro [bastantay]
price el precio [preth-yo]
priest el sacerdote [sathairdotay]
prime minister (man/woman) el primer ministro [preemair]/la primera ministra
printed matter los impresos [eempraysoss]
priority (in driving) la preferencia [prefairenth-ya]
prison la cárcel [karthel]
private privado [preebado]
private bathroom el baño privado [ban-yo]
probably probablemente [probablementay]
problem el problema [problayma]
no problem! ¡con mucho gusto! [moocho goosto]
program(me) el programa
promise: I promise lo prometo [promayto]
pronounce: how is this pronounced? ¿cómo se pronuncia esto? [say pronoonth-ya]
properly (repaired, locked etc) bien [b-yen]
protection factor (of suntan lotion) el factor de protección [protekth-yon]
Protestant (adj) protestante [protestantay]
public convenience los aseos públicos [asay-oss poobleekoss]

public holiday el día de fiesta [day]
pudding (dessert) el postre [pos**t**ray]
pull tirar
pullover el jersey [Hairs**ay**]
puncture el pinchazo [peench**a**tho]
purple morado
purse (for money) el monedero [moned**ai**ro]
(US: handbag) el bolso
push empujar [empooH**ar**]
pushchair la sillita de ruedas [see-y**ee**ta day rw**ay**dass]
put poner [pon**air**]
where can I put ...? ¿dónde puedo poner ...? [d**o**nday pw**ay**do]
could you put us up for the night? ¿podría alojarnos esta noche? [aloH**ar**noss – n**o**chay]
pyjamas el pijama [peeH**a**ma]
Pyrenees los Pirineos [peereen**ay**-oss]

Q

quality la calidad [kaleed**a**]
quarantine la cuarentena [kwarent**ay**na]
quarter la cuarta parte [kw**a**rta p**a**rtay]
quayside: on the quayside en el muelle [mw**ay**-yay]
question la pregunta [preg**oo**nta]
queue la cola
quick rápido
that was quick sí que ha sido rápido [kay a]
what's the quickest way there? ¿cuál es el camino más rápido? [kwal]
fancy a quick drink? ¿te apetece algo rápido de beber? [tay apet**ay**thay – day beb**air**]
quickly rápidamente [rapeedam**e**ntay]
quiet (place, hotel) tranquilo [trank**ee**lo]
quiet! ¡cállese! [k**a**-yaysay]
quite (fairly) bastante [bast**a**ntay]
(very) muy [mwee]
that's quite right eso es cierto [th-y**ai**rto]
quite a lot bastante

R

rabbit el conejo [kon**ay**Ho]
race (for runners, cars) la carrera [karr**ai**ra]
racket (tennis etc) la raqueta [rak**ay**ta]
radiator (of car, in room) el radiador [rad-yad**o**r]
radio la radio [r**a**d-yo]
on the radio por la radio
rail: by rail en tren
railway el ferrocarril
rain la lluvia [y**oo**b-ya]
in the rain bajo la lluvia [b**a**Ho]
it's raining está lloviendo [yob-y**e**ndo]

raincoat el impermeable [eempairmay-**a**blay]
rape la violación [b-yolath-y**o**n]
rare (steak) (muy) p**o**co hecho [mwee – **ay**cho]
rash (on skin) la erupción cutánea [airoopth-y**o**n koot**a**nay-a]
raspberry la frambuesa [frambw**ay**sa]
rat la r**a**ta
rate (for changing money) el cambio [k**a**mb-yo]
rather: it's rather good es bastante bueno [bast**a**ntay bw**ay**no]
I'd rather ... prefiero ... [pref-y**ai**ro]
razor la maquinilla de afeitar [makeen**ee**-ya day afay-eet**a**r]
(electric) la máquina de afeitar eléctrica [m**a**keena]
razor blades las hojas de afeitar [**o**Hass]
read leer [lay-**air**]
ready prepar**a**do
are you ready? ¿estás listo? [l**ee**sto]
I'm not ready yet aún no est**o**y listo [a-**oo**n]

•••••• DIALOGUE ••••••

when will it be ready? ¿cuándo estará listo? [kw**a**ndo]
it should be ready in a couple of days estará listo dentro de un par de días [day]

real verdadero [bairdad**ai**ro]
really realmente [ray-alm**e**ntay]
that's really great eso es estup**e**ndo [**ay**so]
really? (doubt) ¿de verdad? [day baird**a**]
(polite interest) ¿sí?
rearview mirror el (espejo) retrovisor [esp**ay**Ho retrobees**o**r]
reasonable (prices etc) razonable [rathon**a**blay]
receipt el recibo [reth**ee**bo]
recently recientemente [reth-yentem**e**ntay]
reception la recepción [rethepth-y**o**n]
at reception en recepción
reception desk la recepción
receptionist el/la recepcionista [rethepth-yon**ee**sta]
recognize reconocer [rekonoth**air**]
recommend: could you recommend ...? ¿puede usted recomend**a**r ...? [pw**ay**day oost**ay**]
record (music) el disco [d**ee**sko]
red rojo [r**o**Ho]
red wine el vino tinto [b**ee**no t**ee**nto]
refund el reembolso [ray-emb**o**lso]
can I have a refund? ¿puede devolverme el dinero? [pw**ay**day debolb**ai**rmay el deen**ai**ro]
region la zona [th**o**na], la región [reH-y**o**n]
registered: by registered mail por correo certificado

[korr**ay**-o thairteefeek**a**do]
registration number el número de la matrícula [n**oo**mairo day]
relatives los parientes [par-y**e**ntess]
religion la religión [releeH-y**o**n]
remember: I don't remember no recuerdo [rekw**ai**rdo]
I remember recuerdo
do you remember? ¿recuerda? [rekw**ai**rda]
rent (for apartment etc) el alquiler [alkeel**air**]
(verb) alquilar
to/for rent de alquiler

•••••• DIALOGUE ••••••

I'd like to rent a car quisiera alquilar un coche [kees-y**ai**ra]
for how long? ¿por cuánto tiempo? [kw**a**nto t-y**e**mpo]
two days dos días
this is our range ésta es nuestra gama [nw**e**stra]
I'll take the ... me quedo con el ... [may k**ay**do]
is that with unlimited mileage? ¿es con kilometraje ilimitado? [keelometr**a**Hay eeleemeet**a**do]
it is es
can I see your licence please? ¿me deja ver su permiso, por favor? [may d**ay**Ha bair soo pairm**ee**so]
and your passport y su pasaporte [ee soo pasap**o**rtay]
is insurance included? ¿va incluido el seguro? [ba eenkloo-**ee**do]
yes, but you pay the first 50,000 pesetas sí, pero usted paga las primeras cincuenta mil pesetas [p**ai**ro oost**ay** – preem**ai**rass – pes**ay**tass]
can you leave a deposit of ...? ¿puede dejar un depósito de ...? [pw**ay**day d**ay**Har – day]

rented car el coche alquilado [k**o**chay alkeel**a**do]
repair (verb) reparar
can you repair it? ¿puede arreglarlo? [pw**ay**day]
repeat repetir
could you repeat that? ¿puede repetir eso? [pw**ay**day – **ay**so]
reservation la reserva [res**ai**rba]
I'd like to make a reservation quisiera hacer una reserva [kees-y**ai**ra ath**air**]

•••••• DIALOGUE ••••••

I have a reservation tengo una reserva
yes sir, what name please? sí, señor, ¿a qué nombre, por favor? [sen-y**o**r a kay n**o**mbray]

reserve reservar [resairb**a**r]

•••••• DIALOGUE ••••••

can I reserve a table for tonight? ¿puedo reservar una mesa para esta noche? [pw**ay**do – m**ay**sa – n**o**chay]
yes madam, for how many people? sí, señora, ¿para cuántos? [sen-y**o**ra – kw**a**ntoss]
for two para dos
and for what time? ¿y para qué

hora? [kay **o**ra]
for eight o'clock para las **o**cho
and could I have your name please? ¿me dice su nombre, por fav**o**r? [may d**ee**thay soo n**o**mbray]
see **alphabet** for spelling

rest: I need a rest necesito un desc**a**nso [nethes**ee**to]
the rest of the group el r**e**sto del grupo [gr**oo**po]

restaurant el restaurante [restowr**a**ntay]

> Spanish restaurants are categorized by a fork symbol (from 1 to 5 forks according to their quality). You can sit down and have a full meal in a **comedor**, a **cafetería**, a **restaurante** or a **marisquería** – all in addition to the more food-oriented bars, where **tapas** are available. **Comedores** are the places to seek out if your main criteria are price and quantity. Sometimes you will see them attached to a bar (often in a room behind); or as the dining room of a **pensión** or **fonda**, but as often as not they're virtually unmarked and discovered only if you pass an open door. Replacing **comedores** to some extent are **cafeterías**, which the local authorities now grade from one to three cups (the ratings, as with restaurants, seem to be based on facilities offered rather than quality of food). Moving up the scale there are **restaurantes** and **marisquerías**, the latter serving exclusively fish and seafood.

restaurant car el vagón-cafetería [bag**o**n kafetair**ee**-a]

rest room los servicios [sairb**ee**th-yoss]
see **toilet**

retired: I'm retired est**o**y jubilado/jubil**a**da [Hoobeel**a**do]

return (ticket) el billete de ida y vuelta [bee-y**ay**tay day **ee**da ee bw**e**lta]
see **ticket**

reverse charge call la llamada a cobro revertido [yam**a**da – rebert**ee**do]

reverse gear la marcha atr**á**s

revolting asqueroso [askair**o**so]

rib la costilla [kost**ee**-ya]

rice arroz [arr**o**th]

rich (person) rico [r**ee**ko]
(food) sustancial [soostanth-y**a**l]

ridiculous ridículo [reed**ee**koolo]

right (correct) correcto
(not left) derecho
you were right tenía razón [rath**o**n]
that's right eso es [**ay**so]
this can't be right esto no puede ser as**í** [pw**ay**day sair]
right! ¡bien! [b-yen]

is this the right road for ...? ¿es éste el camino correcto para ir a ...? [**e**stay]
on the right a la derecha
turn right gire a la derecha [H**ee**ray]
right-hand drive con el volante a la derecha [bol**a**ntay]
ring (on finger) la sortija [sort**ee**Ha]
I'll ring you te llamaré [tay yamar**ay**]
ring back volver a llamar [bolb**ai**r a yam**a**r]
ripe (fruit) maduro
rip-off: it's a rip-off es un timo
rip-off prices los precios altísimos [pr**ay**th-yoss]
risky arriesgado [arr-yesg**a**do]
river el río
road la carretera [karret**ai**ra]
is this the road for ...? ¿es ésta la carretera que va a ...? [kay ba]
down the road en esta calle [k**a**-yay]
road accident el accidente automovilístico [aktheed**e**ntay owtomobeel**ee**steeko]
road map el mapa de carreteras
roadsign la señal de tráfico [sen-y**a**l day]
rob: I've been robbed ¡me han robado! [may an]
rock la roca
(music) el rock
on the rocks (with ice) con hielo [y**ay**lo]
roll (bread) el bollo [b**o**-yo]
roof el tejado [teH**a**do]
roof rack la baca
room la habitación [abeetath-y**o**n]
in my room en mi habitación

•••••• DIALOGUE ••••••

do you have any rooms? ¿tiene habitaciones? [t-y**ay**nay abeetath-y**o**ness]
for how many people? ¿para cuántos? [kw**a**ntoss]
for one/for two para uno/dos
yes, we have rooms free sí, tenemos habitaciones libres [ten**ay**moss – l**ee**bress]
for how many nights will it be? ¿para cuántas noches? [kw**a**ntass n**o**chess]
just for one night sólo para una noche [**oo**na]
how much is it? ¿cuánto es? [kw**a**nto]
... with bathroom and ... without bathroom ... con baño y ... sin baño [b**a**n-yo – ee seen]
can I see a room with bathroom? ¿me enseña una habitación con baño? [may ensen-ya]
OK, I'll take it vale, me la quedo [b**a**lay may la k**ay**do]

room service el servicio de habitaciones [sairb**ee**th-yo day]
rope la cuerda [kw**ai**rda]
rosé (wine) vino rosado [b**ee**no]
roughly (approximately)

approximadamente [–mentay]
round: **it's my round** es mi turno [toorno]
roundabout (for traffic) la rotonda
round trip ticket el billete de ida y vuelta [bee-yaytay day eeda ee bwelta]
see **ticket**
route la ruta [roota]
what's the best route? ¿cuál es la mejor ruta? [kwal ess la mayHor]
rubber (material) la goma
(eraser) la goma de borrar
rubber band la goma elástica
rubbish (waste) la basura
(poor quality goods) las porquerías [porkairee-ass]
rubbish! (nonsense) ¡tonterías! [tontairee-ass]
rucksack la mochila
rude grosero [grosairo]
ruins las ruinas [rweenass]
rum el ron
rum and coke el ron con coca-cola
run (verb: person) correr [korrair]
how often do the buses run? ¿cada cuánto pasan los autobuses? [kwanto]
I've run out of money se me ha acabado el dinero [say may a – deenairo]
rush hour la hora punta [ora poonta]

S

sad triste [treestay]
saddle (for horse) la silla de montar [see-ya day]
(on bike) el sillín [see-yeen]
safe seguro [segooro]
safety pin el imperdible [eempairdeeblay]
sail la vela [bayla]
sailboard el windsurf
sailboarding el windsurf
salad la ensalada
salad dressing el aliño para la ensalada [aleen-yo]
sale: **for sale** en venta [em baynta]
salmon el salmón [sal-mon]
salt la sal
same: **the same** mismo [meesmo]
the same as this igual que éste [eegwal kay estay]
the same again, please lo mismo otra vez, por favor [beth]
it's all the same to me me es igual [may – eegwal]
sand la arena [arayna]
sandals las sandalias [sandal-yass]
sandwich el sandwich
sanitary napkin la compresa [kompraysa]
sanitary towel la compresa
Saragossa Zaragoza [tharagotha]
sardines las sardinas
Saturday sábado

sauce la salsa
saucepan el cazo [katho]
saucer el platillo [platee-yo]
sauna la sauna [sowna]
sausage la salchicha
say: how do you say ... in Spanish? ¿cómo se dice ... en castellano [say deethay en kastay-yano]
what did he say? ¿que ha dicho? [kay a]
I said ... he dicho ... [ay]
he said ... ha dicho ...
could you say that again? ¿podría repetirlo?
scarf (for neck) la bufanda (for head) el pañuelo [pan-ywaylo]
scenery el paisaje [pa-eesaHay]
schedule (US) el horario [orar-yo]
scheduled flight el vuelo regular [bwaylo regoolar]
school la escuela [eskwayla]
scissors: a pair of scissors las tijeras [teeHairass]
scotch el whisky
Scotch tape® la cinta adhesiva [theenta adeseeba]
Scotland Escocia [eskoth-ya]
Scottish escocés [eskothayss]
I'm Scottish (man/woman) soy escocés/escocesa
scrambled eggs los huevos revueltos [wayboss rebwayltoss]
scratch el rasguño [rasgoon-yo]
screw el tornillo [tornee-yo]
screwdriver el destornillador [destornee-yador]
sea el mar
by the sea junto al mar [Hoonto]
seafood los mariscos
seafood restaurant la marisquería [mareeskairee-a]
seafront el paseo marítimo [pasay-o mareeteemo]
on the seafront en línea de playa [leenay-a day pla-ya]
seagull la gaviota [gab-yota]
search (verb) buscar
seashell la concha marina
seasick: I feel seasick estoy mareado [maray-ado]
I get seasick me mareo [may maray-o]
seaside: by the seaside en la playa [pla-ya]
seat el asiento [as-yento]
is this anyone's seat? ¿es de alguien este asiento? [day alg-yen estay]
seat belt el cinturón de seguridad [theentooron day segooreeda]
sea urchin el erizo de mar [aireetho]
seaweed el alga
secluded apartado
second (adjective) segundo [segoondo]
(of time) el segundo
just a second! ¡un momento!
second class (travel) en segunda clase [klassay]
secondhand de segunda mano [day]

see ver [bair]
can I see? ¿puedo ver? [pwaydo]
have you seen ...? ¿ha visto ...? [a beesto]
I saw him this morning le vi esta mañana [lay bee]
see you! ¡hasta luego! [asta lwaygo]
I see (I understand) ya comprendo
self-catering apartment el apartamento
self-service autoservicio [owtosairbeeth-yo]
sell vender [bendair]
do you sell ...? ¿vende ...? [benday]
Sellotape® la cinta adhesiva [theenta adeseeba]
send enviar [emb-yar]
I want to send this to England quiero enviar esto a Inglaterra [k-yairo emb-yar]
senior citizen el/la pensionista [pens-yoneesta]
separate separado
separated: I'm separated estoy separado/separada
separately (pay, travel) por separado
September septiembre [sept-yembray]
septic séptico
serious serio [sair-yo]
service charge el servicio [sairbeeth-yo]
service station la estacion de servicio [estath-yon day]
serviette la servilleta [sairbee-yayta]
set menu el menu del día [menoo]
several varios [bar-yoss]
Seville Sevilla [sebee-ya]
sew coser [kosair]
could you sew this back on? ¿podría coserme esto? [kosairmay]
sex el sexo
sexy sexy
shade: in the shade a la sombra
shake: let's shake hands choque esa mano [chokay aysa]
shallow (water) poco profundo [profoondo]
shame: what a shame! ¡que lástima! [kay]
shampoo el champú
a shampoo and set un lavado y marcado [labado ee]
share (verb: room, table etc) compartir
sharp (knife) afilado
(taste) ácido [atheedo]
(pain) agudo
shattered (very tired) agotado
shaver la máquina de afeitar [makeena day afay-eetar]
shaving foam la espuma de afeitar
shaving point el enchufe (para la máquina de afeitar) [enchoofay – makeena]
she* ella [ay-ya]
is she here? ¿está (ella) aquí?

[ak**ee**]
sheet (for bed) la sábana
shelf la estantería
[estantair**ee**-a]
shellfish los mariscos
sherry el jerez [Her**e**th]

> The classic Andalucian wine is sherry – **vino de Jerez**. This is served chilled or at **bodega** temperature – a perfect drink to wash down **tapas** – and like everything Spanish, comes in a perplexing variety of forms. The main distinctions are between **fino** or **jerez seco** (dry sherry), **amontillado** [amontee-y**a**do] (medium), and **oloroso** or **jerez dulce** (sweet), and these are the terms you should use to order. Similar – though not identical – are **montilla** [mont**ee**-ya] and **manzanilla** [manthan**ee**-ya], dry, sherry-like wines from the provinces of Córdoba and Huelva. These too are excellent and widely available.

ship el barco
by ship en barco
shirt el camisa
shit! ¡mierda! [m-y**ai**rda]
shock el susto [s**oo**sto]
I got an electric shock me ha dado calambre [may a – kal**a**mbray]
shock-absorber el amortiguador
[amorteegwad**o**r]
shocking escandaloso
shoes los zapatos [thap**a**toss]
a pair of shoes un par de zapatos
shoelaces los cordones para zapatos [kord**o**ness]
shoe polish la crema para los zapatos [kr**ay**ma]
shoe repairer's la zapatería
[thapatair**ee**-a]
shop la tienda [t-y**e**nda]

> Business hours vary from place to place and from season to season. Shops open some time between 9 and 10 a.m. and food shops open earlier than other shops. In winter, they generally close for lunch between 1.30 and 4 p.m. and in summer they re-open later at 5 or 5.30 p.m. They then stay open until 8 p.m. in winter and 9 p.m. in summer. Department stores and hypermarkets usually open from 10 a.m to 9 p.m. and don't close for lunch.

shopping: I'm going shopping voy de compras [boy]
shopping centre el centro comercial [th**e**ntro komairth-y**a**l]
shop window el escaparate
[eskapar**a**tay]
shore la orilla [or**ee**-ya]
short (time, journey) corto
(person) bajo [b**a**Ho]

it's only a short distance queda bastante cerca [kayda bastantay thairka]
shortcut el atajo [ataHo]
shorts los pantalones cortos [pantaloness]
should: what should I do? ¿que hago? [kay ago]
he shouldn't be long no tardará mucho [moocho]
you should have told me debiste habérmelo dicho [debeestay abairmelo]
shoulder el hombro [ombro]
shout (verb) gritar
show (in theatre) el espectáculo [espektakoolo]
could you show me? ¿me lo enseña? [may lo ensen-ya]
shower (in bathroom) la ducha [doocha]
with shower con ducha
shower gel el gel de ducha [Hel]
shut (verb) cerrar [thairrar]
when do you shut? ¿a qué hora cierran? [a kay ora th-yairran]
when do they shut? ¿a qué hora cierran?
they're shut está cerrado [thairrado]
I've shut myself out he cerrado y he dejado la llave dentro [ay – ee ay dayHado la yabay]
shut up! ¡cállese! [ka-yesay]
shutter (on camera) el obturador (on window) la contraventana [kontrabentana]
shy tímido [teemeedo]
sick (ill) enfermo [enfairmo]
I'm going to be sick (vomit) voy a vomitar [boy a bomeetar]
see ill
side el lado
the other side of town al otro lado de la ciudad [day la th-yooda]
side lights las luces de posición [loothess day poseeth-yon]
side salad la ensalada aparte [apartay]
side street la callejuela [ka-yay-Hwayla]
sidewalk la acera [athaira]
see pavement
sight: the sights of ... los lugares de interés de ... [loogaress day eentairess]
sightseeing: we're going sightseeing vamos a hacer un recorrido turístico [bamoss a athair]
sightseeing tour el recorrido turístico
sign (notice) el letrero [letrairo] (roadsign) la señal de tráfico [sen-yal day]
signal: he didn't give a signal no hizo ninguna señal [no eetho]
signature la firma [feerma]
signpost el letrero [letrairo]
silence el silencio [seelenth-yo]
silk la seda [sayda]
silly tonto
silver la plata

silver foil el papel de aluminio [aloom**ee**n-yo]
similar parecido [pareth**ee**do]
simple (easy) sencillo [senth**ee**-yo]
since: since yesterday desde ayer [desday a-y**air**]
since I got here desde que llegamos aquí [kay yeg**a**moss ak**ee**]
sing cant**ar**
singer el/la cantante [kant**a**ntay]
single: a single to ... un billete para ... [bee-y**ay**tay]
I'm single soy soltero [solt**ai**ro]
single bed la cama individual [eendeebeedw**a**l]
single room la habitación individual [abeetath-y**o**n]
sink (in kitchen) el fregadero [fregad**ai**ro]
sister la hermana [airm**a**na]
sister-in-law la cuñada [koon-y**a**da]
sit: can I sit here? ¿puedo sentarme aquí? [pw**ay**do sent**a**rmay ak**ee**]
sit down sentarse [sent**a**rsay]
sit down! ¡siéntese! [s-yentaysay]
is anyone sitting here? ¿está ocupado este asiento? [**e**stay as-yento]
size el tamaño [tam**a**n-yo]
(of clothes) la talla [t**a**-ya]
ski el esquí [esk**ee**]
(verb) esquiar [esk-y**a**r]
a pair of skis un par de esquís [day]
ski boots las botas de esquiar
skiing el esquí [esk**ee**]
we're going skiing vamos a esquiar [b**a**moss – esk-y**a**r]
ski instructor (man/woman) el monitor/la monitora de esquí
ski-lift el telesquí [telesk**ee**]
skin la piel [p-yel]
skin-diving el buceo [booth**ay**-o]
skinny flaco
ski-pants los pantalones de esquí [pantal**o**ness day esk**ee**]
ski-pass el abono
ski pole el bastón de esquí [day]
skirt la falda
ski run la pista de esquí [esk**ee**]
ski slope la pista de esquí
ski wax la cera de esquís [th**ai**ra]
sky el cielo [th-y**ay**lo]
sleep (verb) dormir
did you sleep well? ¿ha dormido bien? [a – b-yen]
I need a good sleep necesito dormir bien [nethes**ee**to]
sleeper (on train) el coche-cama [k**o**chay-k**a**ma]
sleeping bag el saco de dormir [day]
sleeping car el coche-cama [k**o**chay-k**a**ma]
sleeping pill la pastilla para dormir [past**ee**-ya]
sleepy: I'm feeling sleepy tengo sueño [sw**ay**n-yo]

sleeve la m**a**nga
slide (photographic) la diapositiva [d-yaposeet**ee**ba]
slip (under dress) la combinación [kombeenath-y**o**n]
slippery resbaladizo [resbalad**ee**tho]
slow lento
slow down! ¡más desp**a**cio! [desp**a**th-yo]
slowly despacio
could you say it slowly? ¿podría decirlo despacio? [deth**ee**rlo]
very slowly muy despacio [mw**ee**]
small pequeño [pek**e**n-yo]
smell: it smells! (smells bad) ¡apesta!
smile (verb) sonreir [sonray-**ee**r]
smoke el humo [**oo**mo]
do you mind if I smoke? ¿le imp**o**rta si fumo? [lay – f**oo**mo]
I don't smoke no fumo
do you smoke? ¿f**u**ma?
snack: I'd just like a snack quisiera una t**a**pa solamente [kees-y**ai**ra – solam**e**ntay]
sneeze el estorn**u**do
snorkel el tubo de buceo [t**oo**bo day booth**ay**-o]
snow la nieve [n-y**ay**bay]
it's snowing está nev**a**ndo
so: it's so good es tan bueno [bw**ay**no]
not so fast no tan de prisa [pr**ee**sa]
so am I yo también [tamb-y**e**n]
so do I yo también
so-so más o menos [m**ay**noss]
soaking solution (for contact lenses) el líquido preservad**o**r [l**ee**keedo]
soap el jabón [Hab**o**n]
soap powder el jabón en p**o**lvo [em p**o**lbo]
sober sobrio [s**o**br-yo]
sock el calcetín [kalthet**ee**n]
socket (electrical) el enchufe [ench**oo**fay]
soda (water) la soda
sofa el sof**á**
soft (material etc) suave [sw**a**bay]
soft-boiled egg el huevo pas**a**do por agua [w**ay**bo – **a**gwa]
soft drink el refresco
soft lenses las lentes bl**a**ndas [l**e**ntess]
sole (of shoe, of foot) la suela [sw**ay**la]
could you put new soles on these? ¿podría cambiarles las suelas? [kamb-y**a**rless]
some: can I have some water? ¿me da un p**o**co de **a**gua? [may – day]
can I have some rolls? ¿me da unos bollos? [b**o**-yoss]
can I have some? ¿me da un poco?
somebody, someone alguien [**a**lg-yen]
something **a**lgo
something to drink algo de

beber [bebair]
sometimes a veces [baythess]
somewhere en alguna parte [partay]
son el hijo [eeHo]
song la canción [kanth-yon]
son-in-law el yerno [yairno]
soon pronto
I'll be back soon volveré pronto [bolbairay]
as soon as possible lo antes posible [antess poseeblay]
sore: it's sore me duele [may dwaylay]
sore throat el dolor de garganta
sorry: (I'm) sorry perdone [pairdonay]
sorry? (didn't understand) ¿cómo?
sort: what sort of ...? ¿qué clase de ...? [kay klassay day]
soup la sopa
sour (taste) ácido [atheedo]
south el sur [soor]
in the south en el sur
South Africa Sudáfrica
South African (adj) sudafricano
I'm South African (man/woman) soy sudafricano/sudafricana
southeast el sudeste [sood-estay]
southwest el sudoeste [soodo-estay]
souvenir el recuerdo [rekwairdo]
Spain España [espan-ya]
Spaniard (man/woman) el español [espan-yol]/la española
Spanish español
the Spanish los españoles [espan-yoless]
spanner la llave inglesa [yabay eenglaysa]
spare part el repuesto [repwesto]
spare tyre la rueda de repuesto [rwayda day]
spark plug la bujía [booHee-a]
speak: do you speak English? ¿habla inglés? [abla]
I don't speak ... no hablo ... [ablo]

•••••• DIALOGUE ••••••

can I speak to Pablo? ¿puedo hablar con Pablo? [pwaydo]
who's calling ¿quién llama? [k-yen yama]
it's Patricia soy Patricia
I'm sorry, he's not in, can I take a message? lo siento, no está, ¿quiere dejar algún recado? [s-yento – k-yairay dayHar]
no thanks, I'll call back later no gracias, llamaré más tarde [yamaray mass tarday]
please tell him I called por favor, dígale que he llamado [deegalay kay ay yamado]

speciality la especialidad [espeth-yaleeda]
spectacles las gafas
speed la velocidad [belotheeda]
speed limit el límite de velocidad [leemeetay day]
speedometer el velocímetro [belotheemetro]

spell: how do you spell it? ¿cómo se escribe? [say eskr**ee**bay]
see alphabet
spend gast**a**r
spider la araña [ar**a**n-ya]
spin-dryer la secad**o**ra
splinter la astilla [ast**ee**-ya]
spoke (in wheel) el radio [r**a**d-yo]
spoon la cuch**a**ra
sport el deporte [dayp**o**rtay]
sprain: I've sprained my ... me he torcido el ... [may ay torth**ee**do]
spring (season) la primavera [preemab**ai**ra]
(of car, seat) el muelle [mw**ay**-yay]
square (in town) la plaza [pl**a**tha]
stairs las escaleras [eskal**ai**rass]
stale (bread, taste) pas**a**do
stall: the engine keeps stalling el mot**o**r se p**a**ra a c**a**da r**a**to [say]
stamp el sello [s**ay**-yo]

•••••• DIALOGUE ••••••

a stamp for England, please un sello p**a**ra Inglaterra, por fav**o**r
what are you sending? ¿qué es lo que envía? [kay – emb**ee**-a]
this postcard esta post**a**l

> Stamps can be bought from tobacconist's (**estanco**), the Post Office (**Correos**) and sometimes from shops and stalls selling postcards and souvenirs.

standby el vuelo standby [bw**ay**lo]
star la estrella [estr**ay**-ya]
(in film) el/la protagon**i**sta
start el principio [preenth**ee**p-yo]
(verb) comenzar [komenth**a**r]
when does it start? ¿cuándo empieza? [kw**a**ndo emp-**ay**tha]
the car won't start el coche no arr**a**nca [k**o**chay]
starter (of car) el mot**o**r de arranque [arr**a**nkay]
(food) la entr**a**da
starving: I'm starving me muero de hambre [may mw**ai**ro day **a**mbray]
state (in country) el est**a**do
the States (USA) los Est**a**dos Unidos [oon**ee**doss]
station la estación del ferrocarril [estath-y**o**n]
statue la estatua [est**a**twa]
stay: where are you staying? ¿dónde se hospedan? [d**o**nday say osp**ay**dan]
I'm staying at ... me hospedo en ... [may osp**ay**do]
I'd like to stay another two nights me gustaría quedarme otras dos noches [may – ked**a**rmay – n**o**chess]
steak el filete [feel**ay**tay]
steal rob**a**r
my bag has been stolen me han rob**a**do el b**o**lso [may an]
steep (hill) empin**a**do
steering la dirección

[deerekth-y**o**n]
step: on the steps en las escaleras [eskal**ai**rass]
stereo el estéreo [est**ai**ray-o]
sterling las libras esterlinas [estairl**ee**nass]
steward (on plane) el auxiliar de vuelo [owkseel-y**a**r day bw**e**lo]
stewardess la azafata [athaf**a**ta]
sticking plaster la tirita
still: I'm still waiting todavía estoy esperando [todab**ee**-a]
is he still there? ¿está todavía ahí? [a-**ee**]
keep still! ¡quédese quieto! [k**ay**daysay k-y**e**to]
sting: I've been stung algo me ha picado [may a]
stockings las medias [m**ay**d-yass]
stomach el estómago
stomach ache el dolor de estómago [day]
stone (rock) la piedra [p-y**e**dra]
stop (verb) parar
please, stop here (to taxi driver etc) pare aquí, por favor [p**a**ray ak**ee**]
do you stop near ...? ¿para cerca de ...? [th**ai**rka day]
stop doing that! ¡deje de hacer eso! [d**ay**Hay day ath**air** **ay**so]
stopover la escala, la parada
storm la tormenta
straight: it's straight ahead todo derecho [dair**e**cho]
a straight whisky un whisky solo
straightaway en seguida [seg**ee**da]
strange (odd) extraño [estr**a**n-yo]
stranger (man/woman) el forastero [forast**ai**ro]/la forastera
I'm a stranger here no soy de aquí [day ak**ee**]
strap la correa [korr**ay**-a]
strawberry la fresa [fr**ay**sa]
stream el arroyo [arr**o**-yo]
street la calle [k**a**-yay]
on the street en la calle
streetmap el mapa de la ciudad [thyood**a**]
string la cuerda [kw**ai**rda]
strong fuerte [fw**ai**rtay]
stuck atascar
the key's stuck la llave se ha atascado [y**a**bay say a]
student el/la estudiante [estood-y**a**ntay]
stupid estúpido [est**oo**peedo]
subway (US) el metro
suburb el suburbio [soob**oo**rb-yo]
suddenly de repente [rep**e**ntay]
suede el ante [**a**ntay]
sugar el azúcar [ath**oo**kar]
suit el traje [tr**a**Hay]
it doesn't suit me (jacket etc) no me sienta bien [no may s-y**e**nta b-yen]
it suits you te sienta muy bien [tay – mw**ee**]
suitcase la maleta [mal**ay**ta]
summer el verano [bair**a**no]
in the summer en el verano
sun el sol

in the sun en el sol
out of the sun en la sombra
sunbathe tomar el sol
sunblock (cream) la crema protectora [krayma]
sunburn la quemadura de sol [kemadoora]
sunburnt quemado [kemado]
Sunday domingo
sunglasses las gafas de sol
sun lounger la tumbona
sunny: it's sunny hace sol [athay]
sun roof (in car) el techo corredizo [korraydeetho]
sunset la puesta de sol [pwesta day]
sunshade la sombrilla [sombree-ya]
sunshine la luz del sol [looth]
sunstroke la insolación [eensolath-yon]
suntan el bronceado [bronthay-ado]
suntan lotion la loción bronceadora [loth-yon bronthay-adora]
suntanned bronceado
suntan oil el aceite bronceador [athay-eetay]
super fabuloso
supermarket el supermercado [soopairmairkado]
supper la cena [thayna]
supplement (extra charge) el suplemento
sure: are you sure? ¿está seguro?
sure! ¡por supuesto!
[soopwesto]
surname el apellido [apay-yeedo]
swearword la palabrota
sweater el suéter [swetair]
sweatshirt la sudadera [soodadaira]
Sweden Suecia [swayth-ya]
Swedish (adj) sueco [swayko]
sweet (dessert) el postre [postray]
(adj: taste) dulce [doolthay]
(sherry) oloroso
sweets los caramelos [karamayloss]
swelling la hinchazón [eenchathon]
swim (verb) nadar
I'm going for a swim voy a nadar [boy]
let's go for a swim vamos a nadar [bamoss]
swimming costume el bañador [ban-yador]
swimming pool la piscina [peestheena]
swimming trunks el traje de baño [traHay day banyo]
switch el interruptor [eentairooptor]
switch off apagar
switch on encender [enthendair]
swollen inflamado

T

table la mesa [m**ay**sa]
a table for two **u**na mesa p**a**ra dos
tablecloth el mant**e**l
table tennis el ping-p**o**ng
table wine el vino de mesa [b**ee**no day m**ay**sa]
tailback (of traffic) la caravana de coches [karab**a**na day k**o**chess]
tailor el sastre [s**a**stray]
take (lead) coger [koH**air**]
(accept) aceptar [athept**ar**]
can you take me to the airport? ¿me lleva al aeropuerto? [may y**ay**ba al a-airopw**air**to]
do you take credit cards? ¿acepta tarjetas de crédito? [ath**e**pta tarH**ay**tass day kr**ay**deeto]
fine, I'll take it está bien, lo compro [b-yen]
can I take this? (leaflet etc) ¿puedo llevarme esto? [pw**ay**do yeb**a**rmay]
how long does it take? ¿cuánto se tarda? [kw**a**nto say]
it takes three hours se tarda tres horas [**o**rass]
is this seat taken? ¿está ocupado este asiento? [**e**stay as-y**e**nto]
a hamburger to take away **u**na hamburg**ue**sa p**a**ra llevar [yeb**ar**]
can you take a little off here? (to hairdresser) ¿puede quitarme un p**o**co de aquí? [pw**ay**day keet**a**rmay – day ak**ee**]
talcum powder el t**a**lco
talk (verb) hablar [abl**ar**]
tall **a**lto
tampons los tampones [tamp**o**ness]
tan el bronceado [bronthay-**a**do]
to get a tan broncearse [bronthay-**a**rsay]
tank (of car) el depósito [dep**o**seeto]
tap el gr**i**fo
tape (for cassette) la cinta [th**ee**nta]
(sticky) la cinta adhesiva [ades**ee**ba]
tape measure la cinta métrica
tape recorder el casete [kas**e**t]
taste el sab**o**r
can I taste it? ¿puedo probarlo? [pw**ay**do]
taxi el t**a**xi
will you get me a taxi? ¿podría conseguirme un taxi? [konseg**ee**rmay]
where can I find a taxi? ¿dónde puedo coger un taxi? [d**o**nday pw**ay**do koH**air**]

•••••• DIALOGUE ••••••

to the airport/to Hotel Sol please al aeropuerto/al hotel Sol, por fav**o**r [a-airopw**air**to/ot**e**l]
how much will it be? ¿cuánto costar**á**? [kw**a**nto]
1,000 pesetas mil pesetas

[pes**ay**tass]
that's fine, right here, thanks está bien, aquí mismo, gracias [b-yen akee meesmo]

taxi-driver el/la taxista
taxi rank la parada de taxis [day]
tea (drink) el té [tay]
tea for one/two please un té/dos tés, por favor
teabags las bolsas de té
teach: could you teach me? ¿podría enseñarme? [ensen-yarmay]
teacher (primary: man/woman) el maestro [ma-estro]/la maestra
(secondary: man/woman) el profesor/la profesora
team el equipo [ekeepo]
teaspoon la cuchara de té [day tay]
tea towel el paño de cocina [pan-yo day kotheena]
teenager el/la adolescente [adolesthentay]
telegram el telegrama
telephone el teléfono [tel**ay**fono]
see phone
television la televisión [telebees-yon]
tell: could you tell him ...? ¿podría decirle ...? [detheerlay]
temperature (weather) la temperatura [temperatoora]
(fever) la fiebre [f-yebray]
tennis el tenis
tennis ball la pelota de tenis [day]
tennis court la pista de tenis
tennis racket la raqueta de tenis [rak**ay**ta]
tent la tienda de campaña [t-yenda day kampan-ya]
term (at university, school) el trimestre [treemestray]
terminus (rail) la estación terminal [estath-yon tairmeenal]
terrible terrible [terreeblay]
terrific fabuloso [fabooloso]
than* que [kay]
smaller than más pequeño que [pek**ay**n-yo]
thanks, thank you gracias [grath-yass]
thank you very much muchas gracias [moochass]
thanks for the lift gracias por traerme [tra-airmay]
no thanks no gracias

•••••• DIALOGUE ••••••

thanks gracias
that's OK, don't mention it no hay de qué [ī day kay]

that: that man ese hombre [**ay**say ombray]
that woman esa mujer [mooHair]
that one ése
I hope that ... espero que ... [espairo kay]
that's nice (clothes, souvenir etc) es bonito

is that ...? ¿es ése ...? [**ay**say]
that's it (that's right) eso es
the* el, la; (pl) los, las
theatre el teatro [tay-**a**tro]
their* su; (pl) sus [sooss]
theirs* su, sus; (pl) suyos [s**oo**-yoss], suyas; de ellos [day **ay**-yoss], de ellas
them* (things) los, las
(people) les
for them para ellos [**ay**-yoss]/ellas
with them con ellos/ellas
I gave it to them se lo di a ellos/ellas [say]
who? – them ¿quién? – ellos/ellas [k-yen]
then entonces [ent**o**nthess]
there allí [a-y**ee**]
over there allí
up there allí arriba
is/are there ...? ¿hay ...? [ī]
there is/are ... hay ...
there you are (giving something) aquí tiene [ak**ee** t-y**ay**nay]
thermometer el termómetro [tairm**o**metro]
thermos flask el termo [t**ai**rmo]
these: these men estos hombres
these women estas mujeres
can I have these? ¿me puedo llevar éstos? [may pw**ay**do yeb**a**r]
they* (male) ellos [**ay**-yoss]
(female) ellas [**ay**-yass]
thick grueso [grw**ay**so]
(stupid) estúpido [est**oo**peedo]
thief (man/woman) el ladrón/la ladrona
thigh el muslo [m**oo**slo]
thin delgado
thing la cosa
my things mis cosas [meess]
think pensar
I think so creo que sí [kr**ay**-o kay]
I don't think so no lo creo
I'll think about it lo pensaré [pensar**ay**]
third party insurance el seguro contra terceros [tairth**ai**ross]
thirsty: I'm thirsty tengo sed [seth]
this: this man este hombre [**e**stay]
this woman esta mujer
this one éste/ésta
this is my wife ésta es mi mujer
is this ...? ¿es éste/ésta ...?
those: those men aquellos hombres [ak**ay**-yoss]
those women aquellas mujeres [ak**ay**-yass]
which ones? – those ¿cuáles? – aquéllos/aquéllas [kw**a**less]
thread el hilo [**ee**lo]
throat la garganta
throat pastilles las pastillas para la garganta [past**ee**-yass]
through a través de [day]
does it go through ...? (train, bus) ¿pasa por...?
throw (verb) tirar
throw away (verb) tirar
thumb el dedo pulgar [d**ay**do]

thunderstorm la tor**men**ta
Thursday jueves [Hw**ay**bess]
ticket el billete [bee-y**ay**tay]

•••••• DIALOGUE ••••••

a return to Salamanca un billete de ida y vuelta a Salamanca [day **ee**da ee bw**e**lta]
coming back when? ¿cuándo piensa volver? [kw**a**ndo p-y**e**nsa bolb**air**]
today/next Tuesday hoy/el martes que viene [oy/el m**a**rtess kay b-y**ay**nay]
that will be 2,000 pesetas son dos mil pesetas [pes**ay**tass]

ticket office (bus, rail) la taquilla [tak**ee**-ya]
tide la marea [mar**ay**-a]
tie (necktie) la corbata
tight (clothes etc) ajustado [aHoost**a**do]
it's too tight es demasiado estrecho [daymas-y**a**do]
tights los panties
till la caja [k**a**Ha]
time* el tiempo [t-y**e**mpo]
what's the time? ¿qué hora es? [kay **o**ra]
this time esta vez [beth]
last time la última vez [**oo**lteema]
next time la próxima vez
four times cuatro veces [b**e**thess]
timetable el horario [or**ar**-yo]
tin (can) la lata
tinfoil el papel de aluminio [aloom**ee**n-yo]
tin opener el abrelatas
tiny diminuto
tip (to waiter etc) la propina

> In Spain it is customary to leave a tip in restaurants, even though a service charge is included in the bill. Some people also leave tips in bars particularly when they have table service. Taxi drivers are not usually tipped, but often people let them keep the change. Hotel and station porters are tipped. In all but the most rock-bottom establishments, it is customary to leave a small tip: the amount is up to you, though ten per cent of the bill is quite sufficient.

tired cansado
I'm tired estoy cansado/cansada
tissues los Kleenex®
to: to Barcelona/London a Barcelona/Londres
to Spain/England a España/Inglaterra
to the post office a la oficina de Correos
toast (bread) la tostada
today hoy [oy]
toe el dedo del pie [d**ay**do del p-yay]
together junto [H**oo**nto]
we're together (in shop etc) venimos juntos [ben**ee**moss]
can we pay together? ¿podemos pagar todo junto,

por favor? [podaymoss]
toilet los servicios [sairbeeth-yoss]
where is the toilet? ¿dónde están los servicios? [donday]
I have to go to the toilet tengo que ir al servicio [kay]

> Public toilets are rare in Spain. You should take advantage of toilets in bars and restaurants, museums and other tourist places you visit. They're usually marked **damas** and **caballeros**, though you may see the more confusing **señoras** (women) and **señores** (men).

toilet paper el papel higiénico [eeH-yayneeko]
tomato el tomate [tomatay]
tomato juice el zumo de tomate [thoomo]
tomato ketchup el ketchup
tomorrow mañana [man-yana]
tomorrow morning mañana por la mañana
the day after tomorrow pasado mañana
toner (for skin) el tonificador facial [fath-yal]
tongue la lengua [lengwa]
tonic (water) la tónica
tonight esta noche [nochay]
tonsillitis las anginas [anHeenass]
too (excessively) demasiado [demass-yado]
(also) también [tamb-yen]
too hot demasiado caliente [kal-yentay]
too much demasiado
me too yo también
tooth el diente [d-yentay]
toothache el dolor de muelas [day mwaylass]
toothbrush el cepillo de dientes [theepee-yo day d-yentess]
toothpaste la pasta de dientes
top: on top of ... encima de ... [entheema day]
at the top en lo alto
top floor el último piso [oolteemo]
topless topless
torch la linterna [leentairna]
total el total
tour el viaje [b-yaHay]
is there a tour of ...? ¿hay una gira por ...? [ī oona Heera]
tour guide el/la guía turístico [gee-a]
tourist el/la turista
tourist information office la oficina de información turística [ofeetheena day eenformath-yon]
tour operator la agencia de viajes [aHenth-ya day b-yaHess]
towards hacia [ath-ya]
towel la toalla [to-a-ya]
town la ciudad [th-yooda]
in town en el centro [thentro]
just out of town en las afueras de la ciudad [afwairass]

town centre el centro de la ciudad
town hall el ayuntamiento [a-yoontam-y**e**nto]
toy el juguete [Hoog**ay**tay]
track (US) el andén
see **platform**
tracksuit el chándal
traditional tradicional [tradeeth-yon**a**l]
traffic el tráfico
traffic jam el embotellamiento de tráfico [embotayam-y**e**nto day]
traffic lights los semáforos
trailer (for carrying tent etc) el remolque [rem**o**lkay]
(US: caravan) la caravana [karab**a**na]
trailer park el camping
train el tren
by train en tren

•••••• DIALOGUE ••••••

is this the train for ...? ¿es éste el tren para ...? [**e**stay]
sure exacto
no, you want that platform there no, tiene que ir a aquel andén de allí [t-y**ay**nay kay eer a ak**ay**l – day a-y**ee**]

trainers (shoes) las zapatillas de deporte [thapat**ee**-yass day dep**o**rtay]
train station la estación de trenes [estath-y**o**n day tr**ay**ness]
tram el tranvía [tramb**ee**-a]
translate traducir [tradooth**ee**r]
could you translate that? ¿podría traducir eso? [**ay**so]
translation la traducción [tradookth-y**o**n]
translator (man/woman) el traductor/la traductora
trashcan el cubo de la basura [k**oo**bo day la bas**oo**ra]
travel (verb) viajar [b-yaH**a**r]
we're travelling around estamos viajando [b-yaH**a**ndo]
travel agent's la agencia de viajes [aH**e**nth-ya day b-y**a**Hess]
traveller's cheque el cheque de viaje [ch**ay**kay day b-y**a**Hay]
tray la bandeja [band**ay**Ha]
tree el árbol
tremendous tremendo
trendy moderno [mod**ai**rno]
trim: just a trim please (to hairdresser) córtemelo sólo un poco, por favor [k**o**rtaymelo]
trip (excursion) la excursión [eskoors-y**o**n]
I'd like to go on a trip to ... me gustaría hacer una excursión a ... [may – ath**air**]
trolley el carrito
trouble problemas [probl**ay**mass]
I'm having trouble with ... tengo problemas con ...
sorry to trouble you perdone que le moleste [paird**o**nay kay lay mol**e**stay]
trousers los pantalones [pantal**o**ness]
true verdadero [bairdad**ai**ro]
that's not true no es verdad

[baird**a**]
trunk (US) el maletero [malet**ai**ro]
trunks (swimming) el bañador [ban-yad**o**r]
try (verb) intent**a**r
can I have a try? ¿puedo prob**a**rlo? [pw**ay**do]
try on: can I try it on? ¿puedo prob**á**rmelo?
T-shirt la camiseta [kamees**ay**ta]
Tuesday martes [m**a**rtess]
tuna el atún [at**oo**n]
tunnel el túnel [t**oo**nel]
turn: turn left/right gire a la izquierda/derecha [H**ee**ray]
turn off: where do I turn off? ¿dónde me desvío? [d**o**nday may desb**ee**-o]
can you turn the heating off? ¿puede apag**a**r la calefacción? [pw**ay**day – kalefakth-y**o**n]
turn on: can you turn the heating on? ¿puede encender la calefacción? [enthend**ai**r]
turning (in road) el desvío [desb**ee**-o]
TV la tele [t**ay**lay]
tweezers las pinzas [p**ee**nthass]
twice dos veces [b**ay**thess]
twice as much el doble [d**o**blay]
twin beds las c**a**mas gemelas [Haym**ay**lass]
twin room la habitación doble [abeetath-y**o**n d**o**blay]
twist: I've twisted my ankle me he torcido el tobillo [may ay torth**ee**do el tob**ee**-yo]
type el tipo
a different type of ... un tipo diferente de ... [deefair**ay**ntay day]
typical típico
tyre la rueda [rw**ay**da]

U

ugly (person, building) feo [f**ay**-o]
UK el Reino Unido [r**ay**-**ee**no oon**ee**do]
ulcer la úlcera [**oo**lthaira]
umbrella el paraguas [par**a**gwass]
uncle el tío
unconscious inconsciente [eenkonsth-y**e**ntay]
under (in position) debajo de [deb**a**Ho day]
(less than) menos de [m**ay**noss]
underdone (meat) poco hecha [**ay**cha]
underground (railway) el m**e**tro
underpants los calzoncillos [kalthonth**ee**-yoss]
understand: I understand lo entiendo [ent-y**e**ndo]
I don't understand no entiendo
do you understand? ¿entiende usted? [ent-y**e**nday oost**ay**]
unemployed desempleado [desemplay-**a**do]
United States los Est**a**dos Unidos [oon**ee**doss]
university la universidad

[ooneebairseed**a**]
unleaded petrol la gasolina sin plomo [gasol**ee**na seen]
unlimited mileage sin límite de kilometraje [seen l**ee**meetay day keelometr**a**Hay]
unlock abrir [abr**ee**r]
unpack deshacer las maletas [desath**air** lass mal**ay**tass]
until hasta que [**a**sta kay]
unusual poco común [kom**oo**n]
up arriba
up there allí arriba [a-y**ee**]
he's not up yet (not out of bed) todavía no se ha levantado [todab**ee**-a no say a laybant**a**do]
what's up? (what's wrong?) ¿qué pasa? [kay]
upmarket (restaurant, hotel, goods etc) de lujo [day l**oo**Ho]
upset stomach el malestar de estómago
upside down al revés [reb**ay**ss]
upstairs arriba
urgent urgente [oorH**e**ntay]
us*: with us con nosotros
for us para nosotros
USA EEUU, Estados Unidos [oon**ee**doss]
use (verb) usar [oos**a**r]
may I use ...? ¿podría usar ...?
useful útil [**oo**teel]
usual habitual [abeetw**a**l]
the usual (drink etc) lo de siempre [day s-y**e**mpray]

V

vacancy: do you have any vacancies? (hotel) ¿tiene habitaciones libres? [t-y**ay**nay abeetath-y**o**ness l**ee**bress]
see room
vacation las vacaciones [bakath-y**o**ness]
see holiday
vaccination la vacuna [bak**oo**na]
vacuum cleaner la aspiradora
valid (ticket etc) válido [b**a**leedo]
how long is it valid for? ¿hasta cuándo tiene validez? [**a**sta kw**a**ndo t-y**ay**nay baleed**e**th]
valley el valle [b**a**-yay]
valuable (adjective) valioso [bal-y**o**so]
can I leave my valuables here? ¿puedo dejar aquí mis objetos de valor? [pw**ay**do dayH**a**r ak**ee** meess obH**ay**toss day bal**o**r]
value el valor
van la furgoneta [foorgon**ay**ta]
vanilla vainilla [ba-een**ee**-ya]
a vanilla ice cream un helado de vainilla [el**a**do]
vary: it varies depende [dayp**e**nday]
vase el florero [flor**ai**ro]
veal la ternera [tairn**ai**ra]
vegetables las verduras [baird**oo**rass]
vegetarian (man/woman) el vegetariano [beHetar-y**a**no]/la vegetariana

vending machine la máquina [m**a**keena]
very muy [mwee]
very little for me un poquito para mí [pok**ee**to]
I like it very much me gusta mucho [may g**oo**sta m**oo**cho]
vest (under shirt) la camiseta [kamees**ay**ta]
via por
video el video [b**ee**day-o]
view la vista [b**ee**sta]
villa el chalet [chal**ay**]
village el pueblo [pw**ay**blo]
vinegar el vinagre [been**a**gray]
vineyard el viñedo [been-y**ay**do]
visa la visa
visit (verb) visitar [beeseet**a**r]
I'd like to visit Valencia ... me gustaría ir a Valencia [may]
vital: it's vital that ... es de vital importancia que ... [day beet**a**l eemport**a**nth-ya kay]
vodka el vodka [b**o**dka]
voice la voz [both]
voltage el voltaje [bolt**a**Hay]

> The supply is 220V, though anything requiring 240V will work. Most plugs are two round pins: a travel plug is useful.

vomit vomitar [bomeet**a**r]

W

waist la cintura [theent**oo**ra]
waistcoat el chaleco [chal**ay**ko]
wait esperar [espair**a**r]
wait for me espéreme [esp**ai**raymay]
don't wait for me no me espere [may]
can I wait until my wife/partner gets here? ¿puedo esperar hasta que llegue mi mujer/compañero? [pw**ay**do – **a**sta kay y**ay**gay]
can you do it while I wait? ¿puede hacerlo mientras espero? [pw**ay**day ath**ai**rlo m-y**e**ntrass]
could you wait here for me? ¿puede esperarme aquí? [espair**a**rmay ak**ee**]
waiter el camarero [kamar**ai**ro]
waiter! ¡camarero!
waitress la camarera [kamar**ai**ra]
waitress! ¡señorita! [sen-yor**ee**ta]
wake: can you wake me up at 5.30? ¿podría despertarme a las cinco y media? [despert**a**rmay]
wake-up call la llamada para despertar [yam**a**da]
Wales Gales [g**a**less]
walk: is it a long walk? ¿se tarda mucho en llegar andando? [say – m**oo**cho en yeg**a**r]
it's only a short walk está cerca [th**ai**rka]
I'll walk iré andando [eer**ay**]
I'm going for a walk voy a dar una vuelta [boy – bw**e**lta]

Walkman® el walkman® [wo**l**man]
wall (inside) la pared [par**ay**]
(outside) la tapia
wallet la billetera [bee-yet**ai**ra]
wander: I like just wandering around me gusta caminar por ahí [may g**oo**sta – a-**ee**]
want: I want a ... quiero un/una ... [k-y**ai**ro]
I don't want ... no quiero ninguno/ninguna ...
I want to go home quiero irme a casa [**ee**rmay]
I don't want to no quiero
he wants to ... quiere ... [k-y**ai**ray]
what do you want? ¿qué quiere? [kay]
ward (in hospital) la habitación [abeetath-y**o**n]
warm caliente [kal-y**e**ntay]
I'm so warm tengo mucho calor [m**oo**cho]
was*: it was ... era ... [**ai**ra]; estaba ...
wash (verb) lavar [lab**a**r]
can you wash these? ¿puede lavarlos? [pw**ay**day lab**a**rloss]
washer (for bolt etc) la arandela [arand**ay**la]
washhand basin el lavabo [lab**a**bo]
washing (clothes) la ropa sucia [s**oo**th-ya]
washing machine la lavadora [labad**o**ra]
washing powder el detergente [detairH**e**ntay]
washing-up liquid el (detergente) lavavajillas [daytairh**e**ntay lababaH**ee**-yass]
wasp la avispa [ab**ee**spa]
watch (wristwatch) el reloj [rayl**o**H]
will you watch my things for me? ¿puede cuidarme mis cosas? [pw**ay**day kweed**a**rmay meess]
watch out! ¡cuidado! [kweed**a**do]
watch strap la correa [korr**ay**-a]
water el agua [**a**gwa]
may I have some water? ¿me da un poco de agua? [may – day]
waterproof (adjective) impermeable [eempairmay-**a**blay]
waterskiing el esquí acuático [esk**ee** akw**a**teeko]
wave (in sea) la ola
way: it's this way es por aquí [ak**ee**]
it's that way es por allí [a-y**ee**]
is it a long way to ...? ¿queda lejos...? [k**ay**da l**ay**Hoss]
no way! ¡de ninguna manera! [day – man**ai**ra]

•••••• DIALOGUE ••••••

could you tell me the way to ...? podría indicarme el camino a ...? [eendeek**a**rmay]
go straight on until you reach the traffic lights siga recto hasta llegar al semáforo [**a**sta yeg**a**r]
turn left gire a la izquierda

[Heeray]
take the first on the right tome la primera a la derecha [tomay]
see where

we* nosotros, nosotras
weak (person, drink) débil [daybeel]
weather el tiempo [t-yempo]

•••••• DIALOGUE ••••••

what's the weather going to be like? ¿qué tiempo va a hacer? [kay – ba a athair]
it's going to be fine va a hacer bueno [bwayno]
it's going to rain va a llover [yobair]
it'll brighten up later despejará más tarde [despayHara – tarday]

wedding la boda
wedding ring el anillo de casado [anee-yo]
Wednesday miércoles [m-yairkoless]
week la semana
a week (from) today dentro de una semana [day]
a week (from) tomorrow dentro de una semana a partir de mañana [man-yana]
weekend el fin de semana [feen]
at the weekend el fin de semana
weight el peso [payso]
weird extraño [extran-yo]
weirdo: he's a weirdo es un tipo raro
welcome: welcome to ... bienvenido(s) a ... [b-yenbeneedo(ss)]
you're welcome (don't mention it) de nada [day]
well: I don't feel well no me siento bien [may s-yento b-yen]
she's not well no se siente bien [say]
you speak English very well habla inglés muy bien [abla – mwee]
well done! ¡bravo! [brabo]
this one as well éste también [estay tamb-yen]
well well! (surprise) ¡vaya, vaya! [ba-ya]

•••••• DIALOGUE ••••••

how are you? ¿cómo está?
very well, thanks muy bien, gracias [mwee b-yen]
– and you? – ¿y usted? [ee oostay]

well-done (meat) muy hecho [mwee aycho]
Welsh galés [galayss]
I'm Welsh (man/woman) soy galés/galesa
were*: we were estábamos; éramos [airamoss]
you were estabais [estaba-eess]; erais [aira-eess]
they were estaban; eran [airan]
west el oeste [o-estay]
in the west en el oeste
West Indian (adj) antillano [antee-yano]
wet mojado [moHado]

what? ¿qué? [kay]
what's that? ¿qué es eso? [**ay**so]
what should I do? ¿qué hago? [**a**-go]
what a view! ¡qué vista! [b**ee**sta]
what number bus is it? ¿qué autobús es ese? [**ay**say]
wheel la rueda [rw**ay**da]
wheelchair la silla de ruedas [s**ee**-ya day rw**ay**dass]
when? ¿cuándo [kw**a**ndo]
when we get back cuando volvamos [bolb**a**moss]
when's the train/ferry? ¿cuándo es el tren/ferry?
where? ¿dónde? [d**o**nday]
I don't know where it is no sé dónde está [say]

•••••• DIALOGUE ••••••

where is the cathedral? ¿dónde está la catedral?
it's over there está por ahí [a-**ee**]
could you show me where it is on the map? ¿puede enseñarme en el mapa dónde está? [pw**ay**day ensen-y**a**rmay]
it's just here está justo ahí [H**oo**sto a-**ee**]
see way

which: which bus? ¿qué autobús? [kay]

•••••• DIALOGUE ••••••

which one? ¿cuál? [kwal]
that one ese [**ay**say]
this one? éste [**e**stay]
no, that one no, aquél [ak**e**l]

while: while I'm here mientras esté aquí [m-y**e**ntrass est**ay** ak**ee**]
whisky el whisky
white blanco
white wine el vino blanco [b**ee**no]
who? ¿quién? [k-y**e**n]
who is it? ¿quién es?
the man who ... el hombre que... [kay]
whole: the whole week toda la semana
the whole lot todo
whose: whose is this? ¿de quién es esto? [day k-y**e**n]
why? ¿por qué? [kay]
why not? ¿por qué no?
wide ancho
wife: my wife mi mujer [mee mooH**air**]
will*: will you do it for me? ¿puede hacer esto por mí? [pw**ay**day ath**air**]
wind el viento [b-y**e**nto]
window (of house) la ventana [bent**a**na]
(of ticket office, vehicle) la ventanilla [bentan**ee**-ya]
near the window cerca de la ventana [th**air**ka day]
in the window (of shop) en el escaparate [escapar**a**tay]
window seat el asiento junto a la ventana [as-y**e**nto H**oo**nto a la bent**a**na]
windscreen el parabrisas
windscreen wiper el limpiaparabrisas [leemp-ya-

ENGLISH ❖ SPANISH | Wh

parabr**ee**sass]
windsurfing el windsurf
windy: it's so windy hace mucho viento [athay m**oo**cho b-y**e**nto]
wine el vino [b**ee**no]
can we have some more wine? ¿podría traernos más vino? [tra-**ai**rnoss]

> **Vino** (wine) either **tinto** (red) or **blanco** (white) or **rosado/clarete** (rosé), is the invariable accompaniment to every meal and is, as a rule, extremely inexpensive. The most common bottle variety is **Valdepeñas**, a good standard wine from the central plains of New Castile; **Rioja**, from the area round Logroño, is better but a lot more expensive. Both are found all over the country. There are also scores of local wines – some of the best in Catalunya (**Bach**, **Sangre de Toro** and the champagne-like **Cava**) and Galicia (**Ribeiro**, **Fefiñanes** and **Albariño**) – but you'll rarely be given any choice unless you're at a good restaurant. Otherwise, it's whatever comes out of the barrel, or the house-bottled special (ask for **caserio** or **de la casa**). This can be great, it can be lousy, but at least it will be distinctively local.

wine list la lista de vinos [l**ee**sta day b**ee**noss]
winter el invierno [eemb-y**ai**rno]
in the winter en el invierno
winter holiday las vacaciones de invierno [bakath-y**o**nayss day]
wire el alambre [al**a**mbray]
(electric) el cable eléctrico [k**a**blay]
wish: best wishes saludos [sal**oo**doss]
with con
I'm staying with ... est**oy** en c**a**sa de ... [day]
without sin [seen]
witness el/la testigo [test**ee**go]
will you be a witness for me? ¿acepta ser mi testigo? [ath**e**pta sair]
woman la mujer [mooH**air**]
wonderful estupendo [estoop**e**ndo]
won't*: it won't start no arr**a**nca
wood (material) la madera [mad**ai**ra]
woods (forest) el bosque [b**o**skay]
wool la l**a**na
word la pal**a**bra
work el trabajo [trab**a**Ho]
it's not working no funciona [foonth-y**o**na]
I work in ... trabajo en ...
world el mundo [m**oo**ndo]
worry: I'm worried est**oy** preocupado/preocup**a**da [pray-okoop**a**do]

worse: it's worse es peor [pay-**or**]
worst el peor
worth: is it worth a visit? ¿vale la pena visitarlo? [b**a**lay la p**ay**na bees**ee**tarlo]
would: would you give this to ...? ¿le puede dar **e**sto a ...? [lay pw**ay**day]
wrap: could you wrap it up? ¿me lo envuelve? [may lo embw**e**lbay]
wrapping paper el papel de envolver [day embolb**air**]
wrist la muñeca [moon-y**ay**ka]
write escribir [eskreeb**eer**]
could you write it down? ¿puede escribírmelo? [pw**ay**day]
how do you write it? ¿**có**mo se escribe? [say eskr**ee**bay]
writing paper el papel de escribrir
wrong: it's the wrong key no es ésa la llave [**ay**sa la y**a**bay]
this is the wrong train éste no es el tren [**e**stay]
the bill's wrong la cuenta est**á** equivocada [kw**e**nta – ekeebok**a**da]
sorry, wrong number perdone, me he equivoc**a**do de número [paird**o**nay, may ay – day n**oo**mairo]
there's something wrong with ... le p**a**sa **a**lgo a ... [lay]
what's wrong? ¿qué pasa? [kay]

X

X-ray la radiografía [rad-yograf**ee**-a]

Y

yacht el yate [y**a**tay]
yard* (courtyard) el p**a**tio
year el año [**a**n-yo]
yellow amarillo [amar**ee**-yo]
yes sí
yesterday ayer [a-y**air**]
yesterday morning ayer por la mañana [man-y**a**na]
the day before yesterday anteayer [antay-ay**air**]
yet

•••••• DIALOGUE ••••••

is it here yet? ¿est**á** aquí ya? [ak**ee**]
no, not yet no, todavía no [todab**ee**-a]
you'll have to wait a little longer yet todavía tendr**á** que esperar un poquito más [kay espair**ar** oon pok**ee**to]

yobbo el gamberro [gamb**air**ro]
yoghurt el yogur [yog**oo**r]
you* (fam, sing) tú [too]
(pol, sing) usted [oost**ay**]
(fam, pl) vosotros [bos**o**tross]
(pol, pl) ustedes [oost**ay**dess]
this is for you **e**sto es p**a**ra tí/usted
with you contigo/con usted

> In Spanish, when you address people you don't know (especially older people) or those with whom you have a formal relationship, you should use '**usted**' which takes the third person singular of the verb. The plural form of **usted** is **ustedes** and it is used with the third person plural of the verb. If you talk to relatives, friends or younger people you should use '**tú**' or the plural '**vosotros**' when addressing more than one person.

young joven [H**o**ben]
your* (fam, sing) tu; (pl) tus [tooss]
(fam, pl) vuestro [bw**e**stro], vuestra; (pl) vuestros, vuestras
(polite, sing) su; (pl) sus [sooss]
yours* (fam, sing) tuyo [t**oo**-yo], tuya
(fam pl) vuestro [bw**e**stro], vuestra
(polite, sing) suyo [s**oo**-yo], suya; de usted [day oost**ay**]
youth hostel el albergue juvenil [alb**ai**rgay Hoobayn**ee**l]

Z

zero cero [th**ai**ro]
zip la cremallera [krema-y**ai**ra]
could you put a new zip in?
¿podría cambiar la cremallera? [kamb-y**a**r]
zoo el zoo(lógico) [tho(l**o**Heeko)]

Spanish-English

A

a to; at; per; from
abajo [abaHo] downstairs
abierto [ab-yairto] open
abierto de ... a ... open from ... to
abierto las 24 horas del día open 24 hours
abogado m/f lawyer
abonos mpl season tickets
aborrezco [aborethko] I hate
ábrase aquí open here
ábrase en caso de emergencia open in case of emergency
abrebotellas m [abray-botay-yass] bottle-opener
abrelatas m tin opener
abrigo m coat
abrigo de pieles [p-yayless] fur coat
abril m April
abrir to open
abróchense los cinturones fasten your seatbelts
abstenerse de fumar no smoking
abuela f [abwayla] grandmother
abuelo m grandfather
abuelos mpl grandparents
aburrido boring; bored
aburrirse [aboorreersay] to be bored; to get bored
acabar to finish
acabo de ... I have just ...
acantilado m cliff
acceso a ... access to ...
acceso a los andenes to the trains
acceso playa to the beach
acceso prohibido no admittance
accidente m [aktheedentay] accident
tener un accidente to have an accident
accidente de coche [kochay] car accident
accidente de montaña [montan-ya] mountaineering accident
accidente de tráfico road accident
accidente en cadena [kadayna] pile-up
acelerador m [athelairador] accelerator, gas pedal
acelerar [athelairar] to accelerate
acento m [athento] accent
aceptar [atheptar] to accept
acera f [athaira] pavement, sidewalk
acerca de [athairka day] about, concerning
acero m [athairo] steel
acetona f [athaytona] nail polish remover
ácido (m) [atheedo] sour; acid
acompañar [akompan-yar] to accompany
le acompaño en el sentimiento condolences
acondicionador de pelo m [akondeeth-yonador day paylo] hair conditioner
aconsejar [akonsay-Har] to advise

acordarse [akord**a**rsay] to remember
irse a acostar [**ee**rsay] to go to bed

acostar: irse a acostar [**ee**rsay] to go to bed
acostarse [akost**a**rsay] to lie down; to go to bed
al acostarse when you go to bed
actriz f [aktr**ee**th] actress
acuerdo m [akw**ai**rdo] agreement
estoy de acuerdo I agree
de acuerdo OK
adaptador m adaptor
adelantado: por adelantado [adelant**a**do] in advance
adelantar to overtake
adelante [adel**a**ntay] come in
además de [adem**a**ss day] besides, as well as
adentro inside
adiós [ad-y**o**ss] goodbye
admitir to admit, to confess
adolescente m/f [adolesth**e**ntay] teenager
aduana f [ad-w**a**na] customs
aduanero m [adwan**ai**ro] customs officer
aerobús m [a-airob**oo**ss] local train
aerodeslizador m [a-airo-desleethad**o**r] hovercraft
aerolínea f [a-airol**ee**nay-a] airline
aeropuerto m [a-airopw**ai**rto] airport
afeitarse [afay-eet**a**rsay] to shave
aficionado a [afeeth-yon**a**do] keen on
afortunadamente [-m**e**ntay] fortunately
afueras fpl [afw**ai**rass] suburbs
agarrar un colocón to get sozzled
agárrese aquí hold on here
agencia f [a-H**e**nth-ya] agency
agencia de viajes [b-y**a**Hess] travel agency
agenda f [a-H**e**nda] diary
agítese antes de usar(se) shake before use
agosto m August
agradable [agrad**a**blay] pleasant
agradar to please
agradecer [agradeth**ai**r] to thank
agradecido [agradeth**ee**do] grateful
agradezco [agrad**e**thko] I thank
agresivo aggressive
agricultor m farmer
agua f [**a**gwa] water
agua de colonia [kol**o**n-ya] eau de toilette
aguantar: no aguanto ... [agw**a**nto] I can't stand ...
aguja f [ag**oo**Ha] needle
agujero m [agooH**ai**ro] hole
ahora [a-**o**ra] now
aire m [**a-ee**ray] air
aire acondicionado [akondeeth-yon**a**do] air-conditioning
ajedrez m [a-Hedr**e**th] chess
ajustado [a-Hoost**a**do] tight
ala f wing
alambre m [al**a**mbray] wire
alarma f alarm
dar la señal de alarma [sen-y**a**l] to raise the alarm

albergue m [alb**air**gay] country hotel; hostel
albergue juvenil [Hooben**ee**l] youth hostel
albornoz m [albor**no**th] bathrobe
alcohómetro m Breathalyzer®
alegre [al**e**gray] happy
alegro: ¡me alegro de verte! [b**air**tay] nice to see you!
alemán [aláy-m**a**n] German
Alemania f [alem**a**n-ya] Germany
alérgico a [al**air**-Heeko] allergic to
aletas fpl [al**ay**-tass] flippers
alfarería f [alfarair**ee**-a] pottery
alfiler m [alfeel**air**] pin
alfombra f rug, carpet
algo something
algo más something else
algodón m cotton; cotton wool, (US) absorbent cotton
alguien [**a**lg-yen] somebody; anybody
algún some; any
alguno some; any
alianza f [al-y**a**ntha] wedding ring
alicates mpl pliers
alimentación f [aleementath-y**o**n] groceries, foodstuffs
allá: más allá [a-y**a**] further
allí [a-y**ee**] there
almacén m [almath**e**n] department store; warehouse
almohada f [almo-**a**da] pillow
almuerzo m [almw**air**tho] lunch
alojamiento y desayuno [desa-y**oo**no] bed and breakfast
alojamiento m [aloHam-y**e**nto] accommodation
alpinismo m mountaineering
alquilar [alkeel**a**r] to rent; to hire
alquiler m [alkeel**air**] rental
alquiler de barcos boat hire
alquiler de bicicletas [beetheekl**ay**tass] bike hire
alquiler de coches [k**o**chess] car rental
alquiler de esquís [esk**ee**ss] (water-)ski hire
alquiler de sombrillas [sombr**ee**-yass] sunshade hire
alquiler de tablas surfboard hire
alquiler de tumbonas deckchair hire
alquileres rentals
alrededor (de) [alray-day-d**o**r] around
alta costura f haute couture, high fashion
alto high; tall
¡alto! stop!
en lo alto at the top
altura f altitude; height
altura máxima maximum headroom
aluminio m aluminium
amable [am**a**blay] kind
amamantar to breastfeed
amanecer m [amaneth**air**] sunrise, daybreak
amargo bitter
amarillo [amar**ee**-yo] yellow

ambos both
ambulancia f [amboo**la**nth-ya] ambulance
ambulatorio national health clinic
América del Norte f [n**o**rtay] North America
América del Sur [soor] South America
americano American
amiga f friend
amigo m friend
aminorar la marcha to slow down
amor m love
  hacer el amor to make love
amortiguador m [amorteegwad**o**r] shock-absorber
amperio m [amp**ai**r-yo] amp
ampliación f [amplee-ath-y**o**n] enlargement
amplio loose-fitting
ampolla f [amp**o**-ya] blister
analgésico m [anal-H**ay**seeko] painkiller
análisis clínicos mpl clinical tests
anaranjado [anaran-H**a**do] orange
ancho wide
ancho m width, breadth
anchura f width, breadth
¡anda ya! get away!, come off it!
andaluz [andal**oo**th] Andalusian
andar to walk
andén m platform, (US) track
  a los andenes to the trains
anduve [and**oo**bay] I walked
anémico anaemic
anestesia f [anest**ay**s-ya] anaesthetic
anfiteatro m [anfeetay-**a**tro] amphitheatre
angina (de pecho) f [an-H**ee**na] angina
anginas fpl tonsillitis
anillo m [an**ee**-yo] ring
anoche last night
anochecer m [anocheth**air**] nightfall, dusk
ante m suede
anteayer [antay-a-y**air**] the day before yesterday
antepasado m ancestor
antes de before
  antes de que before
antes de ayer [a-y**air**] the day before yesterday
antes de entrar dejen salir let passengers off first
anticonceptivo m [anteekonthept**ee**bo] contraceptive
anticongelante m [anteekon-Hel**a**ntay] antifreeze
anticuado [anteek-w**a**do] out of date
anticuario m antiques dealer
antigüedad: una tienda de antigüedades [t-y**e**nda day anteegway-d**a**dess] an antique shop
antiguo [ant**ee**gwo] ancient
antihistamínico m [antee-eestam**ee**neeko] antihistamine
anulado cancelled
anular to cancel

añadir [an-yad**eer**] to add
año m [**a**n-yo] year
Año Nuevo m [nw**ay**bo] New Year
día de Año Nuevo m [d**ee**-a] New Year's Day
¡feliz Año Nuevo! [fel**ee**th] Happy New Year!
apagar to switch off
apagar los faros to switch off one's lights
apagar luces de cruce headlights off
apagón m power cut
apague el motor switch off your engine
apague las luces switch off your lights
aparato m device
aparatos electrodomésticos electrical appliances
aparcamiento m [aparkam-y**e**nto] car park, (US) parking lot
aparcamiento privado private parking
aparcamiento reservado this parking place reserved
aparcamiento subterráneo underground parking
aparcamiento vigilado supervised parking
aparcar to park
aparecer [apareth**air**] to appear
aparezco [apar**e**thko] I appear
apartamento m apartment
apasionante [apass-yon**a**ntay] thrilling
apearse de [apay-**a**rsay] to get off
apellido m [apay-y**ee**do] surname
apenado distressed, sorry
apenas [ap**ay**nass] scarcely
apenas ... (cuando) [k-w**a**ndo] hardly ... when
apetecer: me apetece [may apet**ay**thay] I feel like
apetito m appetite
apodo m nickname
apoplejía f [apoplay-H**ee**-a] stroke
aprender [aprend**air**] to learn
aprensivo fearful, apprehensive
apresurarse [-**a**rsay] to rush
aproveche: ¡que aproveche! [aprob**ay**-chay] enjoy your meal!
aproximadamente [-m**e**ntay] about
aquel [ak**e**l] that
aquél that (one)
aquella [ak**ay**-ya] that
aquélla that (one)
aquellas [ak**ay**-yass] those
aquéllas those (ones)
aquellos [ak**ay**-yoss] those
aquéllos those (ones)
aquí [ak**ee**] here
aquí tiene [t-y**ay**nay] here you are
árabe [**a**rabay] Arabic
aragonés Aragonese
araña f [ar**a**n-ya] spider
arañazo m [aran-y**a**tho] scratch
árbol m tree
arcén m [arth**e**n] lay-by
ardor de estómago m heartburn

área de servicios m service area, motorway services
arena f [ar**ay**na] sand
Argelia f [arH**ay**lee-a] Algeria
armario m cupboard
armería f [armair**ee**-a] gunsmith's
arqueología f [arkay-oloH**ee**-a] archaeology
arrancar to start up
arreglar to mend; to sort out, to arrange
arrepentido sorry
arriba up; upstairs; on top
arroyo m stream
arte m [**ar**tay] art
artesanía f crafts
artículos de artesanía mpl arts and crafts
artículos de baño [b**a**n-yo] swimwear
artículos de boda wedding presents
artículos de deporte sports goods
artículos de limpieza household cleaning products
artículos de ocasión bargains; second hand goods
artículos de piel leather goods
artículos de playa beachwear
artículos de regalo gifts
artículos de viaje travel goods
artículos para el bebé babywear
artículos para el colegio schoolwear
artista m/f artist
artritis f [-tr**ee**teess] arthritis
asador m restaurant specializing in roast meats and/or fish
ascensor m [asthens**o**r] lift, elevator
asegurar to insure
aseos mpl [as**ay**-oss] toilets, rest room
así like this; like that
así que so (that)
asiático Asian
asiento m [ass-y**e**nto] seat
asma m asthma
aspiradora f hoover®
asqueroso [askair**o**so] disgusting
astigmático long-sighted
asturiano [astoor-y**a**no] Asturian
asustado afraid
asustar to frighten
atacar to attack
atajo m [at**a**Ho] shortcut
ataque m [at**a**kay] attack
ataque al corazón [korath**o**n] heart attack
atascado stuck
atasco (de tráfico) m traffic jam
atención [atenth-y**o**n] please note
¡atención! take care!, caution!
atención al tren beware of trains
ateo [at**ay**-o] atheist
aterrizaje m [atairreeth**a**Hay] landing
aterrizaje forzoso [forth**o**so] emergency landing
aterrizar [atairreeth**a**r] to land
atestado m report

SPANISH ❖ ENGLISH | **Ar**

atletismo m athletics
atracar to assault, to hold up
atracciones turísticas fpl [atrakth-y**o**ness] tourist attractions
atraco a mano armada m hold-up
atractivo attractive
atrás at the back; behind
¡atrás! get back!
la parte de atrás [p**a**rtay] the back
está más atrás it's further back
años atrás years ago
atravesar to go through
atravieso [atrab-y**ay**so] I go through
atreverse [atreb**ai**rsay] to dare
atropellar [atropay-y**a**r] to knock over
atroz [atr**o**th] dreadful
audífono m [owd**ee**fono] hearing aid
aun even
aún [a-**oo**n] still; yet
aunque [a-**oo**nkay] although
autobús m [owtob**oo**ss] bus
autobús sólamente buses only
autocar m coach, bus
auto-estopista m/f [-estop**ee**sta] hitch-hiker
automotor m local short-distance train
automóvil m car
automovilista m/f car driver
autopista f motorway, (US) highway
autopista (de peaje) [pay-**a**Hay] (toll) motorway/highway
auto-servicio m [owto-sairb**ee**th-yo] self-service
autorizada para mayores de 18 años for adults only
autorizada para mayores de 14 años y menores acompañados authorized for those over 14 and young people accompanied by an adult
autorizada para todos los públicos suitable for all
autostop m hitchhiking
hacer autostop to hitchhike
autovía f [-b**ee**-a] dual carriageway, (US) divided highway
AVE m high-speed train Madrid-Seville line
avenida f avenue
avergonzado [abairgonth**a**do] embarrassed
avería f [abair**ee**-a] breakdown
averiado out of order
averiarse [abairee-**a**rsay] to break down
avión m [ab-y**o**n] aeroplane
por avión by air
avisar to inform
aviso m information
aviso a los señores pasajeros passenger information
avispa f wasp
ayer [a-y**ai**r] yesterday
ayer por la mañana [man-y**a**na] yesterday morning
ayer por la tarde [t**a**rday] yesterday afternoon
ayuda f [a-y**oo**da] help
ayudar to help

ayuntamiento m [ayoontam-yento] town hall
azafata f [athafata] air hostess
azul (m) [athool] blue
azul claro light blue
azul marino navy blue

B

baca f roof rack
bahía f [ba-ee-a] bay
bailar [ba-eelar] to dance
ir a bailar to go dancing
baile m [ba-eelay] dance; dancing
bajar [baHar] to go down
bajar de to get off
bajarse [baHarsay] to get off
bajo [baHo] low; short; under(neath)
balcón m balcony
Baleares [balay-aress] Balearics
balón m ball
balón volea [bolay-a] volleyball
baloncesto m [balonthesto] basketball
balonmano m handball
banco m bank; bench
bandeja f [bandayHa] tray
bandera f [bandaira] flag
bañador m [ban-yador] swimming costume
bañarse [ban-yarsay] to go swimming; to have a bath
bañera f [ban-yaira] bathtub
baño m [ban-yo] bathroom; bath
baraja f [baraHa] pack of cards
barato cheap, inexpensive
barba f beard
barbacoa f [barbako-a] barbecue
barbería f [barbairee-a] barber's
barbero m barber
barbilla f [barbee-ya] chin
barca de remos f rowing boat
barcas para alquilar boats to rent
barco m boat
barco de vela sailing boat
barra de labios f [lab-yoss] lipstick
barrio m [barr-yo] district, area
bastante [bastantay] enough
bastante más quite a lot more
bastante menos [maynoss] quite a lot less
basura f litter
bata f dressing gown
bate m [batay] bat
batería f [batairee-a] battery
batería de cocina [kotheena] pots and pans
batín m dressing gown
bautismo m [bowteesmo] christening
bebé m baby
beber [bebair] to drink
bello [bay-yo] beautiful
benvengut [benvengoot] welcome (in Catalan)
besar to kiss
beso m kiss
betún m [betoon] shoe polish
biblioteca f [beebl-yotayka] library; bookcase
bici: ir a dar una vuelta en bici [bwelta en beethee] to go for

a cycle
bicicleta f [beetheekl**ay**ta] bicycle
bien [b-yen] well
¡bien! good!
bien ... bien either ... or ...
o bien ... o bien either ... or ...
bienes mpl [b-y**ay**ness] possessions
¡bienvenido! welcome!
bifurcación f [beefoorkath-y**o**n] fork
bigote m [beeg**o**tay] moustache
billete m [bee-y**ay**tay] ticket
billete de andén platform ticket
billete de banco banknote, (US) bill
billete de ida single ticket, one-way ticket
billete de ida y vuelta [bw**e**lta] return ticket, round trip ticket
blanco (m) white
blusa f blouse
boca f mouth
bocina f [both**ee**na] horn
boda f wedding
bodega f [bod**ay**ga] wine cellar; wine bar
boite f [bwat] night club
bolígrafo m biro®
bolsa f bag; stock exchange
bolsa de plástico plastic bag
bolsa de viaje [b-y**a**Hay] travel bag
bolsillo m [bols**ee**-yo] pocket
bolso m handbag, (US) purse
bomba f bomb
bomberos mpl [bomb**ai**ross] fire brigade
bombilla f [bomb**ee**-ya] light bulb
bombona de gas f camping gas cylinder
bonito (m) nice; tuna fish
bonobús book of 10 reduced-price bus tickets
bordado embroidered
borracho drunk
bosque m [b**o**skay] forest
bota f boot
botas de agua [**a**gwa] wellingtons
botas de esquiar [eskee-**a**r] ski boots
botella f [bot**ay**-ya] bottle
botiquín m [boteek**ee**n] first aid kit
botón m button
botón desatascador coin return button
boxeo m [boks**ay**-o] boxing
boya f buoy
bragas fpl panties
brazo m [br**a**tho] arm
bricolaje m [breekol**a**Hay] DIY
brillar [bree-y**a**r] to shine
brisa f breeze
británico British
brocha de afeitar f [afay-eet**a**r] shaving brush
broche m [br**o**chay] brooch
bronce m [br**o**nthay] bronze
bronceado m [bronthay-**a**do] suntan
bronceador m [bronthay-ad**o**r]

suntan oil/lotion
bronquitis f [bron**kee**teess] bronchitis
brújula f [br**oo**Hoola] compass
Bruselas Brussels
bucear [boothay-**ar**] to (skin-)dive
buceo m [booth**ay**-o] skin-diving
¡buenas! [bw**ay**nass] hello!
bueno [bw**ay**no] good; good-natured
buenas noches goodnight
buenas tardes good evening
buenos días [d**ee**-ass] good morning
bufanda f scarf
bujía f [booH**ee**-a] spark plug
bulto m piece of luggage
burro m donkey
buscar to look for
busqué [boosk**ay**] I looked for
butacas stalls
buzón [booth**o**n] letter box, mail box

C

c/ (calle) street
c/c (cuenta corriente) current account
caballeros mpl [kaba-y**ai**ross] gents, men's rest room
caballo m [kab**a**-yo] horse
cabello m [kab**ay**-yo] hair
cabeza f [kab**e**tha] head
cabida ... personas capacity ... people
cabina telefónica f telephone booth, phone box
cable alargador m [k**a**blay] extension lead
cabra f goat
cabrón m bastard
cacahuetes [kakaw**ay**tess] peanuts
cachondeo m [kachond**ay**-o] laugh
lo digo de cachondeo I'm only joking
cada every
cadena f [kad**ay**na] chain
cadera f [kad**ai**ra] hip
caduca ... expires ...
caer [ka-**air**] to fall
caerse [ka-**air**say] to fall
cafetera f [kafet**ai**ra] coffee pot
cafetería f cafe, bar-type restaurant
caída f [ka-**ee**da] fall
cago: ¡me cago en diez! [d-yayth] for heaven's sake!
caja de cambios f [k**a**Ha] gearbox
caja f [k**a**Ha] cash desk; cashier
caja de ahorros [a-**o**rross] savings bank
cajera f [kaH**ai**ra], **cajero** m cashier
cajero automático [owtom**a**teeko] cash dispenser, (US) automatic teller
calambre m [kal**a**mbray] cramp
calcetines mpl [kalthet**ee**ness] socks
calcetines de algodón cotton socks
calcetines de lana woollen

socks
calculadora f calculator
calefacción f [kalefakth-yon] heating
calefacción central [thentral] central heating
calendario m [-dar-yo] calendar
calidad f quality
caliente [kal-yentay] hot
calle f [ka-yay] street
calle comercial [komairth-yal] shopping street
calle de dirección única [deerekth-yon] one-way street
calle peatonal [pay-atonal] pedestrianized street
calle principal [preentheepal] main street
callejón sin salida m cul-de-sac, dead end
callo m [ka-yo] corn (on foot)
calmante m tranquillizer
calor m heat
hace calor it's warm/hot
calvo bald
calzada deteriorada poor road surface
calzada irregular uneven surface
calzados shoe shop
calzoncillos mpl [kalthonthee-yoss] underpants
cama f bed
cama de campaña [kampan-ya] campbed
cama de matrimonio double bed
cama individual single bed
cámara f camera; inner tube
cámara fotográfica camera
camarera f [kamaraira] waitress; chambermaid
camarero m waiter
camarote m [kamarotay] cabin
cambiar [kamb-yar] to change
cambiarse (de ropa) [kamb-yarsay] to get changed
cambio m change; exchange; exchange rate
cambio de divisas currency exchange
cambio de moneda currency exchange
cambio de sentido junction, take filter lane to exit and cross flow of traffic
caminar to walk
camino m path
camino cerrado (al tráfico) road closed to (traffic)
camino privado private road
camión m lorry, truck
camioneta f van
camisa f shirt
camiseta f T-shirt; vest
camisón m nightdress
campana f bell
camping m camping; campsite; caravan site, (US) trailer park
campo m countryside; pitch; court; field
campo de deportes sports field
campo de futból football ground
campo de golf golf course
Campsa State-owned oil company

canadiense [kanad-y**e**nsay] Canadian
Canal de la Mancha m English Channel
Canarias f [kan**a**r-yass] Canaries
cancelado [kanthel**a**do] cancelled
cancelar [kanthel**a**r] to cancel
cancha f court; pitch
canción f [kanth-y**o**n] song
canguro m/f [kang**oo**ro] baby-sitter
canoso greying; grey
cansado tired
cantar to sing
cantina f buffet
canto m singing
caña f [k**a**n-ya] small glass of beer
caña de pescar fishing rod
capaz: ser capaz (de) [sair kap**a**th] to be able (to)
capazo m [kap**a**tho] carry-cot
capilla f [kap**ee**-ya] chapel
capitán m captain
capó(t) m bonnet, (US) hood
cara f face
caramelos mpl [karam**ay**loss] sweets, candies
caravana f caravan
carburador m carburettor
cárcel f [k**a**rthel] prison
cardenal m bruise
carne f [k**a**rnay] flesh
carné de conducir m [karn**ay** day kondooth**ee**r] driving licence
carnet de identidad m identity card
carnicería f [karneethair**ee**-a] butcher's
caro expensive
carpintería f [karpeentair**ee**-a] joiner's, carpenter's
carrera f [karr**ai**ra] race
carrete m [karr**ay**tay] film (for camera)
carretera f [karret**ai**ra] road
carretera comarcal district highway
carretera cortada road blocked, road closed
carretera de circunvalación by-pass
carretera de doble calzada two-lane road
carretera nacional national highway
carretera principal main highway
carril m lane
carrito m trolley, cart
carrito portaequipajes [porta-aykeep**a**Hess] baggage trolley
carta f letter; menu
cartel m poster
cartelera de espectáculos f [kartel**ai**ra] entertainments guide
cartera f [kart**ai**ra] briefcase; wallet
carterista m pickpocket
cartero m postman, mailman
cartón m cardboard; carton
casa f house
en casa at home
en casa de Juan at Juan's
casa de huéspedes [w**e**spedess] guesthouse

casa de socorro emergency first-aid centre
casado married
casarse [kas**a**rsay] to get married
cascada f waterfall
casi almost
casino m leisure club; casino
caso m case
en caso de que in case
caso urgente [oorHentay] emergency
casete f, cassette f [kas**e**t] cassette
casete m, cassette m cassette player
caspa f dandruff
castaño (m) [kast**a**n-yo] sweet chestnut; brown
castañuelas fpl [kastan-w**ay**lass] castanets
castellano [kastay-y**a**no] Castilian; another word for the Spanish language
Castilla [kast**ee**-ya] Castile
castillo m castle
casualidad: por casualidad [kaswaleed**a**] by chance
Cataluña [katal**oo**n-ya] Catalonia
catarro: tengo catarro I've got a cold
católico (m) Catholic
catorce [kat**o**rthay] fourteen
caucho m [k**ow**cho] rubber
causa f [k**ow**sa] cause
a causa de because of
cayó [ka-y**o**] he fell
caza f [k**a**tha] hunting
cazadora f [kathad**o**ra] bomber jacket, blouson
cazar [kath**a**r] to hunt
cazo m [k**a**tho] saucepan
ceda el paso give way, yield
ceder el paso [thed**air**] to give way
ceja f [th**ay**Ha] eyebrow
celoso [thel**o**so] jealous
cementerio m [thement**air**-yo] cemetery
cena f [th**ay**na] dinner
cenar to have dinner
cenicero m [thayneeth**air**o] ashtray
central telefónica f [thentr**a**l] telephone exchange
centro comercial m [th**e**ntro komairthee-**a**l] shopping centre
centro urbano/ciudad m [th-yood**a**] city/town centre
ceñido [then-y**ee**do] tight-fitting
cepillo m [thep**ee**-yo] brush
cepillo de dientes [d-y**e**ntess] toothbrush
cepillo del pelo hairbrush
cera f [th**ai**ra] wax
cerámica f [thair**a**meeka] ceramics
cerca de [th**ai**rka] near
cercanías m [thairkan**ee**-ass] local short-distance train
cerilla f [thair**ee**-ya] match
cero [th**ai**ro] zero
cerrado [thairr**a**do] closed
cerrado por defunción closed due to bereavement
cerrado por descanso del

personal closed for staff holidays
cerrado por obras/reforma/vacaciones closed for alteration/renovation/holidays
cerradura f [thairradoora] lock
cerramos los ... we close on ...
cerrar [thairrar] to close
cerrar con llave [yabay] to lock
cerrojo m [thairroHo] bolt
certificado m [thairteefeekado] certificate; registered letter
cervecería f [thairbethair-ee-a] bar specializing in beer
cerveza f [thairbaytha] beer
césped m [thesped] lawn
cesta f [thesta] basket
cesto de la compra m shopping basket
CH (casa de huespedes) f [wespedess] boarding house, low-price hostel
chaleco m waistcoat
chalecos salvavidas life-jackets
chalet m [chalay] villa
champú m shampoo
chandal m tracksuit
chaparrón m shower; downpour
chaqueta f [chakayta] cardigan; jacket
chaquetón m [chaketon] jacket; three-quarter length jacket
charcutería f delicatessen
charlar to chat
cheque m [chaykay] cheque, (US) check
cheque de viaje m [day b-yaHay] travellers' cheque
chica f girl
chicle m [cheeklay] chewing gum
chico m boy
chillar [chee-yar] to shout
chino Chinese
chiringuito m [cheereengeeto] open-air bar
chiste m [cheestay] joke
chocar con to run into
chocolate con leche m [chokolatay kon lechay] milk chocolate
chocolate de hacer [athair] plain chocolate
chubasco m sudden short shower
chubasquero m [choobaskairo] cagoule
chupa-chups® m lollipop
Cía. (compañía) company
cicatriz f [theekatreeth] scar
ciclismo m [theekleesmo] cycling
ciclista m/f [theekleesta] cyclist
ciego [th-yaygo] blind
cielo m [th-yaylo] sky
cien [th-yen] hundred
ciencia f [th-yenth-ya] science
ciento ... [th-yento] a hundred and ...
cierren las puertas close the doors
cierro [th-yairro] I close
cigarrillo m [theegarree-yo] cigarette
cinco [theenko] five
cincuenta [theen-kwenta] fifty

cine m [th**ee**nay] cinema
cinta f [th**ee**nta] tape; ribbon
cintura f [theent**oo**ra] waist
cinturón m [theentoor**o**n] belt
cinturón de seguridad seat belt
circo m [th**ee**rko] circus
circulación f [theerkoolath-y**o**n] traffic; circulation
circulación en ambas direcciones two-way traffic
circule despacio drive slowly
circule por la derecha keep to your right
circunvalación f [theerkoonbalath-y**o**n] ring road
cistitis f [theest**ee**teess] cystitis
cita f [th**ee**ta] appointment
ciudad f [thee-oo-d**a**] town, city
claro clear
¡claro! of course!
clase f [kl**a**say] class
clavo m nail
claxon m [kl**a**kson] horn
clima m climate
climatizado [-th**a**do] air-conditioned
clínica f hospital; clinic
cobrador m conductor
cobre m [k**o**bray] copper
cocer [koth**air**] to cook; to boil
coche m [k**o**chay] car
en coche by car
coche-cama m sleeper, sleeping car
cochecito m [kochetheeto] pram
coche comedor dining car
coche de línea [l**ee**nay-a] long-distance bus
coche de niño [n**ee**n-yo] pram; pushchair, baby buggy
coche-restaurante m [-restowr**a**ntay] restaurant car
cocina f [koth**ee**na] kitchen; cooker
cocinar [kotheen**a**r] to cook
cocinera f [kotheen**ai**ra], **cocinero** m cook
código de la circulación m [theerkoolath-y**o**n] highway code
código postal postcode, zip code
codo m elbow
coger [koH**air**] to catch; to take
cojo (m) [k**o**Ho] I catch; I take; person with a limp
cola f tail; queue
hacer cola to queue
colchas fpl bedspreads
colchón m mattress
colchoneta inflable f [eenfl**a**blay] air mattress
colección f [kolekth-y**o**n] collection
colegio m [kol**ay**H-yo] school
colgante m [kolg**a**ntay] pendant
colina f hill
collar m [ko-y**a**r] necklace
colocar to place, to put
color m colour
columna vertebral f spine
combinación f [kombeenath-y**o**n] petticoat
combustible m [komboost**ee**blay] fuel
comedor m dining room
comenzar [komenth**a**r] to begin
comer [kom**air**] to eat

comerciante m [komairth-yantay] shopkeeper; dealer
comida f lunch; food; meal
comidas para llevar take-away meals
comienzo [kom-yentho] I begin
comisaría f police station
comisaría de policía [polee-thee-a] police station
como as; like
¿cómo? pardon?; how?
¿cómo dice? [deethay] pardon?
¿cómo está? how are you?
¿cómo le va? [lay] how are things?
como quieras [k-yairass] it's up to you
compañera f [kompan-yaira] girlfriend
compañero m mate; boyfriend
compañía f [kompan-yee-a] company
compañía aérea [a-airay-a] airline
comparar to compare
compartir to share
completamente [-mentay] completely
completo full, no vacancies
complicado complicated
compra: hacer la compra [athair] to do the shopping
compramos a ... buying rate
comprar to buy
comprender [komprendair] to understand
no comprendo I don't understand
compras: ir de compras to go shopping
compresa m [kompraysa] sanitary towel, sanitary napkin
comprimido efervescente m soluble tablet
comprimidos tablets
computadora f computer
comunicando engaged; busy
con with
concha f shell
concierne [konth-yairnay] it concerns
concierto m [konth-yairto] concert
condición: a condición de que [kondeeth-yon] on condition that
condón m condom
conducir [kondootheer] to drive
conductor m, conductora f driver
conduzca con cuidado drive with care
conduzco [kondoothko] I drive
conejo m [konay-Ho] rabbit
confección f [konfekth-yon] clothing industry
confección de caballero [kaba-yairo] menswear
confección de señoras ladies' fashions
confecciones fpl ready-to-wear clothes
conferencia internacional f [konfairenth-ya eentairnath-yonal] international call
conferencia interurbana long-

distance call
confesar to admit, to confess
confirmar to confirm
confitería f [konfeetair**ee**-a] sweetshop, candy store
conforme [konf**o**rmay] as
estar conforme to agree
conformidad f agreement
congelado [konHayl**a**do] frozen
congelador m [konHaylad**o**r] freezer
congelados mpl [konHayl**a**doss] frozen foods
conjunto m [konH**oo**nto] group; band
conmigo with me
conmoción cerebral f [konmoth-y**o**n thairebr**a**l] concussion
conocer [konoth**air**] to know
conozco [kon**o**thko] I know
conque [konk**ay**] so, so then
conserje m [kons**air**Hay] janitor, porter
conservas fpl jams, preserves
consérvese en sitio fresco store in a cool place
consigna f [kons**ee**g-na] left luggage (office), baggage check
consigna automática left luggage lockers
consigo with himself; with herself; with yourself; with themselves; with yourselves
consulado m consulate
consulta médica surgery, doctor's office
consúmase antes de ... best before ...
contable m/f [kont**a**blay] accountant
contacto: ponerse en contacto con to contact
contado: pagar al contado to pay cash
contagioso [kontaH-y**o**so] contagious
contaminado polluted
contar to count; to tell
contener [konten**air**] to contain
contenido m contents
contento happy
contestar to reply, to answer
contigo with you
continuación: a continuación [konteen-wath-y**o**n] then, next
continuar [konteen-w**a**r] to continue
contorno de cadera m hip measurement
contorno de cintura [theent**oo**ra] waist measurement
contorno de pecho bust/chest measurement
contra against
contradecir [kontradeth**ee**r] to contradict
contraindicaciones fpl contra-indications
contraventanas fpl shutters
control de pasaportes m passport control
convalecencia f [konbaleth**e**nth-ya] convalescence
¡coño! [k**o**n-yo] fuck!
copa f glass
coquetear [koketay-**a**r] to flirt
corazón m [korath**o**n] heart

corbata f tie, necktie
cordero m [kord**ai**ro] lamb
cordones mpl [kord**o**ness] (shoe)laces
correa del ventilador f [korr**ay**-a] fan belt
correo m [korr**ay**-o] mail
correo aéreo [a-**ai**ray-o] airmail
correo urgente [oorH**e**ntay] express
correos m post office
Correos y Telégrafos Post Office
correr [korr**air**] to run
corrida de toros f bullfight
corriente peligrosa dangerous current
corrimiento de tierras danger: landslides
cortadura f cut
cortar to cut
cortarse [kort**a**rsay] to cut oneself
cortaúñas m [korta-**oo**n-yass] nail clippers
corte de pelo m [k**o**rtay] haircut
corte y confección [konfekth-y**o**n] dressmaking
cortina f curtain
corto short
cosa f thing
coser [kos**ai**r] to sew
costa f coast
costar to cost
costilla f [kost**ee**-ya] rib
costumbre f [kost**oo**mbray] custom
cráneo m [kr**a**nay-o] skull
crédito m credit; unit(s)
creer [kray-**air**] to believe
crema f [kr**ay**ma] cream
crema base [b**a**say] foundation cream
crema de belleza [bay-y**ay**tha] cold cream
crema hidratante [eedrat**a**ntay] moisturizer
crema limpiadora [leemp-yad**o**ra] cleansing cream
cremallera f [krema-y**ai**ra] zip, zipper
creyó [kray-y**o**] he believed
crisis nerviosa f [nairb-y**o**sa] nervous breakdown
cristal m [kreest**a**l] crystal; glass
cristalería f glassware
crítica f criticism
criticar to criticize
cruce m [kr**oo**thay] junction, intersection; crossing; crossroads
cruce de ganado danger: cattle crossing
cruce de ciclistas danger: cyclists crossing
crucero m [krooth**ai**ro] cruise
Cruz Roja f [krooth r**o**Ha] Red Cross
cruzar [krooth**a**r] to cross
CTNE f Spanish national telephone company
cuaderno m [kwad**ai**rno] notebook
cuadrado [kwadr**a**do] square
cuadro m [kw**a**dro] painting
de cuadros checked
cual [kwal] which; who
¿cuándo? [kw**a**ndo] when?
¿cuánto? [kw**a**nto] how much?

en cuanto... as soon as...
¡cuánto lo siento! [s-yento] I'm so sorry!
¿cuántos? how many?
cuarenta [kwarenta] forty
cuartel de la guardia civil m civil guard barracks
cuartilla f [kwartee-ya] writing paper
cuarto (m) [kwarto] quarter; fourth; room
cuarto de hora [ora] quarter of an hour
cuarto de baño [ban-yo] bathroom
cuarto de estar sitting room
cuarto piso fourth floor, (US) fifth floor
cuatro [kwatro] four
cuatrocientos [kwatro-th-yentoss] four hundred
cubierta f [koob-yairta] deck
cubierto (m) covered; overcast; meal
cubiertos mpl cutlery
cubo m bucket; cube
cubo de la basura dustbin, trashcan
cucaracha f cockroach
cuchara f spoon
cucharilla f [koocharee-ya] teaspoon
cuchilla de afeitar f [koochee-ya day afay-eetar] razor blade
cuchillería f [koochee-yairee-a] cutlery
cuchillo m [koochee-yo] knife
cuelgue, espere y retire la tarjeta hang up, wait and remove card
cuello m [kway-yo] neck; collar
cuenco m [kwenko] bowl
cuenta f [kwenta] bill; account
cuentas corrientes current accounts
cuento m [kwento] tale
cuerda f [kwairda] rope; string
cuero m [kwairo] leather
cuerpo m [kwairpo] body
cuesta (f) [kwesta] it costs; slope
cueva f [kweba] cave
cuidado (m) [kweedado] take care; look out; care
cuidado con ... caution ...
cuidado con el perro beware of the dog
cuidado con el escalón mind the step
cuidar to look after; to nurse
culebra f snake
culpa f fault, blame; guilt
es culpa mía it's my fault
culturismo m body building
cumplas: ¡que cumplas muchos más! many happy returns!
cumpleaños m [koomplay-an-yoss] birthday
cuna f cot, (US) crib
cuneta f [koonayta] gutter
cuñada f [koon-yada] sister-in-law
cuñado m brother-in-law
cura m priest
curado cured; smoked
curar to cure; to dress
curarse [koorarsay] to heal up
curva f bend; curve

curva peligrosa dangerous bend
cuyo [koo-yo] whose; of which

D

D. (Don) Mr.
damas fpl ladies' toilet, ladies' restroom
danés Danish
danza f [dantha] dancing; dance
daños mpl [dan-yoss] damage
dar to give
dar el visto bueno a [bwayno] to approve
dcha. (derecha) right
de of; from
de 2 metros de alto 2 m high
debajo de [debaHo] under
deber (m) [debair] to have to; to owe; duty
deberes mpl [debairess] homework
débil weak
decepción f [dethepth-yon] disappointment
decepcionado [dethepth-yonado] disappointed
decidir [detheedeer] to decide
décimo [detheemo] tenth
decir [detheer] to say; to tell
declaración f [deklarath-yon] declaration; statement
declarar to declare, to state
dedo m [daydo] finger
dedo del pie [p-yay] toe
defectuoso [defekt-woso] faulty
degustación f [degoostath-yon] café specializing in coffee
dejar [dayHar] to leave; to let
dejar de beber to stop drinking
delante de [delantay] in front of
delantera f [delantaira] front (part)
delantero front
la parte delantera [partay] the front (part)
delgado thin
delicioso [deleeth-yoso] delicious
demás: los demás the others
demasiado [demass-yado] too
demasiados too many
demora f delay
dentadura postiza f [posteetha] dentures
dentista m/f dentist
dentro (de) inside
dentro de dos semanas in two weeks' time
depende [dependay] it depends
dependiente m/f [depend-yentay] shop assistant
deporte m [deportay] sport
deportes de invierno mpl [eemb-yairno] winter sports
deportivo [deporteebo] sports
deportivos mpl trainers
depósito m tank; deposit
deprimido depressed
derecha f right
a la derecha (de) on the right (of)
derecho: todo derecho straight ahead
derribar to wreck, to demolish

desacuerdo m [desak-w**ai**rdo] disagreement
desafortunadamente [-am**e**ntay] unfortunately
desagradable [-d**a**blay] unpleasant
desagradar to displease
desaparecer [desaparayth**ai**r] to disappear
desastre m [des**a**stray] disaster
desayunar [desa-yoon**a**r] to have breakfast
desayuno m [desa-y**oo**no] breakfast
descansar to rest
descarado cheeky
descarrilar to be derailed
descolgar el aparato lift receiver
descubierto [deskoob-y**ai**rto] discovered
descubrir to discover
descuelgue el auricular lift the receiver
descuentos [deskw**e**ntoss] discounts
descuidado [deskweed**a**do] careless
desde (que) [desd**ay**] since
desde luego [lw**ay**go] of course
desear [desay-**a**r] to want; to wish
¿qué desea? [kay des**ay**-a] what can I do for you?
desembarcadero m [desembarkad**ai**ro] quay
desfile de modelos m [desf**ee**lay] fashion show
desgracia: por desgracia [desgr**a**th-ya] unfortunately
deshacer las maletas [dess-ath**ai**r] to unpack
desinfectante m [-t**a**ntay] disinfectant
desmaquillarse [desmakee-y**a**rsay] to remove one's makeup
desmayarse [desmay**a**rsay] to faint
desnudo naked
desobediente [desobayd-y**e**ntay] disobedient
desodorante m [-r**a**ntay] deodorant
desordenado untidy
desorientarse [desor-yent**a**rsay] to lose one's way
despachador automático m ticket machine
despacho de billetes m [bee-y**ay**tess] ticket office
despacio [desp**a**th-yo] slowly
despedirse [desped**ee**rsay] to say goodbye
despegar to take off
despegue m [desp**ay**-gay] take-off
despejado [despayH**a**do] clear
despertador m [despairtad**o**r] alarm clock
despertar to wake
despertarse [-t**a**rsay] to wake up
despierto [desp-y**ai**rto] awake
desprendimiento de terreno danger: landslides
despreocupado [despray-okoop**a**do] thoughtless
después [despw**e**ss] afterwards

después de after
destinatario m addressee
destino m destination
destornillador m [destornee-yador] screwdriver
destruir [destr-weer] to destroy
desvestirse [desbesteersay] to undress
desviación f [desb-yath-yon] diversion
desvío m [desbee-o] detour, diversion
desvío provisional temporary diversion
detener [detenair] to arrest; to stop
detergente en polvo m [detairHentay] washing powder
detergente lavavajillas [lababaHee-yass] washing-up liquid
detestar to detest
detrás (de) behind
devolver [debolbair] to give back; to vomit
di I gave; tell me
día m [dee-a] day
día festivo public holiday
diamante m [d-yamantay] diamond
diapositiva f [d-yaposeeteeba] slide
diario (m) [d-yar-yo] diary; daily newspaper
diarrea f [d-yarray-a] diarrhoea
días azules [athooless] cheap travel days
días festivos public holidays
días laborables weekdays
dibujar [deebooHar] to draw
dibujos animados mpl [deebooHoss] cartoons
diccionario m [deekth-yonar-yo] dictionary
dice [deethay] he/she says; you say
dicho said
¿qué ha dicho? what did you say?; what did he/she say?
diciembre m [deeth-yembray] December
diecinueve [d-yetheenwaybay] nineteen
dieciocho [d-yethee-ocho] eighteen
dieciséis [d-yetheesay-eess] sixteen
diecisiete [d-yethees-yaytay] seventeen
diente m [d-yentay] tooth
dieron [d-yairon] they gave; you gave
dieta f [d-yayta] diet
diez [d-yeth] ten
difícil [deefeetheel] difficult
diga tell me
dígame [deegamay] hello, yes
digo I say
dije [deeHay] I said
dijeron [deeHairon] they said; you said
dijiste [deeHeestay] you said
dijo [deeHo] he/she said; you say
diminuto tiny

Dinamarca f Denmark
dinero m [deen**airo**] money
dinero suelto [sw**e**lto] small change
Dios m [dee-**o**ss] God
¡Dios mío! [m**ee**-o] my God!
dirección f [deerekth-y**o**n] direction; address; steering; management
dirección única one-way traffic
dirección prohibida no entry
director m, **directora** f manager; director; headteacher
dirigir [deereeH**ee**r] to direct; to lead
disco m record
disco compacto compact disc
disco obligatorio parking disk must be displayed
disconformidad f disagreement
discoteca f disco, discotheque
disculparse [deeskoolp**a**rsay] to apologize
disculpe [deesk**oo**lpay] excuse me
disculpen las molestias we apologize for any inconvenience
discurso m speech
discusión f [deeskoos-y**o**n] discussion; argument
discutir to argue
diseñador de modas m [deesen-yad**o**r] fashion designer
distancia f [deest**a**nth-ya] distance
distinto different
distraído [deestra-**ee**do] absent-minded
distribuidor m [deestreebweed**o**r] distributor
distrito postal m postcode, zip code
disuélvase en agua dissolve in water
divertido entertaining; funny
divertirse [deebairt**ee**rsay] to have a good time
divisas fpl foreign currency
divorciado [deeborth-y**a**do] divorced
divorciarse [deeborth-y**a**rsay] to divorce
divorcio m [deeb**o**rth-yo] divorce
doble [d**o**blay] double
doce [d**o**thay] twelve
docena (de) f [doth**ay**na] dozen
dólar m dollar
doler [dol**air**] to hurt
dolor m pain
dolor de cabeza [kab**ay**tha] headache
dolor de garganta sore throat
dolor de muelas toothache
dolor de oídos [o-**ee**doss] earache
doloroso painful
domicilio m [domeeth**ee**l-yo] place of residence; commercial headquarters
domingo m Sunday
domingos y festivos Sundays and public holidays
¡dominguero! [domeeng**air**o] learn to drive!
don Mr
donaciones donations
donde [d**o**nday] where

doña [d**o**n-ya] Miss; Mrs
dorado gold, golden
dormido asleep
dormir to sleep
dormitorio m [dormeet**o**r-yo] bedroom; dormitory
dos two
doscientos [doss-thy**e**ntoss] two hundred
doy I give
droga f drug
droguería f [drogair**ee**-a] drugstore; household cleaning materials
ducha f shower
ducharse [dooch**a**rsay] to have a shower
dudar to doubt; to hesitate
duele [dw**ay**lay] it hurts
dulce [d**oo**lthay] sweet; gentle
dunas fpl sand dunes
durante [door**a**ntay] during
duro (m) hard; tough guy; five peseta coin

E

e and
ebanistería f [ebaneestair**ee**-a] cabinetmaker's
echar to throw
echo de menos a mi ... [dee m**ay**noss] I miss my ...
echar al buzón [booth**o**n] to post, to mail
echar el cerrojo [thairr**o**Ho] to bolt
echar al correo [korr**ay**-o] to post, to mail
echarse la siesta [ech**a**rsay] to have a nap
edad f age
edificio m [edeef**ee**th-yo] building
edredón m quilt, eiderdown; duvet
educado polite
EE.UU. (Estados Unidos) USA
efectivo: en efectivo in cash
eje m [**ay**Hay] axle
eje del cigüeñal [theegwen-y**a**l] crankshaft
ejemplo m [eH**e**mplo] example
por ejemplo for example
el the
él he; him
elástico elastic
electricidad f [elektreetheed**a**] electricity
electricista m [elektreeth**ee**sta] electrician
eléctrico electric
electrodomésticos mpl electrical appliances
elegir [elayH**ee**r] to choose
ella [**ay**-ya] she; her
ellas they; them
ellos they; them
embajada f [embaH**a**da] embassy
embarazada [embarath**a**da] pregnant
embarque m [emb**a**rkay] embarcation
embotellado en ... bottled in ...
embotellamiento m [embotay-yam-y**e**nto] traffic jam
embrague m [embr**a**gay] clutch

embudo m funnel
emergencia f [emairHenth-ya] emergency
emergencias casualty; emergencies
emisión f [emeess-yon] programme; emission; distribution date; issue
emocionante [emoth-yonantay] exciting
empalme m [empalmay] junction
empaquetado m [empaketado] packing
empaste m [empastay] filling
empeorar [empay-orar] to get worse
empezar [empethar] to begin
empinado steep
empleada f [emplay-ada], **empleado** m shop assistant, employee
empujar [empooHar] to push
en in; at; on; by
enagua de medio cuerpo f [enagwa day mayd-yo kwairpo] underskirt
enamorados: día de los enamorados m St Valentine's day
encantado delighted
¡encantado! pleased to meet you!
encantador lovely
encantar to please
encendedor m [enthendedor] lighter
encender [enthendair] to light; to switch on
encender luces de cruce switch headlights on
encendido m [enthendeedo] ignition
enchufe m [enchoofay] plug; socket
encienda las luces switch on your lights
encierro [enth-yairro] bull-running in Pamplona, the bulls loose in the streets
encima [entheema] above
encima de on (top of)
encontrar to find
encontrarse (con/a) [-trarsay] to meet
encuentro (m) [enkwentro] meeting, encounter; I find
enero m [enairo] January
enfadado angry
enfadarse [-darsay] to get angry
enfermedad f [enfairmeda] disease
enfermedad venérea [benairay-a] VD
enfermera f [enfairmaira] nurse
enfermero m male nurse
enfermo [enfairmo] ill
enfrente de [enfrentay] opposite
enhorabuena: ¡enhorabuena! [enorabwayna] congratulations!
dar la enhorabuena a to congratulate
enlace m [enlathay] connection; wedding
enlatados mpl canned food
enorme [enormay] enormous
enseñar [ensen-yar] to teach

entender [entend**air**] to understand
entero [ent**ai**ro] whole
entiendo [ent-y**e**ndo] I understand
entierro m [ent-y**ai**rro] funeral
entonces [ent**o**nthess] then; therefore
entrada f entrance, way in; ticket
entrada por delante entry at the front
entrada libre admission free
entrada gratis admission free
entrar to go in
entre [**e**ntray] among; between
entre sin llamar enter without knocking
entreacto m [entray-**a**kto] intermission
entretanto meanwhile
enviar [emb-y**a**r] to send
envolver [embolb**air**] to wrap up; to involve
equipaje m [ekeep**a**Hay] luggage, baggage
equipaje de mano hand baggage
equipajes mpl left-luggage office, (US) baggage check
equipo m [ek**ee**po] team
equitación f [ekeetath-y**o**n] horse riding
equivocado [ekeebok**a**do] wrong
equivocarse [ekeebok**a**rsay] to make a mistake
equivocarse de número to dial the wrong number
era [air**a**] I/he/she/it was; you were
erais [**ai**ra-eess] you were
éramos we were
eran they were; you were
eras you were
eres you are
erupción f [airoopth-y**o**n] rash; eruption
es he is; you are
ésa [**ay**sa] that one
esa that
ésas those ones
esas those
escala f intermediate stop; scale; ladder
escalera automática f escalator
escaleras fpl stairs
escalón lateral ramp; uneven road surface; no hard shoulder
escandaloso shocking
Escandinavia f Scandinavia
escarcha f frost
escayola f [eska-y**o**la] plaster cast
escocés [eskoth**ay**ss] Scottish
Escocia f [esk**o**th-ya] Scotland
escoger [eskoH**air**] to choose
esconder [eskond**air**] to hide
escribir to write
escrito written
escuchar to listen; to listen to
escuela f [eskw**ay**la] school
escuela de párvulos kindergarten
escurrir a mano to wring by hand
ése [**ay**say] that one
ese that

esencial [esenth-y**a**l] essential
esfuerzo m [esfw**ai**rtho] effort
esmalte de uñas m [esm**a**ltay day **oo**n-yass] nail polish
esmeralda f emerald
eso [**ay**so] that
eso es that's it, that's right
ésos those ones
esos those
espalda f back
espantoso dreadful; frightening
España f [esp**a**n-ya] Spain
español (m) [espan-y**o**l] Spanish; Spaniard
española f Spaniard, Spanish woman/girl
especialista m/f specialist
especialmente [espeth-yalm**e**ntay] especially
espejo m [esp**ay**Ho] mirror
esperar [espair**a**r] to wait; to hope
espere [esp**ai**ray] please wait
¡espéreme! [esp**ai**remay] wait for me!
espere tono más agudo wait for higher pitched tone
espeso [esp**ay**so] thick
esponja f [esp**o**nHa] sponge
esposa f wife
esposo m husband
espuma de afeitar f [afay-eet**a**r] shaving foam
esquí m [esk**ee**] ski; skiing
esquí acuático [akw**a**teeko] waterski; waterskiing
esquiar [eskee-**a**r] to ski
esquina f [esk**ee**na] corner
esta this
ésta this one
estación f [estath-y**o**n] station; season
estación de autobuses [owtob**oo**sess] bus station
estación de servicio [sairb**ee**th-yo] service station
estación de trenes train station
estación principal central station
estacionamiento vigilado supervised parking
estacionamiento limitado restricted parking
estacionarse [estath-yon**a**rsay] to park
estadio de fútbol m [est**a**d-yo] football stadium
Estados Unidos mpl United States
estampado (m) pattern; printed
estanco m tobacconist's
estanque m [est**a**nkay] pond
estaño m [est**a**n-yo] tin; pewter
estar to be
estárter m [est**a**rtair] choke
estas these
éstas these ones
estatua f [est**a**twa] statue
este m [**e**stay] east
este this
éste this one
esterilizado [estaireeleeth**a**do] sterilized
esto this
estómago m stomach
estornudar to sneeze

estos these
éstos these ones
estoy I am
estrecho narrow; tight
Estrecho de Gibraltar m [Heebralt**a**r] Strait of Gibraltar
estrella f [estr**ay**-ya] star
estrellarse contra [estray-y**a**rsay] to run into
estreno m [estr**ay**no] new film release
estreñido [estren-y**ee**do] constipated
estreñimiento m [estren-yeem-y**e**nto] constipation
estropear [estropay-**a**r] to damage
estudiante m/f [estood-y**a**ntay] student
estudiar [estood-y**a**r] to study
estupendo wonderful, great
estúpido stupid
etiqueta f [eteek**ay**ta] label
... **de etiqueta** formal ...
europeo [ay-ooropay-o] European
evidente [ebeed**e**ntay] obvious
exactamente [-m**e**ntay] exactly
¡exacto! exactly!
excelente [esthel**e**ntay] excellent
excepto ... except ...
excepto domingos y festivos except Sundays and holidays
excepto sábados except Saturdays
exceso de equipaje m [esth**ay**so day ekeep**a**Hay] excess baggage
exceso de velocidad [belotheed**a**] speeding
excursión f [eskoors-y**o**n] trip
expedir [esped**ee**r] to dispatch
explicación f [espleekath-y**o**n] explanation
explicar explain
explorar to explore
exportación f [esportath-y**o**n] export
exposición f [esposeeth-y**o**n] exhibition
exprés m slow night train stopping at all stations
expreso m fast train; special delivery
exterior (m) [estairee-**o**r] exterior, outer; foreign; overseas
extintor (de incendios) m [eenth**e**nd-yoss] fire extinguisher
extra 4-star, (US) premium
extranjera f [estranH**ai**ra] foreigner
extranjero (m) [estranH**ai**ro] foreign; abroad; overseas; foreigner
en el extranjero abroad
extraño [estr**a**n-yo] strange

F

fábrica f factory
fabricado por ... made by ...
fácil [f**a**theel] easy
factura f bill; invoice

facturación f [faktoorath-y**o**n] check-in
facturar el equipaje [ekeep**a**Hay] to check in
falda f skirt; hillside
falda pantalón culottes
falso false
falta f lack; mistake; defect; fault
no hace falta que ... [**a**thay] it's not necessary to ...
falta de visibilidad poor visibility
familia f [fam**ee**l-ya] family
famoso famous
farmacia f [farm**a**th-ya] chemist's, pharmacy
farmacia de guardia [gw**a**rd-ya] emergency chemist's/ pharmacy, duty chemist
faro m light; headlight; lighthouse
faro antiniebla [anteen-y**e**bla] fog lamp
favor: a favor de [fab**o**r] in favour of
por favor please
febrero m [febr**airo**] February
fecha f date
fecha de caducidad [kadootheed**a**] expiry date
fecha de caducación [kadookath-y**o**n] expiry date
fecha de nacimiento [natheem-y**e**nto] date of birth
fecha límite de venta sell-by date
¡felices Pascuas y próspero Año Nuevo! [fel**ee**thess p**a**skwass ee pr**o**spairo **a**n-yo nw**ay**bo] merry Christmas and a happy New Year!
felicidad f [feleetheed**a**] happiness
¡felicidades! [feleetheed**a**dess] happy birthday!; congratulations!
felicitar [feleetheet**a**r] to congratulate
feliz [fel**ee**th] happy
¡feliz cumpleaños! [koomplay-**a**n-yoss] happy birthday!
feo [f**ay**-o] ugly
feria de ... ... fair
ferias fpl [f**air**-yass] fair
ferretería f [fairraytair**ee**-a] hardware store
ferrobús m local short-distance train
ferrocarril m railway, railroad
festividad f celebration
festivos bank holidays, public holidays
fibras naturales [natoor**a**less] natural fibres
fiebre f [f-y**e**bray] fever
fiebre del heno [**ay**no] hay fever
fiesta f public holiday; party
fiesta de ... feast of ...
fiesta nacional [nath-yon**a**l] bullfighting
fila f row
filtro m filter
fin m [feen] end; purpose
a fin de que [day kay] so that
fin de semana weekend
fin de serie [s**air**-yay]

discontinued articles
final m [feen**a**l] end
final de autopista end of motorway/highway
fingir [feenHeer] to pretend
fino fine; delicate
firma f signature; company
firmar to sign
firme deslizante slippery surface
firme en mal estado bad surface
flaco skinny
flequillo m [flek**ee**-yo] fringe
flor f flower
floristería f florist
flotador m rubber ring
flotadores mpl [flotad**o**ress] lifebelts
folleto m [fo-y**ay**to] leaflet
fonda f (simple) restaurant; boarding house
fondo m bottom; background
en el fondo (de) at the bottom (of)
fontanero m [fontan**ai**ro] plumber
footing m jogging
forma f form
en forma fit
foto f photograph
hacer fotos to take photographs
fotografía f photograph; photography
fotografiar [fotograf-y**a**r] to photograph
fotógrafo m photographer
fotómetro m light meter
francamente [-m**e**ntay] frankly
francés [franth**ay**ss] French
Francia f [fr**a**nth-ya] France
franqueo m [frank**ay**-o] postage
fregadero m sink
fregar: fregar los platos to do the washing up
freír [fray-**ee**r] to fry
frenar [fren**a**r] to brake
freno m [fr**ay**no] brake
freno de mano handbrake
frente f [fr**e**ntay] forehead
fresco fresh
frigorífico m fridge
frío [fr**ee**-o] cold
hace frío [**a**thay] it's cold
frontera f [front**ai**ra] border
frutería f fruit shop/store; greengrocer
fue [fway] he/she/it went; he/she/it was; you went; you were
fuego m [fw**ay**go] fire
¿tiene fuego? have you got a light?
fuegos artificiales [arteefeeth-y**a**less] fireworks
fuente f [fw**e**ntay] fountain; source; font
fuera [fw**ai**ra] outside; he/she/it was; he/she/it went; you were; you went
fuera de servicio out of order
fuera de apart from
fuera de horas punta off-peak hours
fuerais [fw**ai**ra-eess] you were; you went
fuéramos [fw**ai**ramoss] we were;

we went
fueran [fw**ai**ran] they were; they went; you were; you went
fueras [fw**ai**rass] you were; you went
fueron [fw**ai**ron] they were; they went; you were; you went
fuerte [fw**ai**rtay] strong; loud
fuerza f [fw**ai**rtha] force; strength
fui [fwee] I was; I went
fuimos [fw**ee**moss] we were; we went
fuiste [fw**ee**stay] you were; you went
fuisteis [fw**ee**stay-eess] you were; you went
fumadores smoking
fumar to smoke
funcionar [foonkth-yon**a**r] to work
funcionario m [foonkth-yon**a**r-yo] civil servant
funeraria f undertaker's
furgón m van
furgoneta f van
furioso [foor-y**o**so] furious
furúnculo m abscess; boil
fusible m [foos**ee**blay] fuse
fútbol m football
futuro (m) [foot**oo**ro] future

G

gabardina f raincoat
gafas fpl glasses, eyeglasses
gafas de sol sunglasses
gafas de bucear [boothay-**a**r] goggles
galería f [galair**ee**-a] gallery
galería de arte [day **a**rtay] art gallery
galerías fpl store
Gales m [g**a**less] Wales
galés Welsh
gallego [ga-y**ay**-go] Galician
ganar to win; to earn
ganga f bargain
ganso m goose
garaje m [gar**a**Hay] garage
garantía f guarantee
garganta f throat
gas-oil m diesel
gasóleo m [gas**o**lay-o] diesel
gasolina f petrol, fuel
gasolina normal two star petrol, (US) regular (gas)
gasolina super four star petrol, (US) premium (gas)
gasolinera f [gasoleen**ai**ra] petrol/gas station, filling station
gastar to spend
gato m cat; jack
gemelos mpl [Haym**ay**loss] twins; cufflinks
generalmente [Henairalm**e**ntay] generally; usually
¡genial! [Hayn-y**a**l] great!, fantastic!
genio: tener mal genio [H**ay**n-yo] to be bad-tempered
gente f [H**e**ntay] people
gerente m [Hair**e**ntay] manager
¡gilipollas! [Heeleep**o**-yass] stupid idiot!

gimnasia f [Heemn**a**s-ya] gymnastics
gimnasio m gymnasium
ginecólogo m [Heenek**o**logo] gynaecologist
girar [Heer**a**r] to turn
giro [H**ee**ro] money order; turn
gitano m [Heet**a**no] gypsy
glorieta f [glor-y**ay**ta] roundabout
gobierno m [gob-y**ai**rno] government
gol m goal
Golfo de Vizcaya m [beethk**a**-ya] Bay of Biscay
golpe m [g**o**lpay] blow
de golpe all of a sudden
golpear [golpay-**a**r] to hit
goma f rubber; glue
goma elástica rubber band
gordo fat
gorra f cap
gorro m bonnet, cap
gorro de baño [b**a**n-yo] bathing cap
gorro de ducha shower cap
gota f drop
gotera f [got**ai**ra] leak
gracias [gr**a**th-yass] thank you
gracias, igualmente [eegwalm**e**ntay] thank you, the same to you
gracioso [grath-y**o**so] funny
grados mpl degrees
gramática f grammar
gramo m gramme
Gran Bretaña f [bret**a**n-ya] Great Britain
grande [gr**a**nday] big, large
grandes rebajas [reb**a**Hass] sales
grandes almacenes mpl [almath**ay**ness] large department store
granizo m [gran**ee**tho] hail
granja f [gr**a**nHa] farm
granjero m [granH**ai**ro] farmer
grano m spot
grasa f fat
grasiento [grass-y**e**nto] greasy
graso greasy
gratificación f [grateefeekath-y**o**n] reward; tip
gratis free
grave [gr**a**bay] serious
gravilla f [grab**ee**-ya] loose chippings
Grecia f [gr**e**th-ya] Greece
grifo m tap, (US) faucet
gripe f [gr**ee**pay] flu
gris grey
gritar to shout
grosero [gros**ai**ro] rude
grúa f [gr**oo**-a] tow truck, breakdown lorry; crane
grueso [grw**ay**so] thick
grupo m group
grupo sanguíneo [sang**ee**nay-o] blood group
guante m [gw**a**ntay] glove
guapo [gw**a**po] handsome
guardacostas m/f [gwardak**o**stass] coastguard
guardar [gward**a**r] to keep; to put away
guardarropa m [gwardarr**o**pa] cloakroom, (US) checkroom
guardería (infantil) f [gwardair**ee**-a (infant**ee**l)] crèche; nursery

school
guárdese en sitio fresco keep in a cool place
guardia civil m/f [gward-ya theebeel] police; policeman/policewoman
guateque m [gwatay-kay] party
guerra f [gairra] war
guerra civil civil war
guía m/f [gee-a] guide
guía telefónica f phone book, telephone directory
guía turística tourist guide
guisar [geesar] to cook
guitarra f [geetarra] guitar
gustar to please
me gusta ... I like ...
gusto: mucho gusto pleased to meet you!
con mucho gusto certainly, with great pleasure
el gusto es mío how do you do, it is a pleasure

H

h is not pronounced in Spanish

ha he/she/it has; you have
habéis [abay-eess] you have
habilidoso skilful
habitación f [abeetath-yon] room
habitación doble [doblay] double room
habitación individual [eendeebeedwal] single room
habitación con dos camas twin room
habitar to live
hablador talkative
hablar to speak
hable aquí speak here
habrá there will be; he/she/it will have; you will have
habrán they will have; you will have
habrás you will have
habré [abray] I will have
habréis [abray-eess] you will have
habremos we will have
habría [abree-a] I would have; he/she/it would have; you would have
habríais [abree-a-eess] you would have
habríamos [abree-amoss] we would have
habrían [abree-an] they would have; you would have
habrías [abree-ass] you would have
hace [athay]: hace ... días ... days ago
hace calor it is hot
hacer [athair] to make; to do
hacerse [athairsay] to become
hacia [ath-ya] towards
hago I do; I make
hambre: tengo hambre [ambray] I'm hungry
hamburguesería f [amboorgaysairee-a] restaurant selling hamburgers, hot dogs
han [an] they have; you have
haré [aray] I will do

h is not pronounced in Spanish

harto: estar harto (de) [**a**rto] to be fed up (with)
has [ass] you have
hasta [**a**sta] even; until
hasta que [kay] until
¡hasta la vista! see you!
¡hasta luego! [lw**ay**go] cheerio!; see you later!
¡hasta mañana! [man-y**a**na] see you tomorrow!
¡hasta pronto! see you soon!
hay [I] there is; there are
hay ... we sell ...
haya [**ī**-a] I have; he/she/it has; you have
haz [ath] do; make
he [ay] I have
hecho m [**ay**-cho] fact
hecho made; done
hecho a la medida made-to-measure
helada f frost
heladería f [eladair**ee**-a] ice-cream parlour
helado f [el**a**do] ice-cream
helar to freeze
hembra female
hemos we have
herida f [air**ee**da] wound
herido injured
hermana f [airm**a**no] sister
hermano m brother
hermoso [airm**o**so] beautiful
herramientas fpl [airram-y**e**ntass] tools
hervir [airb**ee**r] to boil
hice [**ee**thay] I made; I did
hidratante: crema hidratante f [eedrat**a**ntay] moisturizer
hidropedales mpl [eedroped**a**less] pedalos
hielo m [**yay**lo] ice
hierba f [**yai**rba] grass
hierro m [**yai**rro] iron
hija f [**ee**Ha] daughter
hijo m son
hilo m thread
hipermercado [eepairmairk**a**do] hypermarket
hipo m hiccups
hipódromo m horse-racing track
historia f [eest**o**r-ya] history; story
hizo [**ee**tho] he/she made; he/she did; you made; you did
hogar m home; household goods
hoja f [**o**Ha] leaf; sheet of paper
hoja de afeitar [day afay-eet**a**r] razor blade
¡hola! hello!, hi!
hombre m [**o**mbray] man
¡hombre! hey there!; you bet; oh come on!
hombre de negocios [neg**o**th-yoss] businessman
hombro m shoulder
hondo deep
honrado honest
hora f [**o**ra] hour
¿qué hora es? what time is it?
hora local local time
horario m [or**a**r-yo] timetable,

(US) schedule
horario de autobuses [owtob**oo**sess] bus timetable/ schedule
horario de invierno [eemb-y**ai**rno] winter timetable/schedule
horario de recogidas [rekoH**ee**dass] collection times
horario de trenes train timetable/schedule
horario de verano summer timetable/schedule
horas de consulta surgery hours, (US) office hours (of doctor)
horas de oficina [ofeeth**ee**na] opening hours
horas de visita visiting hours
horas punta rush hour
hormiga f ant
horno m oven
horquilla f [ork**ee**-ya] hairpin
hospedarse [osped**a**rsay] to stay
hostal m [ost**a**l] restaurant specializing in regional dishes; boarding house
hostal-residencia m [reseed**e**nth-ya] long-stay boarding house
hostería f [ostair**ee**-a] restaurant specializing in regional dishes
hotel-residencia m residential hotel
hoy [oy] today
HR (hostal-residencia) m boarding house where no meals are served, often lower-priced, residential hotel
hube [**oo**bay] I had
hubieron [oob-y**ai**ron] they had; you had
hubimos [oob**ee**moss] we had
hubiste [oob**ee**stay] you had
hubisteis [oob**ee**stay-eess] you had
hubo [**oo**bo] he/she/it had; you had; there was/were
huelga f [w**e**lga] strike
hueso m [w**ay**so] bone
huésped m/f [w**e**sped] guest
huevo m [w**ay**bo] egg
humedad m humidity, dampness
húmedo damp
humo m smoke
humor m humour
hundirse [oond**ee**rsay] to sink
hurto m theft

I

idéntico (a/que) identical (to)
idioma m [eed-y**o**ma] language
idiota m/f [eed-y**o**ta] idiot
iglesia f [eegl**ay**s-ya] church
igual [eegw**a**l] equal; like
me da igual it's all the same to me
imbécil (m) [eemb**ay**theel] nutter; stupid
impaciente [eempath-y**e**ntay] impatient
imperdible m [eempaird**ee**blay] safety pin
impermeable (m) [eempairmay-**a**blay] waterproof; raincoat

importación f [eemportath-**yon**] imported goods
importante [eemport**a**ntay] important
importar: no importa it doesn't matter
¿le importa si ...? do you mind if ...?
importe m [eemp**o**rtay] amount
importe del billete [bee-y**ay**tay] fare
importe total total due
imposible [eemposee**e**blay] impossible
impreso m [eempr**ay**so] form
impuesto m [eempw**e**sto] tax
incendiar [eenthend-y**a**r] to set fire to
incendio m [eenth**e**nd-yo] fire (blaze)
incluido [eenkl-w**ee**do] included
incluso even
increíble [eenkray-**ee**blay] incredible
indemnizar [eendemneeth**a**r] to compensate
independiente [eendepend-yentay] independent
indicaciones fpl instructions for use
indicador m indicator
indicador de nivel gauge
indicar to indicate
indicativos provinciales area codes
indicativos de paises country codes
indignado indignant
indispuesto [eendeespw**e**sto] unwell
infantil children's
infarto m heart attack
infectarse [eenfekt**a**rsay] to become infected
inflamado swollen
inflamarse [eenflam**a**rsay] to swell
influenciar [eenflwenth-y**a**r] to influence
información f [eenformath-y**o**n] information
información de vuelos [bw**ay**loss] flight information
información turística tourist information
información y turismo tourist information office
informar to inform
informarse (de/sobre) [-m**a**rsay (day/s**o**bray)] to get information (on/about)
infracción f [eenfrakth-y**o**n] offence
Inglaterra f [eenglat**ai**rra] England
inglés (m) [een-gl**ay**ss] English; Englishman
inglesa f Englishwoman
ingresos mpl deposits; income
iniciales fpl [eeneeth-y**a**less] initials
inmediatamente [eenmed-yatam**e**ntay] immediately
inocente [eenoth**e**ntay] innocent
insertar monedas insert coins
inserte moneda insert coin
insistir to insist
insolación f [eensolath-y**o**n]

sunstroke
instituto de belleza m [bay-yaytha] beauty salon
instrucciones de lavado mpl washing instructions
inteligente [eenteleeHentay] intelligent
intentar to try
interés m [eentairayss] interest
interesante [eentairesantay] interesting
interior (m) [eentairee-or] interior, inner; domestic, home
intermedio (m) [eentairmayd-yo] intermediate; intermission, interval
intermitente m [eentairmeetentay] indicator
interruptor m switch
interurbana long-distance
intoxicación alimenticia f [eentokseekath-yon aleementeeth-ya] food poisoning
introduzca moneda insert coin
introduzca el dinero exacto insert exact amount
introduzca la tarjeta y marque insert card and dial
inútil useless, pointless
invierno m [eemb-yairno] winter
invitada f, **invitado** m guest
invitar to invite
inyección f [eenyekth-yon] injection
ir to go
ir de paseo [pasay-o] to go for a walk
Irlanda f [eerlanda] Ireland
Irlanda del Norte [nortay] Northern Ireland
irlandés (m) [eerlandayss] Irish; Irishman
irlandesa f Irishwoman
irse [eersay] to go away
isla f island
Islas Canarias fpl [kanar-yass] Canary Islands
itinerario m [eeteenairar-yo] itinerary
IVA (impuesto sobre el valor añadido) [eeba] VAT
izq. (izquierda) left
izquierda f [eethk-yairda] left
a la izquierda (de) on the left (of)

J

jabón m [Habon] soap
jabón de afeitar [afay-eetar] shaving soap
jamonería f [Hamonairee-a] hams (shop)
jarabe m [Harabay] syrup
jardín m [Hardeen] garden
jardines públicos [Hardeeness] park, public gardens
jarra f [Harra] jug
jarrón m [Harron] vase
jefe m [Hayfay] boss
jefe de tren guard
jersey m [Hairsay-ee] jumper
jersey de cuello alto [kway-yo] polo neck jumper
¡Jesús! [Haysooss] bless you!
¡joder! [Hodair] hell!

joven (m/f) [H**o**ben] young; young man; young woman
joyas fpl [H**o**yass] jewellery
joyería f [Hoyair**ee**-a] jewellery; jeweller's
judío [Hood**ee**-o] Jewish
juego (m) [Hw**ay**go] game; I play
jueves m [w**ay**bess] Thursday
jugar [Hoog**a**r] to play
juguete m [Hoog**ay**tay] toy
juguetería f [Hoogaytair**ee**-a] toy shop
juicio m [Hw**ee**th-yo] judgement; opinion; reason
julio m [H**oo**l-yo] July
junio m [H**oo**n-yo] June
junto (a) [H**oo**nto] next (to)
juntos together
justo [H**oo**sto] just

K

kiosko de periódicos m [k-y**o**sko day pairee-**o**deekoss] newsagent's, newsstand
kiosko de prensa newsagent's, newsstand

L

la the; her; it
labio m [l**a**b-yo] lip
laborables [labor**a**bless] weekdays, working days
laca f hair spray
lado m side
  al lado de beside, next to
ladrillo m [ladr**ee**-yo] brick
ladrón m thief
lagartija f [lagart**ee**Ha] lizard
lago m lake
lámpara f lamp
lana f wool
lana pura pure wool
lanas al peso wool sold by weight
lápiz m [l**a**peeth] pencil
lápiz de ojos [**o**Hoss] eyeliner
largo (m) length; long
  a lo largo de along
largura f length
las the; them; you
  las que ... the ones that ...
lástima: es una lástima it's a pity
lastimarse la espalda [lasteem**a**rsay] to hurt one's back
lata f can; nuisance
latón m brass
lavabo m [lab**a**bo] washbasin
lavabos toilets, rest room
lavado m [lab**a**do] washing
lavadora f [labad**o**ra] washing machine
lavandería f [labandair**ee**-a] laundry
lavandería automática [owtom**a**teeka] launderette, laundromat
lavaplatos m [labapl**a**toss] dishwasher
lavar [lab**a**r] to wash
lavar a mano wash by hand
lavar en seco dry clean
lavar la ropa to do the washing
lavarse [lab**a**rsay] to wash

lavar separadamente wash separately
laxante m [laks**a**ntay] laxative
le [lay] him; her; you
lección f [lekth-y**o**n] lesson
leche f [l**e**chay] milk
leche limpiadora f [leemp-yad**o**ra] skin cleanser
lechería f [lechair**ee**-a] dairy shop; dairy produce
leer [lay-**air**] to read
lejía f [leH**ee**-a] bleach
lejos [l**ay**Hoss] far away
lejos de far from
lencería f [lenthair**ee**-a] drapery
lentillas fpl [lent**ee**-yass] contact lenses
lentillas blandas soft lenses
lentillas duras hard lenses
lentillas porosas gas permeable lenses
lento slow
leotardos mpl [lay-ot**a**rdoss] tights, pantyhose
les them; you
letra f letter; banker's draft
levantar [lebant**a**r] to raise, to lift
levantarse [lebant**a**rsay] to get up
ley f [l**ay**-ee] law
libra f pound
libre [l**ee**bray] free; vacant
libre de impuestos duty-free
librería f [leebrair**ee**-a] bookshop, bookstore
libreta de ahorros f [leebr**ay**ta day a-**o**rross] savings account book
libreta de direcciones [deerekth-y**o**ness] address book
libro m book
libro de frases phrase book
libros de bolsillo [bols**ee**-yo] paperbacks
líder m [l**ee**dair] leader
ligero [leeH**ai**ro] light
lima de uñas f [**oo**n-yass] nailfile
límite f [l**ee**meetay] limit
límite de altura maximum height
límite de peso [p**ay**so] weight limit
límite de velocidad [day belotheed**a**d] speed limit
limpiaparabrisas m [leemp-yaparabr**ee**sass] windscreen wiper
limpiar [leemp-y**a**r] to clean
limpieza f [leemp-y**ay**tha] cleanliness; cleaning
limpieza de coches car wash
limpieza en seco dry-cleaning
limpio [l**ee**mp-yo] clean
línea f [l**ee**nay-a] line
linterna f [leent**ai**rna] torch
lío m [l**ee**-o] mess
liquidación f [leekeedath-y**o**n] sale
liquidación total clearance sale
liso flat; plain; straight
lista f list
lista de correos [korr**ay**-oss] poste restante, (US) general delivery
lista de espera [esp**ai**ra] standby

listo clever; ready
litera f [leet**air**a] couchette
litro m litre
llamada f [yam**a**da] call
llamada a cobro revertido [rebairt**ee**do] reverse charge call
llamar [yam**a**r] to call; to name
llamar por teléfono [tel**ay**fono] to call, to phone
llamarse [yam**a**rsay] to be called
llame a la puerta please knock
llame al timbre please ring
llame antes de entrar knock before entering
llamo: me llamo ... [may y**a**mo] my name is ...
llave f [y**a**bay] key; spanner
llave inglesa [eengl**ay**sa] spanner
llegada f [yayg**a**da] arrival
llegadas internacionales international arrivals
llegadas nacionales domestic arrivals
llegar [yeg**a**r] to arrive; to get to
llegué [yeg**ay**] I arrived
llenar [yen**a**r] to fill
llenar el depósito to fill up
lleno [y**ay**no] full
llevar [yeb**a**r] to carry; to take; to bring; to give a lift to
llevar a juicio [Hw**ee**th-yo] to prosecute
llevarse [yeb**a**rsay] to take away
llorar [yor**a**r] to cry
llover [yob**air**] to rain
lloviendo: está lloviendo [yob-y**e**ndo] it's raining
llovizna f [yob**ee**thna] drizzle
llueve [y-w**ay**-bay] it is raining
lluvia f [y**oo**b-ya] rain
lo it; the
localidad f place
localidades tickets
loción antimosquitos f [loth-y**o**n anteemosk**ee**toss] insect repellent
loción bronceadora [bronthay-ad**o**ra] suntan lotion
loción para después del afeitado [despw**e**ss del afay-eet**a**do] after-shave
loco (m) mad; madman
locomotora f engine
locutorio telefónico m telephone booth
Londres [l**o**ndress] London
longitud f [lonHeet**oo**] length
los the
los que ... the ones that ...
loza f [l**o**tha] crockery
luces de posición fpl [l**oo**thess day poseeth-y**o**n] sidelights
luces traseras [tras**air**ass] rear lights
luego [lw**ay**go] then
luego que after
lugar m place
en lugar de instead of
lugar de veraneo [bairan**ay**-o] summer resort
lugares de interés places of interest
lujo m [l**oo**Ho] luxury
lujoso luxurious
luna f moon

lunes m [l**oo**ness] Monday
luz f [looth] light
luz de carretera main beam
luz de cruce [kr**oo**thay] dipped headlights

M

machista m male chauvinist, sexist
madera f [mad**ai**ra] wood
madre f [m**a**dray] mother
madrileño [madreel**ay**n-yo] from Madrid, Madrid
madrugada f small hours
maduro ripe
maestra f [ma-**e**stra], **maestro** m primary school teacher
mal (m) badly; unwell, ill, sick; evil
¡maldita sea! [s**ay**-a] damn!
maleducado rude
malentendido m misunderstanding
maleta f suitcase
hacer las maletas to pack
maletero m [malet**ai**ro] boot, (US) trunk
mal genio m [H**ay**n-yo] bad temper
mal humor m bad mood; bad temper; anger
Mallorca [ma-y**o**rka] Majorca
malo bad
mamá f mum
manantial m [manant-y**a**l] spring
mancha f stain
mandar to send; to order
mandíbula f jaw
manera: de esta manera [man**ai**ra] in this way
de manera que so (that)
mano f hand
manoplas fpl mittens
manta f blanket
mantel m tablecloth
mantelerías fpl [mantelair**ee**-ass] table linen
mantenga limpia España keep Spain tidy
mantenga limpia la ciudad keep our city tidy
manténgase en sitio fresco store in a cool place
manténgase alejado de los niños keep out of the reach of children
manual de conversación m [manw**a**l day konbairsath-y**o**n] phrasebook
mañana (f) [man-y**a**na] morning; tomorrow
por la mañana in the morning
¡hasta mañana! see you tomorrow!
mañana por la mañana tomorrow morning
mañana por la tarde [t**a**rday] tomorrow afternoon; tomorrow evening
mapa m map
mapa de carreteras road map
mapa de recorrido network map
maquillaje m [makee-y**a**Hay] make-up
maquillarse [makee-y**a**rsay] to put one's makeup on

máquina de afeitar eléctrica f [m**a**keena day afay-eet**a**r] electric shaver
máquina de escribir typewriter
máquina de fotos camera
máquina tragaperras [m**a**keena] slot machine
maquinaria f [makeen**a**r-ya] machinery
maquinilla de afeitar f [makeen**ee**-ya] razor
mar m sea
la mar de ... lots of ...; very ...
maravilloso [marabee-y**o**so] marvellous
marca registrada f [reHeestr**a**da] registered trade mark
marcar to dial
marcar el número dial the number
marcha f gear
marcha atrás reverse gear
marcharse [march**a**rsay] to go away
marea f [mar**ay**-a] tide
mareado [maray-**a**do] sick; merry, drunk
mares: a mares loads
marica m poofter
marido m husband
mariposa f butterfly; fairy, pansy
marisquería f [mareeskair**ee**-a] shellfish restaurant
marque ... dial ...
marrón brown
marroquinería f [marrokeen-air**ee**-a] fancy leather goods
Marruecos m [marrw**ay**-koss] Morocco
martes m [m**a**rtess] Tuesday
martes de carnaval Shrove Tuesday
martillo m [mart**ee**-yo] hammer
marzo m [m**a**rtho] March
más more
más de more than
más pequeño smaller
el más caro the most expensive
ya no más no more
más o menos [m**ay**noss] more or less
matar to kill
matrícula f number plate; registration; registration fees
máximo personas maximum number of people
mayo m [m**a**-yo] May
mayor [may**o**r] adult; bigger; older; biggest; oldest
la mayor parte (de) [p**a**rtay] most (of)
mayor de edad of age, adult
mayoría: la mayoría [mayor**ee**-a] most
me me; myself
me duele aquí [dw**ay**lay] I have a pain here
mecánico m mechanic
mechas fpl highlights
media docena (de) f [doth**ay**na] half a dozen
media hora f half an hour
media pensión f [pens-y**o**n] half board, (US) European plan
mediano [mayd-y**a**no] medium;

average
medianoche f [mayd-yan**o**chay] midnight
medias fpl [m**ay**d-yass] stockings
ir/pagar a medias to go Dutch
medias panty tights, pantyhose
medicina f [medeeth**ee**na] medicine
médico m [m**ay**deeko] doctor
médico general [Hay-nair**a**l] GP
medida: a medida que as
medida del cuello f [kw**ay**-yo] collar size
medio m [m**ay**d-yo] middle
por medio de by (means of)
medio: de tamaño medio medium-sized
medio billete m [bee-y**ay**tay] half(-price ticket)
medio litro half a litre
mediodía m [mayd-yod**ee**-a] midday
medir to measure
medusa f jellyfish
mejor [mayH**o**r] best; better
mejorar [mayHor**a**r] to improve
mejoría f [mayHor**ee**-a] recovery
mencionar [menth-yon**a**r] to mention
menor [men**o**r] smaller; younger; smallest; youngest
menor de edad minor
menos [m**ay**noss] less; fewest; least
a menos que unless
menudo tiny, minute
a menudo often
menú turístico m set menu
mercadillo m [mairkad**ee**-yo] street market
mercado m market
mercado cubierto [koob-y**ai**rto] indoor market
mercado de divisas exchange rates
mercería f [mairthair**ee**-a] haberdashery
merendar to have an afternoon snack
merendero m [mairend**ai**ro] open-air café
merienda f [mair-y**e**nda] tea, afternoon snack
mes m month
mesa f table
mesón m inn
meta [m**ay**ta] goal
metro m metre; underground, (US) subway
mezquita f [methk**ee**ta] mosque
mí me
mi my
mía [m**ee**-a] mine
microbús m minibus
miedo m [m-y**ay**do] fear
tengo miedo (de/a) I'm afraid (of)
mientras [m-yentrass] while
mientras que whereas
mientras tanto meanwhile
miércoles m [m-y**ai**rkoless] Wednesday
miércoles de ceniza [then**ee**tha] Ash Wednesday
¡mierda! [m-y**ai**rda] shit
mil [meel] thousand
militar m serviceman

millón m [mee-y**o**n] million
minifalda f mini-skirt
ministerio de ... ministry of ...
minúsculo tiny
minusválido (m) disabled; disabled person
minuto m minute
mío [m**ee**-o] mine
miope [m-y**o**pay] short-sighted
mirador m scenic view, vantage point
mirar to look (at)
mis my
misa f mass
mismo same
mitad f half
mitad de precio [pr**ay**th-yo] half price
mobilette f [mobeel**e**ttay] moped
mochila f rucksack
moda f fashion
de moda fashionable
moda jóvenes [H**o**bayness] young fashions
moda juvenil [Hoobayn**ee**l] young fashions
modas caballeros [kaba-y**ai**ross] men's fashions
modas niños/niñas [n**ee**n-yoss] children's fashions
modas pre-mamá maternity fashions
modas señora ladies' fashions
modelo m model; design; style
moderno [mod**ai**rno] modern
modista f dressmaker; fashion designer
modisto m fashion designer
modo: de modo que so (that)
modo de empleo instructions for use
mojado [moH**a**do] wet
moldeado con secador de mano [molday-**a**do] blow-dry
molestar to disturb; to bother
molesto annoying
monedas fpl coins
monedero m [moned**ai**ro] purse
montacargas m service lift, service elevator
montaña f [mont**a**n-ya] mountain
montañismo m [montan-y**ee**smo] climbing
montar to get in; to ride; to assemble
montar a caballo [kab**a**-yo] to go horse-riding
montar en bici [b**ee**thee] to cycle
moquetas fpl [mok**ay**tass] carpets
morado purple
mordedura f bite
moreno [mor**ay**no] dark-haired
morir to die
moros mpl Moors
morriña: tengo morriña [morr**ee**n-ya] I'm homesick
mosca f fly
mostrador m counter
mostrador (de equipajes) [day ekeep**a**Hess] check-in
mostrar to show
moto f motorbike
motora f motorboat
mover [mob**ai**r] to move
mozo m [m**o**tho] porter

muchacha f girl
muchacho m boy
muchas gracias [gr**a**th-yass] thank you very much
muchísimas gracias thank you very much indeed
muchísimo enormously, a great deal
mucho much; a lot; a lot of
mucho más a lot more
mucho menos [m**ay**noss] a lot less
muchos/muchas a lot; a lot of; many
muebles mpl [mw**ay**bless] furniture
muela f [mw**ay**la] back tooth
muela del juicio [Hw**ee**th-yo] wisdom tooth
muelle m [mw**ay**-yay] spring; quay
muerte f [mw**air**tay] death
muerto [mw**air**to] dead
mujer f [mooH**air**] woman; wife
muletas fpl crutches
multa f fine; parking ticket
multa por uso indebido penalty for misuse
mundo m world
muñeca f [moon-y**e**ka] wrist; doll
muro m wall
músculo m muscle
museo m [moos**ay**-o] museum
museo de arte [**a**rtay] art gallery
música f music
muslo m thigh
musulmán Muslim
muy [mwee] very
muy bien [b-yen] very well

N

N (carretera nacional) national highway
nacido [nath**ee**do] born
nacimiento m [natheem-y**e**nto] birth
nacional [nath-yon**a**l] domestic
nacionalidad f [nath-yonaleed**a**] nationality
nada nothing
de nada you're welcome, don't mention it
nada que declarar nothing to declare
nadar to swim
nadie [n**a**d-yay] nobody
naranja f [nar**a**nHa] orange
nariz f [nar**ee**th] nose
natación f [natath-y**o**n] swimming
naturaleza f [natooral**ay**tha] nature
naturalmente [-m**e**ntay] naturally; of course
náusea: siento náuseas [s-y**e**nto n**ow**say-ass] I feel sick
navaja f [nab**a**Ha] penknife
Navidad f Christmas
¡feliz Navidad! [fel**ee**th] merry Christmas!
neblina f mist
necesario [nethes**a**r-yo] necessary
necesitar: necesito ... [nethes**ee**to] I need ...

negar to deny
negativo (m) negative
negocio m [negoth-yo] business
negro (m) black; furious
nena f [nayna] baby girl; little girl
nene m [naynay] baby boy; little boy
nervioso [nairb-yoso] nervous
neumático m [nay-oomateeko] tyre
neumáticos - se reparan, se arreglan tyres repaired
neurótico [nay-ooroteeko] neurotic
nevar to snow
ni neither, nor
ni ... ni ... neither ... nor ...
niebla f [n-yebla] fog
nieta f [n-yayta] granddaughter
nieto m grandson
nieva [n-yayba] it is snowing
nieve f [n-yaybay] snow
ningún [neengoon] nobody; none; not one; no ...
en ningún sitio [seet-yo] nowhere
ninguno nobody; none; not one; no ...
niña f [neen-ya] child
niñera f [neen-yaira] nanny
niño m [neen-yo] child
nivel del aceite m [athay-eetay] oil level
no no; not
no admite plancha do not iron
no aparcar no parking
no aparcar, llamamos grúa illegally parked vehicles will be towed away
no contiene alcohol does not contain alcohol
no entrada por detrás no entry at the rear
no exceda la dosis indicada do not exceed the stated dose
no fumadores no smoking
no funciona out of order
no hay de qué [no I day kay] you are welcome
no hay localidades sold out
no molestar do not disturb
no para en ... does not stop in ...
no ... pero sí not ... but
no pisar el césped keep off the grass
no recomendada para menores de 18 años not recommended for those under 18 years of age
no se admiten caravanas no caravans allowed
no se admiten devoluciones no refunds given
no se admiten perros no dogs allowed
no tocar please do not touch
no utilizar lejía do not bleach
noche f [nochay] night
esta noche tonight
por la noche at night
nochebuena f [nochay-bwayna] Christmas Eve
nochevieja f [nochay-b-yayHa] New Year's Eve
nombre m [nombray] name

nombre de soltera [solt**ai**ra] maiden name
nombre de pila first name
nordeste m [nord**e**stay] north-east
normal (m) [norm**a**l] normal; lower grade petrol, (US) regular
normalmente [-m**e**ntay] usually
noroeste m [noro-**e**stay] north-west
norte m [n**o**rtay] north
al norte de la ciudad north of the town
Noruega f [norw**ay**ga] Norway
nos us; ourselves
nosotras, nosotros we; us
noticias fpl [not**ee**th-yass] news
novecientos [nobay-th-y**e**ntoss] nine hundred
novela f novel
noveno [nob**ay**no] ninth
noventa ninety
novia f [n**o**b-ya] girlfriend; fiancée; bride
noviembre m [nob-y**e**mbray] November
novillada f [nobee-y**a**da] bullfight featuring young bulls
novio m [n**o**b-yo] boyfriend; fiancé; groom
nube f [n**oo**bay] cloud
nublado cloudy
nuboso cloudy
nuera f [nw**ai**ra] daughter-in-law
nuestra [nw**e**stra], **nuestras, nuestro, nuestros** our
Nueva York [nw**ay**ba] New York
nueve [nw**ay**bay] nine
nuevo new
número m [n**oo**mairo] number
número de teléfono phone number
número (de calzado) [day kalth**a**do] (shoe) size
nunca never

O

o or
o ... o ... either ... or ...
objeción f [ob-Heth-y**o**n] objection
objetar [obHayt**a**r] to object
objetivo m [obHayt**ee**bo] lens; objective
objetos de escritorio [obH**ay**toss day eskreet**o**r-yo] office supplies
objetos perdidos lost property, lost and found
obra f work; play
obras fpl roadworks
obstruido [obstr-w**ee**do] blocked
obturador m shutter
ocasión f [okass-y**o**n] occasion; opportunity; bargain
de ocasión second hand
occidental [oktheedent**a**l] Western
ochenta eighty
ocho eight
ocho días mpl [d**ee**-ass] week
ochocientos [ochoth-y**e**ntoss] eight hundred
octavo eighth

octubre m [okt**oo**bray] October
oculista [okool**ee**sta] optician
ocupado engaged; occupied; busy
ocupantes del coche mpl [okoop**a**ntess del k**o**chay] passengers
odiar [od-y**a**r] to hate
oeste m [o-**e**stay] west
al oeste de la ciudad west of the town
ofender [ofend**air**] to offend
oferta (especial) f [of**air**ta (espeth-y**a**l)] special offer
oficina f [ofeeth**ee**na] office
oficina de reclamaciones [reklamath-y**o**ness] complaints department
oficina de registros [reH**ee**stross] registrar's office
oficina de turismo tourist information office
oficina de objetos perdidos [obH**ay**toss] lost property office, lost and found
oficina de información y turismo [eenformath-y**o**n] tourist information office
oficina de correos [korr**ay**-oss] post office
oficina de correos y telégrafos post office and telegrams
oficinista m/f [ofeetheen**ee**sta] office worker
oficio m [of**ee**th-yo] job
ofrecer [ofreth**air**] to offer
oído (m) [o-**ee**do] ear; hearing; heard
¡oiga! [**oy**ga] listen here!; excuse me!
oigo I hear
oír [o-**ee**r] to hear
ojo m [**o**Ho] eye
ojo al tren beware of the train
ola f wave; fashion
ola de calor heatwave
oler [ol**air**] to smell
olor m smell
olvidar to forget
omnibús m local short-distance train
once [**o**nthay] eleven
operadora f operator
operarse [opair**a**rsay] to have an operation; to come about
oportunidad f chance, opportunity
oportunidades bargains
óptica f optician's
óptico m optician
optimista optimistic
orden m order
ordenador m computer
oreja f [or**ay**-Ha] ear
organizar [organeeth**a**r] to organize
orgulloso [orgoo-y**o**so] proud
orilla f [or**ee**-ya] shore
oro m gold
orquesta f [ork**e**sta] orchestra
os you; to you
oscuro dark
otoño m [ot**o**n-yo] autumn, (US) fall
otorrinolaringólogo ear, nose and throat specialist
otra vez [bayth] again
otro another (one); other

oveja f [ob**ay**Ha] sheep
oye [**o**-yay] he/she hears; you hear; listen

P

p (paseo) street; parking
paciente [path-y**e**ntay] patient
pacotilla: de pacotilla [pakot**ee**-ya] rubbishy; second-rate
padecer de [padeth**air**] to suffer from
padecer del corazón [korath**o**n] to have a heart condition
padre m [p**a**dray] father
padres mpl parents
pagadero payable
pagar to pay
página f [p**a**Heena] page
páginas amarillas [amar**ee**-yass] yellow pages
pagos mpl deposits
pague el importe exacto (please tender) exact money
país m [pa-**ee**ss] country
País Vasco Basque Country
País de Gales: el País de Gales [g**a**less] Wales
paisaje m [pa-ees**a**Hay] scenery
pájaro m [p**a**Haro] bird
pala f spade
palabra f word
palacio m [pal**a**th-yo] palace
palacio real [ray-**a**l] royal palace
palacio de congresos conference hall
Palacio de Justicia [Hoost**ee**th-ya] Law Courts
Palacio de la Opera opera house
palanca de velocidades f [belotheed**a**dess] gear lever
palco m box (at theatre)
palomitas de maíz fpl [ma-**ee**th] popcorn
palos de golf mpl golf clubs
pan m bread
panadería f [panadair**ee**-a] baker's
pantalla f [pant**a**-ya] screen
pantalón corto m shorts
pantalones mpl [pantal**o**ness] trousers, (US) pants
pantalones cortos mpl shorts
pantalones vaqueros [bak**air**oss] jeans
panties mpl tights
pantorrilla f [pantorr**ee**-ya] calf
pañal m [pan-y**a**l] nappy, (US) diaper
pañería f [pan-yair**ee**-a] drapery
pañuelo m [panw**ay**lo] handkerchief; scarf
pañuelo (de cabeza) [day kab**ay**tha] (head)scarf
papá m dad
papel m [pap**e**l] paper; rôle
papel celo® [th**ay**lo] sellotape®, Scotch tape®
papel de envolver [embolb**air**] wrapping paper
papel de escribir writing paper
papel de plata silver foil
papel higiénico [eeH-y**ay**neeko] toilet paper
papelera f litter; litter bin
papelería f [papelair**ee**-a]

stationery, stationer's
papeles pintados mpl wallpaper
paquete m [pak**ay**tay] packet
par m pair
para for; in order to
para automáticas for automatic washing machines
para que [kay] in order that
para uso del personal staff only
para uso externo not to be taken internally
parabrisas m windscreen
paracaidismo m [paraka-eed**ee**smo] parachuting
parachoques m [parach**o**kess] bumper, (US) fender
parada f stop
parada de autobuses bus stop
parada de taxis taxi rank
parador m hotel restaurant; luxury hotel
parador nacional [nath-yon**a**l] state-owned hotel, often a historic building which has been restored
paraguas m [par**a**gwass] umbrella
parar to stop
parecer [pareth**air**] to seem; to resemble
parecido [pareth**ee**do] similar
pared f [par**ay**d] wall
pareja f [par**ay**-Ha] pair; couple
parezco [par**e**thko] I seem
pariente m/f [par-y**e**ntay] relative
parking m car park, (US) parking lot
paro: en paro unemployed
parque m [p**a**rkay] park
parque de atracciones [atrakth-y**o**ness] amusement park
parque de bomberos [bomb**air**oss] fire station
parque de recreo [rekr**ay**-o] amusement park
parque infantil children's park; playpen
parrilla f [parr**ee**-ya] grill
parte f [p**a**rtay] part
en todas partes everywhere
en otra parte elsewhere
en alguna parte somewhere
¿de parte de quién? [day k-yen] who's calling?
parte antigua [ant**ee**gwa] old town
parte meteorológico m [maytay-orol**o**Heeko] weather forecast
particular private
partida f game
partido m match
pasado last
la semana pasada last week
pasado mañana the day after tomorrow
pasado de moda out of fashion
poco pasado rare
pasador m hairslide
pasaje m [pas**a**Hay] plane ticket
pasajero m [pasaH**air**o] passenger
pasajeros de tránsito transit passengers
pasaporte m [pasap**o**rtay] passport
pasaportes passport control
pasar to pass; to overtake;

to happen
pasar la aduana [ad-**wa**na] to go through customs
pasarlo bien [b-yen] to enjoy oneself
pasarlo bomba to have a great time
pasatiempo m [pasat-**ye**mpo] hobby
Pascua [p**a**sk-wa] Easter
pasear [pasay-**ar**] to go for a walk
pasen enter; cross, walk
paseo m [pas**ay**-o] walk; drive; ride
paseo de ... ... avenue
pasillo m [pas**ee**-yo] corridor
paso m passage; pass; step
estar de paso to be passing through
paso a nivel level crossing, (US) grade crossing
paso de cebra [th**ay**bra] zebra crossing
paso de contador unit
paso de peatones [pay-at**o**ness] pedestrian crossing
paso subterráneo pedestrian underpass
pasta de dientes f [d-**ye**ntess] toothpaste
pastelería f [pastelair**ee**-a] cake shop
pastilla f [past**ee**-ya] tablet
pastillas para la garganta throat pastilles
patatas fritas chips, French fries; crisps, potato chips
patinaje m [pateen**a**Hay] skating
patinar to skid; to skate
patio de butacas m stalls
peaje m [pay-**a**Hay] toll
peatón m [pay-at**o**n] pedestrian
peatón, camine por la izquierda pedestrians keep to the left
peatón, circula por tu izquierda pedestrians keep to the left
peatonal pedestrian
peatones pedestrians
peatones, caminen por la izquierda pedestrians keep to the left
pecho m chest; breast
pedazo m [ped**a**tho] piece
pediatra m/f [pedee-**a**tra] pediatrician
pedir to order; to ask for
pedir disculpas to apologize
pedir hora [**o**ra] to make an appointment
peinar [pay-een**ar**] to comb
peinarse [pay-een**ar**say] to comb one's hair
peine m [p**ay**-**ee**nay] comb
pelea f [pel**ay**-a] fight
peletería f [peletair**ee**-a] furs, furrier
película f film, movie
película en color colour film
película en versión original [bairs-y**o**n oreeHeen**al**] film in the original language
peligro m danger
peligro de incendio danger: fire hazard
peligro deslizamientos slippery road surface
peligroso dangerous

es peligroso bañarse danger: no swimming
es peligroso asomarse al exterior do not lean out
pelirrojo [peleerr**o**Ho] redheaded
pelo m [p**ay**lo] hair
me está tomando el pelo you're pulling my leg
pelón bald
pelota f ball
peluca f wig
peluquería f [pelookair**ee**-a] hairdresser's
peluquería de caballeros [kaba-y**ai**ross] gent's hairdresser's
peluquería de señoras ladies' salon
peluquera f [pelook**ai**ra], peluquero m hairdresser
pena f [p**ay**na] grief, sorrow
¡qué pena! [kay] what a pity!
pendiente de pago outstanding
pendientes mpl [pend-y**e**ntess] earrings
pene m [p**ay**nay] penis
penicilina f [peneetheel**ee**na] penicillin
pensar to think
pensión f [pens-y**o**n] guesthouse, boarding house; pension
pensión completa [kompl**ay**ta] full board, (US) American plan
pensionista m [pens-yon**ee**sta] old-age pensioner
peor [pay-**o**r] worse; worst
pequeño (m) [pek**ay**n-yo] small; child
percha f [p**ai**rcha] coathanger
perder [paird**ai**r] to lose; to miss
perderse [paird**ai**rsay] to get lost
pérdida f loss
perdón sorry, excuse me; pardon, pardon me
perezoso [paireth**o**so] lazy
perfecto [pairf**e**kto] perfect
perfumería f [pairfoomair**ee**-a] perfumes (shop)
periódico m [pairee-**o**deeko] newspaper
periodista m [pair-yod**ee**sta] journalist
período m [pair**ee**-odo] period
perla f [p**ai**rla] pearl
permanente f [pairman**e**ntay] perm
permiso m [pairm**ee**so] licence
permitido allowed
permitir to allow
pero [p**ai**ro] but
perra: no tengo una perra I'm broke
perro m [p**ai**rro] dog
persona f [pairs**o**na] person
persuadir [pairswad**ee**r] to persuade
pesadilla f [pesad**ee**-ya] nightmare
pesado heavy
pésame: dar el pésame [p**ay**samay] to offer one's condolences
pesar weight
a pesar de que despite the fact that

a pesar de in spite of
pesca f fishing
ir de pesca to go fishing
pescadería f [peskadairee-a] fishmonger's
pescar to fish; to catch out
peso m [payso] weight
peso neto net weight
peso máximo maximum weight
pestañas fpl [pestan-yass] eyelashes
petición de mano f [peteeth-yon] engagement
pez m [peth] fish
picadura f bite
picante [peekantay] hot
picar to sting; to itch
picor m itch
pidió [peed-yo] he/she asked for; you asked for
pie m [p-yay] foot
a pie on foot
piedra f [p-yedra] stone
piedra preciosa [preth-yosa] precious stone
piel f [p-yayl] skin
pienso [p-yenso] I think
pierna f [p-yairna] leg
pieza de repuesto f [p-yaytha day repwesto] spare part
piezas de recambio [rekamb-yo] spares
pijama m [peeHama] pyjamas
pila f battery; pile
píldora f pill
piloto m pilot
pilotos mpl rear lights
pincel m [peenthayl] paint brush
pinchazo m [peenchatho] puncture
pintar to paint
pintura f painting; paint
pinza de la ropa f clothes peg
pinzas fpl [peenthass] tweezers
piña f [peen-ya] pineapple
pipa f pipe
piragua f [peeragwa] canoe
piragüismo m [peeragweesmo] canoeing
Pirineos mpl [peereenay-oss] Pyrenees
piscina f [peestheena] swimming pool
piscina cubierta [koob-yairta] indoor swimming pool
piso m floor; flat, apartment
piso amueblado [amweblado] furnished apartment
piso bajo [baHo] ground floor, (US) first floor
piso sin amueblar [amweblar] unfurnished apartment
pista f track; clue
pista de baile [ba-eelay] dance floor
pista de patinaje [pateenaHay] skating rink
pista de tenis tennis court
pistas de esquí [eskee] ski runs
pistola f gun
plancha f iron
planchar to iron
plano (m) flat; map
planta f plant; floor
planta baja [baHa] ground floor
planta primera [preemaira] first floor, (US) second floor

planta sótano lower floor; basement
planta superior [soopair-y**o**r] upper floor
plástico (m) plastic
plata f silver
plateado [platay-**a**do] silver
platillo m [plat**ee**-yo] saucer
plato m plate; dish, course
playa f [pl**a**-ya] beach
playeras fpl [pla-y**ai**rass] trainers
plaza f [pl**a**tha] square; seat
en plaza current prices
plaza de abastos marketplace
plaza de toros bullring
plazas libres [l**ee**bress] seats available
pluma f pen; feather
población f [poblath-y**o**n] village; town; population
pobre [p**o**bray] poor
poco little
poco profundo shallow
pocos few
unos pocos a few
poder (m) [pod**ai**r] to be able to; power
podrido rotten
policía f [poleeth**ee**-a] police
policía m/f policeman; policewoman
policía municipal f [mooneetheep**a**l] municipal police
polideportivo m sports centre
polígono industrial m industrial estate
política f politics
político political
póliza de seguros f insurance policy
polo m ice lolly
polvos mpl powder
pomada f ointment
pon put
poner [pon**ai**r] to put
ponerse en marcha [pon**ai**rsay] to set off
ponerse en pie [p-yay] to stand up
poney m pony
pongo I put
poquito: un poquito [pok**ee**to] a little bit
por by; through; for
por allí [a-y**ee**] over there
por fin at last
por lo que [kay] for which reason
por lo menos [m**ay**noss] at least
por qué [kay] why
por semana per week
por si in case
por ciento [th-y**e**nto] per cent
por favor please
por favor, use un carrito please take a trolley
por favor, use una cesta please take a basket
porcelana f [porthel**a**na] porcelain
porque [p**o**rkay] because
portaequipajes m [porta-ekeep**a**Hess] luggage rack
portátil [port**a**teel] portable
portero m [port**ai**ro] porter;

doorman; goalkeeper
portugués [portoog**ay**ss] Portuguese
posada f inn
posible [pos**ee**blay] possible
postal f postcard
precaución f [prekowth-y**o**n] caution
precio m [pr**e**th-yo] price
precioso [preth-y**o**so] beautiful; precious
precio unidad unit price
precios fijos [f**ee**Hoss] fixed prices
preferencia f [prefair**e**nth-ya] right of way; preference
preferir [prefair**ee**r] to prefer
prefijo m [pref**ee**Ho] dialling code, area code
pregunta f question
preguntar to ask
prendas fpl clothing
prensa f press; newspapers
preocupado [pray-okoop**a**do] worried
preocupes: ¡no te preocupes! [no tay pray-ok**oo**pess] don't worry
preparar to prepare
prepararse [prepar**a**rsay] to get ready
presentar to introduce
preservativo m [presairbat**ee**bo] condom
presión f [press-y**o**n] pressure
presión de los neumáticos [nay-oom**a**teekoss] tyre pressure
prestado: pedir prestado to borrow
prestar to lend
prima f cousin
primavera f [preemab**ai**ra] spring
primer [preem**air**] first
primer piso m first floor, (US) second floor
primer plato m first course
primera (clase) f [kl**a**say] first class
primero first
primeros auxilios [owk-s**ee**l-yoss] first-aid post
primo m cousin
princesa f [preenth**ay**sa] princess
principal [preentheep**a**l] main
príncipe m [pr**ee**ntheepay] prince
principiante m/f [preentheep-y**a**ntay] beginner
principio m [preenth**ee**p-yo] beginning
principio de autopista start of motorway/highway
prioridad de paso priority
prioridad a la derecha give way/yield to vehicles coming from your right
prisa: darse prisa [d**a**rsay] to hurry
¡dese prisa! [d**ay**say] hurry up!
privado private
probablemente [probablem**e**ntay] probably
probador m fitting room
probar to try
probarse to try on

problema m problem
procesiones de Semana Santa fpl [prothess-y**o**ness] Holy Week processions
producido en ... produce of ...
producto preparado con ingredientes naturales product prepared using natural ingredients
productos alimenticios [aleementeeth-yoss] foodstuffs
productos de belleza [bay-y**ay**tha] beauty products
profesor m, **profesora** f teacher; lecturer
profundidad f depth
profundo deep
programa infantil m children's programme
prohibida la entrada a menores de ... no admission for those under ... years of age
prohibida su reproducción copyright reserved
prohibida su venta not for sale
prohibida la entrada no entry, no admission
prohibido [pro-eeb**ee**do] prohibited, forbidden; no
prohibido acampar no camping
prohibido adelantar no overtaking, no passing
prohibido aparcar no parking
prohibido aparcar excepto carga y descarga no parking except for loading and unloading
prohibido asomarse do not lean out
prohibido asomarse a la ventana do not lean out of the window
prohibido asomarse a la ventanilla do not lean out of the window
prohibido bañarse no swimming
prohibido cambiar de sentido no U-turns
prohibido cantar no singing
prohibido el paso no entry; no trespassing
prohibido encender fuego no campfires
prohibido escupir no spitting
prohibido estacionar no parking
prohibido fijar carteles stick no bills
prohibido fumar no smoking
prohibido girar a la izquierda no left turn
prohibido hablar con el conductor do not speak to the driver
prohibido hacer auto-stop no hitch-hiking
prohibido hacer sonar el claxon/la bocina do not sound your horn
prohibido pescar no fishing
prohibido pisar el césped keep off the grass
prohibido pisar la hierba keep off the grass
prohibido tirar basura no litter
prohibido tirar escombros no dumping
prohibido tocar la bocina/el claxon do not sound

your horn
prohibido tomar fotografías no photographs
prometer [prometair] to promise
prometida f fiancée
prometido (m) engaged; fiancé
pronóstico del tiempo m [t-yempo] weather forecast
pronto soon
¡hasta pronto! [asta] see you soon!
llegar pronto [yegar] to be early
pronunciar [pronoonth-yar] to pronounce
propiedad privada private property
propietario m [prop-yetar-yo] owner
propina f tip
propósito: a propósito deliberately
proteger [protay-Hair] to protect
provecho: ¡buen provecho! [bwen probay-cho] enjoy your meal!
provincia f [probeenth-ya] district
provocar to cause
próximo next
la semana próxima next week
prudente [proodentay] careful
prueba de alcoholemia f [pr-wayba day alko-olaym-ya] breath test
pts (pesetas) pesetas
pub bar in which no meals are served, often higher priced and disco music played
público (m) public; audience
pueblo m [pweblo] village; people
puede [pwayday] he/she can; you can
puede ser [sair] maybe
puedo [pwaydo] I can
puente m [pwentay] bridge
puente aéreo [a-airay-o] shuttle plane
puente de fuerte pendiente humpbacked bridge
puente de peaje [pay-aHay] toll bridge
puente romano Roman bridge
puerta f [pwairta] door; gate
por la otra puerta use other door
puerta de embarque [embarkay] gate
puerta nº. gate no.
puerto m harbour; pass; port
puerto deportivo marina
puerto de montaña [montan-ya] (mountain) pass
pues [pwayss] since; so
puesta de sol f [pwesta] sunset
puesto de periódicos [pairee-odeekoss] newspaper kiosk
puesto de socorro m first-aid post
puesto que [kay] since
pulga f flea
pulmones mpl lungs
pulmonía f [poolmonee-a] pneumonia
pulse botón para cruzar press button to cross
pulsera f [poolsaira] bracelet

pulso m pulse
puntual: llegar puntual [poont-wal] to arrive on time
punto de vista m point of view
punto: hacer punto [athair] to knit
¡puñeta! [poon-yayta] hell!
¡vete a hacer puñetas! [baytay a athair] bugger off!
pura lana virgen [beerHen] pure new wool
puro m cigar
puse [poosay] I put

Q

que [kay] who; that; which; than
que ... o que whether ... or
¿qué? what?
¿qué hay? [I] how's things?
¿qué tal?, mucho gusto how do you do?, nice to meet you
¡qué va! no way!
quedarse [kedarsay] to stay
quedarse con to keep
quedarse sin gasolina to run out of petrol/gas
quejarse [kayHarsay] to complain
quemadura f [kemadoora] burn
quemadura de sol sunburn
quemar [kemar] to burn
quemarse [kemarsay] to burn oneself
querer [kerair] to love; to want
querido [kaireedo] dear
¿quién? [k-yen] who?
quiero [k-yairo] I want; I love
no quiero I don't want to
quince [keenthay] fifteen
quince días [dee-ass] fortnight
quinientos [keen-yentoss] five hundred
quinto [keento] fifth
quiosco m [k-yosko] kiosk
quisiera [keess-yaira] I would like; he/she would like; you would like
quiso [keeso] he/she wanted; you wanted
quitaesmalte m [keeta-esmaltay] nail polish remover
quitar [keetar] to remove
quizá(s) [keetha(ss)] maybe

R

rabioso [rab-yoso] furious
R.A.C.E (Real Automóvil Club de España) Spanish Royal Automobile Club
ración f [rath-yon] portion
radiador m [rad-yador] radiator
radio m [rad-yo] spoke
radio f radio
radiografía f [rad-yografee-a] X-ray
rápidamente [-mentay] quickly
rápido fast
rápido m train stopping at many stations
raqueta de tenis f [rakayta] tennis racket
raro rare; strange
rata f rat
ratón m mouse
rayas: a rayas [ra-yass] striped

razón f [rath**o**n] reason; rate
razón aquí apply within
tiene razón you're right
razonable [rathon**a**blay] reasonable
rea sale
realmente [ray-alm**e**ntay] really
rebajado [rebaH**a**do] reduced
rebajas fpl [reb**a**Hass] reductions, sale
rebajas de verano [bair**a**no] summer sale
rebanada f slice
recado m message
recepción f [rethepth-y**o**n] reception
recepcionista m/f [rethepth-yon**ee**sta] receptionist
receta f [reth**ay**ta] recipe; prescription
con receta médica only available on prescription
recetar [rethayt**a**r] to prescribe
recibir [retheeb**ee**r] to receive
recibo m [reth**ee**bo] receipt
recién [reth-y**e**n] recently
recién pintado wet paint
reclamación de equipajes f [reklamath-y**o**n day ekeep**a**Hess] baggage claim
reclamaciones fpl [reklamath-y**o**ness] complaints
recoger [rekoH**ai**r] to collect; to pick up
recogida de equipajes f [rekoH**ee**da] baggage claim
recoja su ticket take your ticket
recomendar to recommend
reconocer [rekonoth**ai**r] to recognize; to examine
recordar to remember
recorrido m journey
recto straight
recuerdo (m) [rekw**ai**rdo] souvenir; I remember
red f network; net
redondo round
reduzca la velocidad reduce speed now
reembolsar [ray-embols**a**r] to refund
reembolsos refunds
reestreno [ray-estr**ay**no] re-release (of a classic movie)
regalo m present
regatear [regatay-**a**r] to haggle
régimen m [**ray**-Heemen] diet
registrar [reHeestr**a**r] to search
regla f rule; period
registro de equipajes m [reH**ee**stro day ekeep**a**Hess] check in
registros sanitarios government health certificate
regresar to return
reina f [r**ay-ee**na] queen
Reino Unido m United Kingdom
reír [ray-**ee**r] to laugh
rejoneador m [reHonay-ad**o**r] bullfighter on horseback
relajarse [relaH**a**rsay] to relax
rellenar [ray-yayn**a**r] to fill in
reloj m [ray-l**o**H] watch; clock
reloj de pulsera [pools**ai**ra] (wrist)watch
relojería f [ray-loHair**ee**-a] watches and clocks

remar to row
remite m [rem**ee**tay] sender's name and address
remitente m/f [remeet**e**ntay] sender
remo m [r**ay**mo] oar
remolque m [rem**o**lkay] trailer
remonte m [rem**o**ntay] ski tow
Renacimiento m [renatheem-y**e**nto] Renaissance
RENFE (Red Nacional de Ferrocarriles Españoles) Spanish Railways/Railroad
reparación f [reparath-y**o**n] repair(s)
reparación de calzado shoe repairs
reparaciones faults service
reparar to repair
repente: de repente [rep**e**ntay] suddenly
repetir to repeat
replicar to reply
reponerse [repon**air**say] to recover
reposar to rest
representante m/f [repraysent**an**tay] representative, agent
repuestos mpl [repw**e**stoss] spare parts
repugnante [repoogn**a**ntay] disgusting
resaca f hangover
resbaladizo [resbalad**ee**tho] slippery
resbalar to slip
rescatar to rescue
reserva f [res**air**ba] reservation
reserva de asientos seat reservation
reservado reserved
reservado el derecho de admisión the management reserve the right to refuse admission
reservado socios members only
reservar to reserve; to book
reservas fpl reservations
resfriado m [resfree-**a**do] cold
respirar to breathe
responder [respond**air**] to answer
responsable [respons**a**blay] responsible
respuesta f [respw**e**sta] answer
resto m rest
retales mpl [ret**a**less] remnants
retrasado late
retrasado mental mentally handicapped
retraso m delay
retrete m [retr**ay**tay] toilets, (US) rest rooms
reumatismo m [ray-oomat**ee**smo] rheumatism
reunión f [ray-oon-y**o**n] meeting
revelado m film processing
revelar to develop; to reveal
revisar to check
revisor m ticket collector
revista m magazine
rey m [ray] king
Reyes: día de los Reyes m [d**ee**-a day loss r**ay**-ess] 6th of January, Epiphany
rico rich
ridículo ridiculous

rímel m mascara
rincón m corner
riñón m [reen-**yon**] kidney
río m [**ree**-o] river
rizado [reeth**a**do] curly
robar to steal
robo m theft
roca f rock
rodilla f [rod**ee**-ya] knee
rojo [**ro**Ho] red
románico romanesque
rómpase en caso de emergencia break in case of emergency
romper to break
ropa f clothes
ropa confeccionada ready-to-wear clothes
ropa de caballeros [kaba-**yai**ross] men's clothes
ropa de cama bed linen
ropa de señoras ladies' clothes
ropa infantil children's clothes
ropa interior f [eentair-y**o**r] underwear
ropa sucia [s**oo**th-ya] laundry
rosa (f) pink; rose
roto broken
rotulador m felt-tip pen
rubéola f [roob**ay**-ola] German measles
rubí m [roob**ee**] ruby
rubio [**roo**b-yo] blond
rueda f [rw**ay**da] wheel
rueda de repuesto f [repwesto] spare wheel
ruedo m bullring
ruego [rw**ay**go] I request
ruido m [rw**ee**do] noise
ruidoso [rweed**o**so] noisy
ruinas fpl [rw**ee**nass] ruins
rulo m roller, curler
rulot(a) f caravan, (US) trailer
ruta f route

S

S.A. (Sociedad Anónima) PLC, Inc
sábado m Saturday
sábana f sheet
saber [sab**air**] to know
saber a to taste of
sabor m taste
sabroso tasty
sacacorchos m [sakak**o**rchoss] corkscrew
sacar to take out; to get out
sacar un billete [bee-y**ay**tay] to buy a ticket
saco de dormir m sleeping bag
sal (f) salt; leave
sala f room; hall
sala climatizada air conditioned
sala de baile [b**a**-**ee**lay] dance hall
sala de cine [th**ee**nay] cinema, movie theater
sala de conciertos [konth-y**air**toss] concert hall
sala de embarque [emb**a**rkay] departure lounge
sala de espera [esp**air**a] waiting room
sala de exposiciones [esposeeth-y**o**ness] exhibition hall
sala de tránsito transit lounge
sala X X-rated cinema

salado salty
saldar to sell at a reduced price
saldo m clearance; balance
saldos sales
sales de baño fpl [saless day ban-yo] bath salts
salgo I leave
salida f exit; departure
salida ciudad take this direction to leave the city
salida de ambulancias ambulance exit
salida de autopista end of motorway/highway; motorway exit
salida de camiones heavy goods vehicle exit, works exit
salida de emergencia [aymairHenth-ya] emergency exit
salida de fábrica factory exit
salida de incendios fire exit
salida de socorro f emergency exit
salidas fpl departures
salidas de noche night life
salidas internacionales international departures
salidas nacionales domestic departures
salir to go out; to leave
salón m lounge
salón de belleza [bay-yaytha] beauty salon
salón de demostraciones exhibition hall
salón de peluquería [pelookairee-a] hairdressing salon
saltar to jump
salud f [saloo] health
¡salud! cheers!
saludar to greet
saludos best wishes
salvo que [kay] except that
sandalias fpl [sandal-yass] sandals
San Fermín [fairmeen] July 7th, when the 'encierro' happens
sangrar to bleed
sangre f [sangray] blood
sano healthy
Santiago [sant-yago] July 25th, a national holiday
sarampión m [saramp-yon] measles
sartén f frying pan
sastre m [sastray] tailor
se [say] himself; herself; itself; yourself; themselves; yourselves; oneself
sé [say] I know
no sé I don't know
se aceptan tarjetas de crédito we accept credit cards
se alquila for hire, to rent
se alquila piso flat to let, apartment for rent
se alquilan habitaciones rooms to rent
se alquilan hidropedales pedalos for hire
se alquilan sombrillas parasols for hire
se alquilan tumbonas deckchairs for hire

se habla inglés English spoken
se hacen fotocopias photocopying service
se necesita ... ... needed
se precisa ... ... needed
se prohibe ... ... forbidden
se prohibe fumar no smoking
se prohibe hablar con el conductor do not speak to the driver
se prohibe la entrada no entry, no admittance
se prohibe tirar basura no litter
se ruega please ...
se ruega desalojen su habitación antes de las doce please vacate your room by 12 noon
se ruega no ... please do not ...
se ruega no aparcar no parking please
se ruega no molestar please do not disturb
se ruega pagar en caja please pay at the desk
se vende for sale
secador de pelo m [paylo] hair dryer
secadores mpl dryers
secar to dry
secarse el pelo [sekarsay] to dry one's hair, to have a blow-dry
sección f [sekth-yon] department
seco dry
secretaria f, secretario m secretary
secreto secret
sed: tengo sed [seth] I'm thirsty
seda f silk
seda natural pure silk
seguida: en seguida [segeeda] immediately, right away
seguir [segeer] to follow
según according to
segunda clase f [klasay] second class
segundo (m) second
de segunda mano second-hand
segundo piso m second floor, (US) third floor
segundo plato m main course
seguridad f [segooreeda] safety; security
seguro (m) safe; sure; insurance
seguro de viaje m [b-yaHay] travel insurance
seis [say-eess] six
seiscientos [say-eess-th-yentoss] six hundred
sello m [say-yo] stamp
semáforos mpl traffic lights
semana f week
Semana Santa Holy Week
semanarios mpl weeklies
sencillo [senthee-yo] simple
sensible [senseeblay] sensitive
sentar: sentar bien (a) [b-yen] to suit
sentarse [sentarsay] to sit down
sentido m direction; sense; meaning
sentir to feel
señal de tráfico f [sen-yal day trafeeko] roadsign

señas fpl [s**e**n-yass] address
señor [sen-y**o**r] gentleman, man; sir
el señor Brown Mr Brown
señora f [sen-y**o**ra] lady, woman; madam
la señora Brown Mrs Brown
señoras fpl ladies' toilet, ladies' room; ladies' department
señores mpl [sen-y**o**ress] gents' toilet, men's room
señorita f [sen-yor**ee**ta] young lady, young woman; miss
la señorita Brown Miss Brown
separado separate; separated
por separado separately
septiembre m [sept-y**e**mbray] September
séptimo seventh
sequía f [sek**ee**-a] drought
ser [sair] to be
a no ser que unless
serio [s**air**-yo] serious
servicio m [sairb**ee**th-yo] service; toilet
servicio a través de operadora operator-connected calls
servicio automático direct dialling
servicio de habitaciones room service
servicio de fotocopias photocopying service
servicio (no) incluido service charge (not) included
servicios mpl [sairb**ee**th-yoss] toilets, (US) rest rooms
servicios de rescate mountain rescue
servicios de socorro emergency services
servilleta f [sairbee-y**ay**ta] serviette
servir [sairb**ee**r] to serve
sesenta [says**e**nta] sixty
sesión continua continuous showing
sesión de noche late showing
sesión de tarde early showing
setecientos [saytay-th-y**e**ntoss] seven hundred
setenta [set**e**nta] seventy
sexto [s**e**sto] sixth
si [see] if
sí [see] yes; oneself; herself; itself; yourself; themselves; yourselves; each other
si no otherwise
SIDA m AIDS
sido been
siempre [s-y**e**mpray] always
siempre que [kay] whenever; so long as
siento [s-y**e**nto] I sit down; I feel; I regret
lo siento I'm sorry
siete [s-y**ay**tay] seven
siga adelante straight ahead
siglo m century
siglo de oro XVI-XVII century
significar to mean
siguiente [seeg-y**e**ntay] next
el día siguiente [d**ee**-a] the day after
silencio m [seel**e**nth-yo] silence
silla f [s**ee**-ya] chair
silla de ruedas [rw**ay**dass]

wheelchair
sillita de ruedas [see-y**ee**ta] pushchair, buggy
sillón m [see-y**o**n] armchair
similar (a) similar (to)
simpático nice
sin [seen] without
sin duda undoubtedly
sin embargo however
sin plomo unleaded
sinagoga f synagogue
sincero [seenth**ai**ro] sincere
sino but
sino que [kay] but
siquiera [seek-y**ai**ra] even if
sírvase [s**ee**rbasay] please
sírvase coger una cesta please take a basket
sírvase frío serve cold
sírvase usted mismo help yourself
sitio m [s**ee**t-yo] place
en ningún sitio [neen-g**oo**n] nowhere
smoking m dinner jacket
sobrar to be left over; to be too many
sobre (m) [s**o**bray] envelope; on; above
sobrecarga [sobrayk**a**rga] excess weight; extra charge
sobrina f niece
sobrino m nephew
sobrio [s**o**br-yo] sober
sociedad f [soth-yayd**a**] society; company
socio m [s**o**th-yo] associate; member
socorrer [sokor**air**] to help
socorrista mf lifeguard
¡socorro! help!
sois [soyss] you are
sol m sun
al sol in the sun
solamente [solam**e**ntay] only
soleado [solay-**a**do] sunny
solo alone
sólo only
no sólo ... sino también [tamb-y**e**n] not only ... but also
sólo carga y descarga loading and offloading only
sólo laborables weekdays only
sólo monedas de nueva emisión only new coins
sólo motos motorcycles only
solo para residentes (del hotel) hotel patrons only
soltero (m) [solt**ai**ro] single; bachelor
solterón m bachelor
solterona f spinster
solución ... gotas solution ... drops
sombra f shade; shadow
sombra de ojos [**o**Hoss] eye shadow
sombrero m [sombr**ai**ro] hat
sombrilla f [sombr**ee**-ya] parasol
somnífero m [somn**ee**fairo] sleeping pill
somos we are
son they are; you are
sonreír [sonray-**ee**r] to smile
sordo deaf
sorprendente [sorprend**e**ntay] surprising
sorpresa f surprise

sortija f [sorteeHa] ring
sótano m basement
soy [soy] I am
sport: de sport casual
Sr (Señor) Mr
Sra (Señora) Mrs
Sres (Señores) Messrs
Srta (Señorita) Miss
starter m choke
stop m stop sign
su [soo] his; her; its; their; your
suave [swabay] soft
subir to go up; to get on; to get in; to put up
subtitulada sub-titled
subtítulos mpl subtitles
suburbios mpl [sooboorb-yoss] suburbs
suceder [soothedair] to happen
sucio [sooth-yo] dirty
sucursal f branch
sudar to sweat
Suecia f [swayth-ya] Sweden
sueco [swayko] Swedish
suegra f [swaygra] mother-in-law
suegro m father-in-law
suela f [swayla] sole
suelo (m) floor; I am used to
suelto m [swelto] change
sueño m [swayn-yo] dream; I dream
  tener sueño to be sleepy
suerte f [swairtay] luck
  por suerte luckily, fortunately
  ¡buena suerte! [bwayna] good luck!
suéter m [swaytair] sweater
suficiente: es suficiente [soofeeth-yentay] that's enough
sugerencias de presentación serving suggestions
Suiza f [sweetha] Switzerland
sujetador m [sooHay-tador] bra
sumar to add
supe [soopay] I knew
súper soopair] four-star petrol, (US) premium (gas); supermarket
supermercado m [soopairmairkado] supermarket
supuesto: por supuesto [soopwesto] of course
sur m south
  al sur de south of
sureste m [soorestay] south-east
suroeste m [sooro-estay] south-west
surtido m assortment
sus [sooss] his; her; its; their; your
susto m shock
susurrar to whisper
sutil subtle
suyo [soo-yo] his; hers; its; theirs; yours

T

T.V.E. (Television Española) Spanish Television
Tabacalera SA Spanish tobacco monopoly
tabaco m tobacco
tabla de surf f surfboard

tabla de windsurf sailboard
tablero de instrumentos m dashboard
tablón de anuncios m notice board, (US) bulletin board
tablón de información [tablon day eenformath-yon] indicator board
tacón m heel
tacones altos [takoness] high heels
tacones planos flat heels
TAF m slow diesel train
Tajo m [taHo] Tagus
tal such
con tal (de) que provided that
tal vez [bayth] maybe
talco m talcum powder
TALGO m fast diesel train, luxury train (supplement required)
talla f [ta-ya] size
tallas sueltas odd sizes
tallas grandes large sizes
taller (de reparaciones) m [ta-yair (day reparath-yoness)] garage
talón m heel
talón de equipajes [ekeepaHess] baggage slip
talonario de cheques m [talonar-yo day chekess] cheque book
tamaño m [taman-yo] size
también [tamb-yen] also
yo también me too
tampoco neither, nor
yo tampoco me neither
tan: tan bonito so beautiful
tan pronto como as soon as
tancat closed (in Catalan)
tanto (m) so much; point
tanto ... como ... both ... and ...
tantos so many
tapa f lid
tapas fpl savoury snacks, tapas
tapón m plug
taquilla f [takee-ya] ticket office
tarde (f) [tarday] afternoon; evening; late
a las tres de la tarde at 3 p.m.
esta tarde this afternoon, this evening
por la tarde in the evening
llegar tarde [yegar] to be late
tarifa f charge, charges
tarifa especial estudiante [espeth-yal estood-yantay] student reduced rate
tarifa normal standard rate
tarifa reducida [redootheeda] reduced rate
tarifas de servicio fares
tarjeta f [tarHayta] card
tarjeta bancaria cheque card
tarjeta de crédito credit card
tarjeta de embarque [embarkay] boarding pass
tarjeta de transporte público [transportay] travel card
tarjeta postal postcard
tarjeta telefónica phonecard
tauromaquia f [towromak-ya] bullfighting
taxista m/f taxi driver
taza f [tatha] cup
te [tay] you; yourself
teatro m [tay-atro] theatre

techo m ceiling
teclado m keyboard
tejado m [teHado] roof
tejanos mpl [teHanoss] jeans
tejidos mpl [teHeedoss] materials, fabrics
tela f [tayla] material; dosh
tele f [taylay] TV
telecabina f cable car
teleférico m cable car
telefonear [telefonay-ar] to telephone
teléfono m telephone
teléfono interurbano long-distance phone
teléfonos para casos urgentes emergency telephone numbers
telesilla m [telesee-ya] chairlift
telesquí m [teleskee] ski lift
televisor m television (set)
temer [temair] to fear
temor m fear
tempestad f storm
temporada f season
temprano early
ten hold
tenedor m fork
tener [tenair] to have
tener derecho to have the right
tener prisa to be in a hurry
tener prioridad [pree-oreeda] to have right of way
tener que [kay] to have to
tengo que I have to, I must
¡tenga cuidado! [kweedado] be careful!
tenis m tennis
tensión f [tens-yon] blood pressure
teñirse el pelo [ten-yeersay el paylo] to dye one's hair, to have one's hair dyed
TER m fast luxury diesel trains, a supplement is required
tercer piso m [tairthair] third floor, (US) fourth floor
tercero [tairthairo] third
tercio m [tairth-yo] third
terciopelo m [tairth-yopaylo] velvet
terco stubborn
terminal f [tairmeenal] terminus; terminal
terminal nacional domestic terminal
terminar to finish
termo m thermos flask
termómetro m thermometer
test del embarazo [embaratho] pregnancy test
testigo m witness
tetera f [tetaira] teapot
tfno (teléfono) telephone
ti [tee] you
tía f [tee-a] aunt; bird, woman
tibio [teeb-yo] lukewarm
tiburón m shark
tiempo m [t-yempo] time; weather
a tiempo on time
tiempo de recreo [rekray-o] leisure
tiempo libre [leebray] free time
tienda f [t-yenda] shop, store; tent

esta tienda se translada a ... business is transferred to ...
tienda de artículos de piel [p-yayl] leather goods shop
tienda de artículos de regalo gift shop
tienda de comestibles [komesteebless] grocer's
tienda de deportes [deportess] sports shop
tienda de discos record shop
tienda de electrodomésticos electrical goods shop
tienda de lanas woollen goods shop
tienda de muebles [mwaybless] furniture shop
tienda de regalos gift shop
tienda de ultramarinos grocer's
tienda de vinos y licores off-licence, (US) liquor store
tienda libre de impuestos [leebray day eempwestoss] duty-free shop
tiendas: ir de tiendas to go shopping
tiene que [t-yaynay kay] he must
¿tiene ...? have you got ...?
tierra f [t-yairra] earth
tijeras fpl [teeHairass] scissors
timbre m [teembray] bell
timbre de alarma alarm bell
tímido shy
tintorería f [teentoraireea-a] dry-cleaner's
tío m [tee-o] uncle; bloke, guy
tipo de cambio m [kamb-yo] exchange rate
tirar to pull; to throw; to throw away
tirita f Elastoplast®, Bandaid®
toalla f [to-a-ya] towel
toalla de baño [ban-yo] bath towel
tobillo m [tobee-yo] ankle
tocadiscos m record player
tocar to touch; to play
todavía [todabee-a] still; yet
todavía no not yet
todo all, every; everything
todos los días every day
todo derecho straight on
todo seguido [segeedo] straight ahead
todos everyone
tomamos la tensión we take your blood pressure
tomar to take
tomar el sol to sunbathe
tomavistas m cine-camera
tome usted take
tómese antes de las comidas to be taken before meals
tómese después de las comidas to be taken after meals
tómese ... veces al día to be taken ... times per day
tonelada f tonne
tono m dialling tone; shade
tonto silly
torcer [torthair] to twist; to sprain
torcerse un tobillo [oon tobee-yo] to twist one's ankle
torero m [torairo] bullfighter
tormenta f storm
tormentoso stormy
tornillo m [tornee-yo] screw

toro m bull
toros mpl bullfighting
torpe [torpay] clumsy
torre f [torray] tower
tos f cough
toser [tosair] to cough
tosferina f [tosfaireena] whooping cough
total: en total altogether
totalmente [-mentay] absolutely
tóxico [tokseeko] poisonous
trabajador [trabaHador] industrious
trabajar [trabajar] to work
trabajo m [trabaHo] work
traducir [tradootheer] to translate
traer [tra-air] to bring
tragar to swallow
traigo [tra-eego] I bring
traje [traHay] I brought
traje m suit; dress
traje de baño [ban-yo] swimming costume
traje de noche [nochay] evening dress
traje de señora lady's suit
traje típico traditional regional costume
tranquilizante [trankeeleethantay] tranquillizer
tranquilizarse [trankeeleetharsay] to calm down
tranquilo [trankeelo] quiet
transbordo m transfer; change
hacer transbordo en ... change at ...
transferencia f [transfairenth-ya] transfer
tras after
trasero (m) [trasairo] bottom; back; rear
tratar to treat
través: a través de across, through
travieso [trab-yayso] mischievous
trece [traythay] thirteen
treinta [tray-eenta] thirty
tren m [tren] train
tren de carga goods train
trenes de cercanías [treness day thairkanee-ass] local trains, suburban trains
tren de lavado automático car wash
tren de pasajeros [pasaHaiross] passenger train
tren directo through train
tren tranvía [tranbee-a] stopping train
tres [tress] three
tres cuartos de hora mpl three quarters of an hour
trescientos [tress-th-yentoss] three hundred
tripulación f [treepoolath-yon] crew
triste [treestay] sad
tristeza f [treestaytha] sadness
tronco m body; buddy
tropezar [tropethar] to trip
trozo (de) m [trotho (day)] piece (of)
trueno m [trwayno] thunder
tu [too] your
tú [too] you
tú mismo yourself

tubería f [toobair**ee**-a] pipe
tubo de escape m [esk**a**pay] exhaust
tubo de respirar snorkel
tuerza [tw**air**tha] turn
tumbona f deck chair
túnel m tunnel
Túnez m [t**oo**neth] Tunisia
turista m/f tourist
turno m turn; round
es mi turno it's my turn/ round
turrón m [toorr**o**n] nougat
tus [tooss] your
tuyo [t**oo**yo] yours

U

u [oo] or
Ud (usted) [oost**ay**] you (sing)
Uds (ustedes) [oost**ay**dess] you (plural)
úlcera (de estómago) f [**oo**lthaira] (stomach) ulcer
últimamente [oolteemam**e**ntay] recently, lately
último last; latest
últimos días [d**ee**-ass] last days
ultramarinos m grocer's
un [oon] a
una [**oo**na] a
unas some
uno one; someone
unos some; a few
uña f [**oo**n-ya] fingernail
urbana local
urbanización f [oorbaneethath-y**o**n] housing estate
urgencias [oorHenth-yass] casualty department, emergencies
usado used; secondhand
usar to use
uso use
el uso del tabaco es perjudicial para su salud smoking can damage your health
uso externo not to be taken internally
uso obligatorio cinturón de seguridad seatbelts must be worn
Usted [oost**ay**] you
Ustedes [oost**ay**dess] you
útil useful
utilice sólo moneda fraccionaria small change only

V

> **v** is pronounced more like a **b** than an English **v**

va he/she/it goes; you go
vaca f cow
vacaciones fpl [bakath-y**o**ness] holiday, vacation
vacío [bath**ee**-o] empty
vacuna f vaccination
vacunarse [bakoon**a**rsay] to be vaccinated
vado permanente no parking at any time
vagón m carriage
vagón restaurante [restowr**a**ntay] restaurant car

v is pronounced more like a **b** than an English **v**

vagón de literas [leet**air**ass] sleeping car
vainilla f [ba-een**ee**-ya] vanilla
vais [ba-eess] you go
vajilla f [baH**ee**-ya] crockery
vale [b**a**lay] OK
valer [bal**air**] to be worth
valiente [bal-**y**entay] brave
valla f [b**a**-ya] fence
valle m [b**a**-yay] valley
valores mpl [bal**o**ress] securities
válvula f valve
vamos we go
van they go; you go
vapor m steamer
vaqueros mpl [bak**air**oss] jeans; cowboys
varicela f [bareeth**ay**-la] chickenpox
varios [b**a**r-yoss] several
varón m male
varonil manly
vas you go
vasco Basque
Vascongadas fpl the Basque country
vaso m glass
vaya [b**a**-ya] go; I/he/she go; you go
¡vaya por Dios! [d**ee**-oss] oh Christ!
¡váyase! [b**a**-yasay] go away!
¡váyase a paseo! [pas**ay**-o] get lost!
Vd (usted) [oost**ay**] you (sing)
Vds (ustedes) you (plural)
ve [bay] go; he/she sees; you see
veces: a veces [b**ay**thess] sometimes
vecino m [beth**ee**no] neighbour
vehículos pesados heavy vehicles
veinte [b**ay-ee**ntay] twenty
vejiga f [beH**ee**ga] bladder
vela f [b**ay**la] candle; sail
velero m [bel**air**o] sailing boat
velocidad f [belotheed**a**] speed
velocidad controlada por radar radar speed checks
velocidad limitada speed limits apply
velocidades fpl [belotheed**a**dess] gears
velocímetro m [beloth**ee**metro] speedometer
ven [ben] come; they see; you see
vena f [b**ay**na] vein
venda f bandage
vendar to dress (wound)
vendemos a ... selling rate
vender [bend**air**] to sell
veneno m [ben**ay**no] poison
vengo I come
venir to come
venta f sale
de venta aquí on sale here
venta de localidades tickets (on sale)
venta de sellos stamps sold here
ventana f window
ventanilla f [bentan**ee**-ya]

window; ticket office
ventas a crédito credit terms available
ventas a plazos hire purchase, (US) installment plan
ventas al contado cash sales
ventilador m fan
ver [bair] to see; to watch
veraneante m [bairanay-**a**ntay] holidaymaker, vacationer
veranear [bairanay-**a**r] to holiday
verano m [bair**a**no] summer
verbena f [bairb**ay**na] open-air dance
verdad f [baird**a**] truth
¿de verdad? is that so?
¿verdad? don't you?; do you?; isn't he?; is he? etc
verdadero [bairdad**ai**ro] true
verde (m) [b**ai**rday] green
versión f [bairs-y**o**n] version
en versión original in the original language
vestido m dress
vestir to dress
de vestir formal
vestirse [best**ee**rsay] to get dressed
vestuarios mpl [bestw**a**r-yoss] fitting rooms
vez f [bayth] time
una vez once
en vez de instead of
vi [bee] I saw
vía aérea: por vía aérea by air mail
vía oral orally
vía rectal per rectum
viajar [b-yaH**a**r] to travel
viaje m [b-y**a**Hay] journey
¡buen viaje! [bwen] have a good trip!
viaje de negocios [neg**o**th-yoss] business trip
viaje de novios [n**o**b-yoss] honeymoon
viaje organizado [organeeth**a**do] package tour
viajero m [b-yaH**ai**ro] passenger
vida f life
vidrio m [b**ee**dr-yo] glass
viejo [b-y**ay**Ho] old
viene: la semana que viene [b-y**ay**nay] next week
viento m [b-y**e**nto] wind
vientre m [b-y**e**ntray] stomach
viernes [b-y**ai**rness] Friday
Viernes Santo m Good Friday
vine [b**ee**nay] I came
vinos y licores wines and spirits
viñedo [been-y**ay**do] vineyard
violación f [b-yolath-y**o**n] rape
violar [b-yol**a**r] to rape
violento [b-yol**e**nto] violent; embarrassing, awkward
sentirse violento to feel awkward
visado m visa
visita f visit
visita con guía [g**ee**-a] guided tour
visitante m/f [beeseet**a**ntay] visitor
visitar to visit
visor m viewfinder

víspera f [beespaira] the day before
vista f view
¡hasta la vista! see you!
vista turística scenic view
visto seen
viuda f [b-yooda] widow
viudo m widower
vivir to live
vivo alive; I live
VO (versión original) original language
volante m [bolantay] steering wheel
volar to fly
voltaje [boltaHay] voltage
volver [bolbair] to come back
volver a hacer algo to do something again
volver a casa to go home
vomitar to vomit
vosotras, vosotros you
v.o. subtitulada version in the original language with subtitles
voy I go
voz f [both] voice
vuelo m [bwaylo] flight
vuelo nacional [nath-yonal] domestic flight
vuelo regular scheduled flight
vuelta f [bwelta] change
la vuelta al colegio [kolay-Hyo] back to school
vuelvo [bwelbo] I return
vuestra [bwestra], vuestras, vuestro, vuestros your; yours

W

wáter [batair] toilet, rest room

Y

y [ee] and
ya already
ya está there you are
ya ... ya sometimes ... sometimes
ya que [kay] since
yerno m [yairno] son-in-law
yo I; me
yo mismo myself

Z

zapatería f [thapataireee-a] shoe shop/store
zapatero m [thapatairo] cobbler; shoe repairer
zapatillas fpl [thapatee-yass] slippers
zapatos mpl [thapatoss] shoes
zona f [thona] area
zona de avalanchas frequent avalanches
zona monumental historic monuments
zona (reservada) para peatones pedestrian precinct
zona azul [athool] restricted parking area, permit holders only
zona de servicios [sairbeeth-yoss] service area
zurdo [thoordo] left-handed

Menu Reader:

Food

aceite [ath**ay**-eetay] oil
aceite de oliva [day ol**ee**ba] olive oil
aceitunas [athay-eet**oo**nass] olives
aceitunas aliñadas [aleen-y**a**dass] olives with salad dressing
aceitunas negras black olives
aceitunas rellenas [ray-y**ay**nass] stuffed olives
aceitunas verdes [b**ai**rdess] green olives
acelgas [ath**e**lgass] chard, spinach beet
achicoria [acheek**o**r-ya] chicory
aguacate [agwak**a**tay] avocado
aguja de ternera [ag**oo**Ha day tairn**ai**ra] veal for stewing
ahumados [a-oom**a**doss] smoked fish
ahumados variados [baree-**a**doss] smoked fish
ajillo [aH**ee**-yo] garlic
ajo [**a**Ho] garlic
alaju [al**a**-Hoo] nougat-type sweet made from walnuts or pine nuts, toasted breadcrumbs and honey
albahaca [alba-**a**ka] basil
albaricoque [albareek**o**kay] apricot
albóndigas meatballs
albóndigas de lomo [day] pork meatballs
alcachofas artichokes
alcachofas en vinagreta [beenagr**ay**ta] artichokes in vinaigrette dressing
alcachofas a la andaluza [andal**oo**tha] artichokes with ham and bacon
alcachofas a la romana artichokes in batter
alcaparras capers
aliñada [aleen-y**a**da] with salad dressing
ali oli garlic mayonnaise
almejas [alm**ay**-Hass] clams
almejas a la buena mujer [bw**ay**na mooH**air**] clams stewed with chillies, white wine, lemon and herbs
almejas a la marinera [mareen**ai**ra] clams stewed in white wine and parsley
almejas a la valenciana [balenth-y**a**na] clams in a white wine sauce
almejas al natural [natoor**a**l] live clams
almejas en salsa verde [b**ai**rday] clams in parsley and white wine sauce
almejas naturales [natoor**a**less] live clams
almendra almond
alubias [al**oo**b-yass] beans
alubias blancas white kidney beans
alubias rojas [r**o**Hass] red kidney beans
ancas de rana frogs' legs
ancas de rana albuferena [alboofair**ay**na] frogs' legs in a sauce made from chicken soup, mushrooms and paprika
anchoas [anch**o**-ass] anchovies

anchoas a la barquera [bark**ai**ra] marinated anchovies with capers
anguila [ang**ee**la] eel
anguila ahumada [a-oom**a**da] smoked eel
angulas baby eels
angulas al all-i-pebre [all-ee-p**e**bray] baby eels with garlic and black pepper
añojo [an-y**o**Ho] veal
apio [**a**p-yo] celery
arenques frescos [ar**e**nkess] fresh herrings
arroz [arr**o**th] rice
arroz a la cubana boiled rice with fried eggs and either bananas or tomato sauce
arroz a la emperatriz [empairatr**ee**th] rice with milk, apricots, truffles, raisins, Cointreau and gelatine
arroz a la turca [t**oo**rka] boiled rice with curry sauce, onions and tomatoes
arroz a la valenciana [balenth-y**a**na] paella
arroz blanco boiled white rice
arroz con leche [l**e**chay] rice pudding
asado roast
asados roast meats
asadurilla [asadoor**ee**-ya] lambs' liver stew
atún [at**oo**n] tuna
atún al horno [**o**rno] baked tuna
avellana [abay-y**a**na] hazelnut
aves [**a**bess] poultry
azafrán [athafr**a**n] saffron
azúcar [ath**oo**kar] sugar

bacalao a la catalana [bakal**a**-o] cod with ham, almond, garlic and parsley
bacalao al ajo arriero [**a**Ho arr-y**ai**ro] cod with garlic, peppers and chillies
bacalao a la vizcaína [beethka-**ee**na] cod served with ham, peppers and chillies
bacalao al pil pil [peel] cod cooked in olive oil
baveresa de coco [babair**ay**sa day] cold coconut sweet
becadas snipe
becadas a la vizcaína [beethka-**ee**na] snipe served with bacon, onion and sherry sauce
becadas asadas baked snipe
berenjena [bairenH**ay**na] aubergine, eggplant
berenjenas a la mallorquina [ma-york**ee**na] aubergines/eggplants with garlic mayonnaise
berza [b**ai**rtha] cabbage
besugo bream
besugo al horno [al **o**rno] baked sea bream
besugo asado baked sea bream
besugo mechado sea bream stuffed with ham and bacon
bien hecho [b-yen **e**cho] well done
bistec a la riojana [r-yoH**a**na]

steak with fried red peppers
bistec de ternera [tairn**ai**ra] veal steak
bizcocho [beethk**o**cho] sponge finger
bocadillo [bokad**ee**-yo] sandwich, snack
bogavante [bogab**a**ntay] lobster
bollo [b**o**-yo] roll
bomba helada [el**a**da] baked alaska
bonito tuna
bonito al horno [**o**rno] baked tuna
boquerones en vinagre [bokair**o**ness en been**a**gray] anchovies in vinaigrette
boquerones fritos fried fresh anchovies
brandada de bacalao [bakal**a**-o] creamy cod purée
brazo de gitano [br**a**tho day Heet**a**no] swiss roll
brevas [br**e**bass] figs
broqueta de riñones [brok**e**ta day reen-y**o**ness] kidney kebabs
buey [boo-**ay**] beef
buñuelos [boon-yw**ay**loss] light fried pastry
buñuelos de bacalao [bakal**a**-o] fried pastry containing flaked, dried, salted cod
buñuelos de cuaresma rellenos [day kwar**e**sma ray-y**ay**noss] light fried pastries with chocolate and cream
butifarra Catalan sausage – contains bacon
butifarra con rovellons [robay-y**o**ns] Catalan sausage with mushrooms
butifarra con setas Catalan sausage with mushrooms
buvangos rellenos [boob**a**ngoss ray-y**ay**noss] stuffed courgettes/zucchini

cabello de ángel [kab**ay**-yo day] sweet pumpkin filling (used in cakes)
cabracho mullet
cabrito asado roast kid
cacahuetes [kakaw**ay**tess] peanuts
cachelada [kachel**a**da] pork stew with eggs, tomato, onion and boiled potatoes
cachelos [kach**ay**loss] boiled potatoes served with spicy sausage and bacon
calabacines [kalabath**ee**ness] courgettes, zucchini; marrow
calabaza [kalab**a**tha] pumpkin
calamares a la romana [kalam**a**ress] squid rings fried in batter
calamares en su tinta [t**ee**nta] squid cooked in their ink
calamares fritos fried squid
caldeirada [kalday-eer**a**da] fish soup
caldera de dátiles de mar [kald**ai**ra day d**a**teeless] seafood stew
caldereta de cordero a la pastora [kaldair**ay**ta day kord**ai**ro] lamb and vegetable stew

caldereta gallega [ga-y**ay**ga] vegetable stew
caldo clear soup
caldo de gallina [ga-y**ee**na] chicken soup
caldo de perdiz [paird**ee**th] partridge soup
caldo de pescado clear fish soup
caldo gallego [ga-y**ay**go] clear soup with green vegetables, beans and pork
caldo guanche [gw**a**nchay] soup made from potatoes, onions, tomatoes and courgettes/zucchini
callos a la madrileña [k**a**-yoss a la madreel**e**n-ya] tripe cooked with chillies
camarones [kamar**o**ness] baby prawns
canela [kan**ay**la] cinnamon
canelones [kanel**o**ness] canneloni
cangrejo [kangr**ay**-Ho] crab
cangrejos de río river crabs
caracoles [karak**o**less] snails
caracoles a la madrileña [madreel**e**n-ya] snails cooked with chillies
carbonada de buey [boo-**ay**] beef cooked in beer
cardo type of thistle, eaten as a vegetable
carne [k**a**rnay] meat
carne de cerdo [th**ai**rdo] pork
carne de membrillo [membr**ee**-yo] quince jelly (dessert)
carne de vaca [b**a**ka] beef
carne picada minced meat
carnero [karn**ai**ro] mutton
carnes [k**a**rness] meat; meat dishes
carro de queso [k**ay**so] cheese board
carta menu
castaña [kast**a**n-ya] chestnut
caza [k**a**tha] game
cazuela [kathw**ay**la] casserole
cazuela de chichas meat casserole
cazuela de hígado [**ee**gado] liver casserole
cebolla [theb**o**-ya] onion
cebolletas [thebo-y**e**tass] spring onions
cecina [theth**ee**na] dry cured meat
centollo [thent**o**-yo] spider crab
centollo relleno [ray-y**ay**no] spider crab cooked in its shell
cerdo [th**ai**rdo] pork, pig
cereza [thair**ay**tha] cherry
cesta de frutas [th**e**sta day fr**oo**tass] a selection of fresh fruit
champiñón a la crema [champeen-y**o**n – kr**ay**ma] mushrooms in cream sauce
champiñón al ajillo [aH**ee**-yo] mushrooms fried with garlic
champiñón a la plancha grilled mushrooms
champiñones [champeen-y**o**ness] mushrooms
chanfaina [chanf**a**-**ee**na] rice

and black pudding stew
chanfaina castellana [kastay-y**a**na] rice and sheeps' liver stew
changurro spider crab cooked in its shell
chanquetes [chank**ay**tess] fish (like whitebait)
chateaubrian [chatobr**ee**-an] thick steak
chicharros horse mackerel
chipirones [cheepeer**o**ness] baby squid
chipirones en su tinta [t**ee**nta] baby squid cooked in their ink
chipirones rellenos [ray-y**ay**noss] stuffed baby squid
chirimoyas [cheereem**o**-yass] custard apples
chocos squid
chocos con habas [**a**bass] squid with broad beans
chorizo [chor**ee**tho] spicy red sausage
chuleta [chool**ay**ta] chop
chuleta de buey [day boo-**ay**] beef chop
chuleta de cerdo [th**ai**rdo] pork chop
chuleta de cerdo empanada breaded pork chop
chuleta de cordero [kord**airo**] lamb chop
chuleta de ternera [tairn**aira**] veal chop
chuleta de ternera empanada breaded veal chop
chuletas de gamo venison chops
chuletas de lomo ahumado [a-oom**a**do] smoked pork chops
chuletas de venado [ben**a**do] venison chops
chuletitas de cordero [day kord**ai**ro] small lamb chops
chuletón large chop
chuletón de ternera a la diable roja [d-y**a**blay r**o**Ha] large, grilled, breaded veal chop
churros fried pastry strips
cigala [theeg**a**la] crayfish
cigalas a la parrilla [parr**ee**-ya] grilled crayfish
cigalas cocidas [koth**ee**dass] boiled crayfish
ciruela [theerw**ay**la] plum, greengage
ciruelas pasas prunes
civet de liebre [theeb**e**t day l-y**ay**bray] marinated hare
coca amb pinxes [k**o**ka am p**ee**nsess] sardine pie
cochinillo asado [kocheen**ee**-yo] roast sucking pig
cocido [koth**ee**do] stew made from meat, chickpeas and vegetables
cocido castellano/madrileño [kastay-y**a**no/madreel**e**n-yo] stew made from meat, chickpeas, vegetables etc
cocochas (de merluza) [mairl**oo**tha] hakes' gills
cóctel de bogavante [bogab**a**ntay] lobster cocktail
cóctel de gambas prawn

cocktail
cóctel de langostinos king prawn cocktail
cóctel de mariscos seafood cocktail
codillo de cerdo con chucrut [kod**ee**-yo day th**ai**rdo kon chookr**oo**t] pigs' trotters with sauerkraut
codoñate [kodon-y**a**tay] cake made with chestnuts, honey and quince
codoñate de nueces [nw**ay**thess] cake made with walnuts
codornices [kodorn**ee**thess] quail
codornices con uvas [**oo**bass] quail stewed with grapes
codornices estofadas braised quail
col cabbage
coles de Bruselas [k**o**less day broos**ay**lass] Brussels sprouts
coliflor cauliflower
coliflor con bechamel cauliflower cheese
comino cumin
conejo [kon**ay**-Ho] rabbit
conejo encebollado [enthebo-y**a**do] rabbit served with onions
conejo estofado braised rabbit
congrio [k**o**ngr-yo] conger eel
consomé al jerez [konsom**ay** al H**ai**reth] consommé with sherry
consomé con yema [y**ay**ma] consommé with egg yolk
consomé de ave [**a**bay] chicken consommé
consomé de pollo [p**o**-yo] chicken consommé
contra de ternera con guisantes [tairn**ai**ra kon gees**a**ntess] veal stew with peas
contrafilete de ternera [kontrafeel**ay**tay day] veal fillet
copa de helado [el**a**do] assorted ice cream served in a stemmed glass
cordero [kord**ai**ro] lamb
cordero chilindrón lamb stew with onion, tomato, peppers and eggs
corvina [korb**ee**na] Mediterranean fish, similar to sea bass
costillas de cerdo [kost**ee**-yas day th**ai**rdo] pork ribs
costillas de cerdo con chucrut [chookr**oo**t] pork ribs with sauerkraut
crema catalana [kr**ay**ma] crème caramel
cremada dessert made from egg, sugar and milk
crema de cangrejos [kr**ay**ma day kangr**ay**-Hoss] cream of crab soup
crema de espárragos cream of asparagus soup
crema de espinacas cream of spinach soup
crema de legumbres/verduras [leg**oo**mbrays/baird**oo**rass] cream of vegetable soup
crep(e) pancake
crep(e)s imperiales [eempair-y**a**less] crêpe suzette

criadillas [kree-ad**ee**-yass] bulls' testicles; truffles (edible fungus); root vegetable
criadillas de ternera [tairn**ai**ra] calves' testicles
criadillas de tierra [t-y**ai**rra] truffles (edible fungus)
criadillas en salsa verde [b**ai**rday] root vegetable in parsley sauce
crocante [krok**a**ntay] ice cream with chopped nuts
croquetas [krok**ay**tass] croquettes
crudo raw
cuajada [kwaH**a**da] junket, curds

dátiles [d**a**teeless] dates
dátiles de mar shellfish
delicias de queso [del**ee**th-yass day k**ay**so] cheese croquettes
dulce de membrillo [d**oo**lthay day membr**ee**-yo] quince jelly

embutidos cured pork sausages
embutidos de la tierra [t-y**ai**rra] local sausages
empanada gallega [ga-y**ay**ga] pie with chicken, chorizo sausage, peppers, ham, onions and tuna
empanada santiaguesa [sant-yag**ay**sa] fish pie
empanado in breadcrumbs
empanadillas [empanad**ee**-yass] small pies
empanadillas de chorizo [chor**ee**tho] small pies filled with spicy sausage
endivias [end**ee**b-yass] endive
ensaimada mallorquina [ensa-eem**a**da ma-york**ee**na] large, spiral-shaped bun
ensalada salad
ensalada de frutas fruit salad
ensalada ilustrada mixed salad
ensalada mixta [m**ee**sta] mixed salad
ensalada simple [s**ee**mplay] green salad
ensaladilla [ensalad**ee**-ya] Spanish salad
ensaladilla rusa [r**oo**sa] Russian salad
entrantes [entr**a**ntess] entrées, starters
entrecot a la parrilla [entrek**o**t – parr**ee**-ya] grilled entrecôte steak
entrecot a la pimienta [peem-y**e**nta] entrecôte in black pepper sauce
entremés [entrem**ay**ss] hors d'œuvre, starter
entremeses [entrem**ay**sess] hors d'œuvres
entremeses de la casa hors d'œuvres – house speciality
entremeses variados [bar-y**a**doss] assorted hors d'œuvres
escabeche de ... [eskab**e**chay] marinated ...
escalibada flaked cod and vegetable salad (Catalan dish)
escalope a la milanesa [eskal**o**pay] breaded veal escalope with cheese

escalope a la parrilla [parree-ya] grilled veal
escalope a la plancha grilled veal
escalope Cordon Bleu veal escalope with ham and cheese
escalope de cerdo [thairdo] pork escalope
escalope de lomo de cerdo escalope of fillet of pork
escalope de ternera [tairnaira] veal escalope
escalopines al vino de Marsala [eskalopeeness – beeno] veal escalopes cooked in wine
escalopines de ternera [tairnaira] veal escalopes
escarola endive
espadín a la toledana kebab
espaguetis italiana [espagayteess eetal-yana] spaghetti
espárragos asparagus
espárragos calientes [kal-yentess] grilled asparagus with béchamel sauce
espárragos dos salsas asparagus with mayonnaise and vinagrette dressing
espárragos en vinagreta [beenagrayta] asparagus in vinaigrette dressing
espárragos trigueros [treegayross] green asparagus
especia [espayth-ya] spice
especialidad speciality
espina fishbone
espinacas spinach
espinazo de cerdo con patatas [espeenatho day thairdo] pork ribs with potatoes
espuma de jamón [day Hamon] boiled ham mousse
estofado stew; stewed
estofado de liebre [l-yaybray] hare stew
estofado de liebre con níscalos hare stew with wild mushrooms
estofados stews
estragón tarragon

fabada (asturiana) [astoor-yana] bean stew with red sausage, black pudding and pork
fabricación: de fabricación casera homemade
faisán [fa-eesan] pheasant
faisán trufado [troofado] pheasant with truffles
farinato fried sausage
fiambres [f-yambress] cold meats, cold cuts
fideos [feeday-oss] thin pasta; noodles; vermicelli
filete [feelaytay] steak; fillet
filete a la parrilla [parree-ya] grilled beef steak
filete a la plancha grilled beef steak
filete de cerdo [thairdo] pork steak
filete de ternera [tairnaira] veal steak
flan crème caramel
flan con nata crème caramel with whipped cream
flan de café [day kafay] coffee-

flavoured crème caramel
flan de caramelo [karam**ay**lo] crème caramel
flan (quemado) al ron [kem**a**do] crème caramel with rum
frambuesa [frambw**ay**sa] raspberry
fresa [fr**ay**sa] strawberry
fresas con nata strawberries and cream
fritanga al modo de Alicante [day aleek**a**ntay] dish of fried peppers, tuna and garlic
frito fried
fritos de la casa fried hors d'œuvres – house speciality
fritos variados [bar-y**a**doss] fried hors d'œuvres
fruta fruit
frutas en almíbar fruit in syrup
fruta variada [bar-y**a**da] assorted fresh fruit

gachas manchegas type of sweet or savoury porridge
galleta [ga-y**ay**ta] biscuit
gallina a la cairatraca [ga-y**ee**na a la ka-eeratr**a**ka] stewed chicken
gallina en pepitoria [pepeet**o**r-ya] stewed chicken with peppers, onions and tomato
gamba prawn
gambas a la americana prawns with brandy and garlic
gambas al ajillo [aH**ee**-yo] prawns with garlic
gambas a la plancha grilled prawns
gambas cocidas [koth**ee**dass] boiled prawns
gambas en gabardina prawns in batter
gambas rebozadas [reboth**a**dass] prawns in batter
garbanzos [garb**a**nthoss] chickpeas
garbanzos a la catalana chickpeas with sausage, boiled eggs and pine nuts
gazpacho andaluz [gathp**a**cho andal**oo**th] cold soup made from tomatoes, onions, garlic, peppers and cucumber
gazpacho manchego rabbit stew with tomato and garlic, sometimes also with partridge meat
gelatina [Helat**ee**na] jelly
gratén de ... ... au gratin
grelo turnip
guisado de cordero [gees**a**do day kord**ai**ro] stewed lamb
guisado de costillas de ternera [kostee-y**a**ss day tairn**ai**ra] rib of veal stew
guisado de ternera stewed veal
guisantes [gees**a**ntess] peas

habas [**a**bass] broad beans
habas fritas fried young broad beans
habichuelas [abeechw**ay**lass] haricot beans; white kidney beans
hamburguesa [amboorg**ay**sa] hamburger

harina [ar**ee**na] flour
helado [el**a**do] ice cream
helado de caramelo [karam**ay**lo] caramel ice cream
helado de mantecado dairy ice cream
helado de nata dairy ice cream
helado de vainilla [ba-een**ee**-ya] vanilla ice cream
hierbas [**yair**bass] herbs
hígado [**ee**gado] liver
hígado de ternera estofado [tairn**air**a] braised calves' liver
hígado encebollado [enthebo-y**a**do] liver in an onion sauce
hígado estofado braised liver
higos [**ee**goss] figs
higos secos dried figs
hornazo [orn**a**tho] Easter cake
horno: al horno baked
huevo [w**ay**bo] egg
huevo duro [d**oo**ro] hard-boiled egg
huevo hilado [eel**a**do] shredded boiled eggs used as a garnish
huevo pasado por agua [**a**g-wa] boiled egg
huevos a la española [espan-y**o**la] fried eggs
huevos a la flamenca baked eggs with sausage, tomato, peas, asparagus and peppers
huevos cocidos [koth**ee**doss] hard-boiled eggs
huevos con picadillo [peekad**ee**-yo] eggs with minced sausage meat
huevos duros con mayonesa [ma-yon**ay**sa] egg mayonnaise
huevos escalfados poached eggs
huevos fritos fried eggs
huevos fritos con chorizo [chor**ee**tho] fried eggs with Spanish sausage
huevos pasados por agua [**a**g-wa] boiled eggs
huevos rellenos [ray-y**ay**noss] stuffed eggs
huevos revueltos [rebw**e**ltoss] scrambled eggs

incluye pan, postre y vino includes bread, dessert and wine
IVA no incluido VAT not included

jamón [Ham**o**n] ham
jamón con huevo hilado [w**ay**bo eel**a**do] ham with shredded egg garnish
jamón de Jabugo [day Hab**oo**go] jamón ibérico from Jabugo, Huelva
jamón ibérico [eeb**air**eeko] Spanish ham
jamón serrano [sairr**a**no] cured ham, similar to Parma ham
jamón York boiled ham
jarrete de ternera [Harr**ay**tay day tairn**air**a] veal hock
jeta [H**e**ta] pigs' cheeks
jeta rebozada [rebothada] pigs' cheek in batter
judías [Hood**ee**-ass] beans

judías verdes [b**ai**rdess] green beans
judías verdes a la española [espan-y**o**la] French bean stew
judías verdes al natural [natoor**a**l] plain green beans
judías verdes con jamón [Ham**o**n] French beans with ham
judiones [Hood-y**o**ness] broad beans

lacón con grelos bacon with turnip tops
langosta lobster
langosta a la americana lobster with brandy and garlic
langosta a la catalana lobster with mushrooms and ham in a white sauce
langosta con mahonesa [ma-on**ay**sa] lobster with mayonnaise
langosta fría con mayonesa cold lobster with mayonnaise
langosta gratinada lobster au gratin
langostinos a la plancha grilled king prawns
langostinos dos salsas king prawns cooked in two sauces
laurel [lowr**e**l] bay leaves
lebrato hare
leche frita [lechay fr**ee**ta] slices of thick custard fried in breadcrumbs
leche merengada cold milk with meringues and cinnamon
lechuga [lech**oo**ga] lettuce
lengua [l**e**ngwa] tongue
lengua de buey [boo-**ay**] ox tongue
lenguado a la parrilla [lengw**a**do a la parr**ee**-ya] grilled sole
lenguado a la plancha grilled sole
lenguado a la romana sole in batter
lenguado al chacolí con hongos [**o**ngoss] sole with mushrooms and white wine
lenguado frito fried sole
lenguado grillado [gree-y**a**do] grilled sole
lenguado menie/meuniere [men-y**ai**r] sole meunière – sole coated in flour, fried and served with butter, lemon juice and parsley
lenguado rebozado [reboth**a**do] sole in batter
lentejas [lent**ay**-Hass] lentils
lentejas aliñadas [aleen-y**a**dass] lentils in vinaigrette dressing
lentejas onubenses [onoob**e**nsess] lentils with spicy sausage, onion and garlic
liba rebozada [reboth**a**da] sea bass fried in batter
liebre estofada [l-y**ay**bray] stewed hare
lima [l**ee**ma] lime
limón lemon

lombarda red cabbage
lomo curado [koor**a**do] cured pork sausage
lomo de liebre [l-y**ay**bray] loin of hare
lonchas de jamón [Ham**o**n] slices of cured ham
longaniza [longan**ee**tha] cooked Spanish sausage
lubina a la cantábrica sea bass with garlic, lemon juice and white wine
lubina a la marinera [mareen**ai**ra] sea bass in a parsley sauce

macarrones [makarr**o**ness] macaroni
macarrones gratinados macaroni cheese
macedonia de fruta [mathed**o**n-ya] fruit salad
maduro [mad**oo**ro] ripe
magdalena [magdal**ay**na] muffin
magras con tomate [tom**a**tay] slices of cured ham with tomato
mahonesa [ma-on**ay**sa] mayonnaise
maíz [ma-**ee**th] sweetcorn
mandarinas tangerines
manises [man**ee**sess] peanuts
manitas de cordero [kord**ai**ro] leg of lamb
manos de cerdo [th**ai**rdo] pigs' trotters
mantecadas small sponge cakes
mantecado vanilla ice cream
mantequilla [mantek**ee**-ya] butter
manzana [manth**a**na] apple
manzanas a la malvasía [malbass**ee**-a] apples in syrup
manzanas asadas baked apples
mariscada cold mixed shellfish
mariscos seafood
mariscos del día fresh shellfish
mariscos del tiempo [t-y**e**mpo] seasonal shellfish
marmitako tuna and vegetable stew
mayonesa [ma-yon**ay**sa] mayonnaise
mazapán [mathap**a**n] marzipan
medallones de anguila [meda-y**o**ness day ang**ee**la] eel steaks
medallones de merluza [mairl**oo**tha] hake steaks
mejillones [may-Hee-y**o**ness] mussels
mejillones a la marinera [mareen**ai**ra] mussels in wine sauce with garlic and parsley
mejillones con salsa mussels with tomato and herb sauce
melocotón peach
melocotones en almíbar [melokot**o**ness] peaches in syrup
melón melon
melón al calisay [kalees**i**] melon with a spirit or liqueur poured over it

melón con jamón [Hamon] melon with cured ham
membrillo [membree-yo] quince
menestra de legumbres [legoombress] vegetable stew made from pulses
menestra de verduras [bairdoorass] vegetable stew
menú [menoo] set menu
menú de la casa fixed price menu
menú del día today's set menu
merluza a la castellana [mairlootha – kastay-yana] hake with clams, prawns, linseeds, eggs and chilli
merluza a la cazuela [kathwayla] hake casserole
merluza al ajo arriero [aHo arr-yairo] hake with garlic and chillies
merluza a la riojana [r-yoHana] hake with chillies
merluza a la romana hake steaks in batter
merluza a la vasca [baska] hake in a garlic sauce
merluza caldo corto hake with vegetable sauce
merluza en salsa verde [bairday] hake in parsley and white wine sauce
merluza fría [free-a] cold hake
merluza frita fried hake
merluza koskera [koskaira] hake in a garlic sauce
merluza (lomos de) con angulas y almejas [ee almay-Hass] hake fillet with baby eels and clams
mermelada [mairmelada] jam; marmalade
mero [mairo] grouper (fish)
mero a la levantina [lebanteena] grouper with lemon juice and rosemary
mero en salsa verde [bairday] grouper with garlic, parsley and white wine sauce
miel [m-yel] honey
mojete [moHay-tay] 'dipping' sauce for bread, usually made from vegetables
mojojones [moHoHoness] mussels
mollejas con setas [mo-yay-Hass] lambs' gizzards with mushrooms
mollejas de ternera [tairnaira] calves' sweetbreads
mora blackberry
morcilla [morthee-ya] black pudding, blood sausage
morcilla de ternera [tairnaira] black pudding made from calves' blood
morros de cerdo [thairdo] pigs' cheeks
morros de vaca [day baka] cows' cheeks
morros de vaca pastora cows' cheeks with vegetables
mortadela salami-type sausage
morteruelo [mortair-waylo] breaded minced liver
mostaza [mostatha] mustard

mousse de limón lemon mousse
mújol guisado [m**oo**Hol gees**a**do] red mullet

nabo turnip
naranja [nar**a**nHa] orange
nata cream
nata batida whipped cream
natillas [nat**ee**-yass] cold custard with cinnamon
natillas de chocolate [chokol**a**tay] cold custard with chocolate
níscalos wild mushrooms
nísperos [n**ee**spaiross] medlars – fruit similar to crab apple
nueces [nw**ay**thess] walnuts
nuez [nwayth] nut
ñoquis [n-y**o**keess] potato gnocchi

oca en adobo marinaded goose
orejas de cerdo [or**ay**-Has day th**ai**rdo] pigs' ears
orejas y pie de cerdo [ee p-yay] pigs' ears and trotters
ostra oyster
otros mariscos según precios en plaza other shellfish, depending on current prices

pa amb tomaquet bread spread with olive oil and tomato sauce
paella [pa-**ay**-ya] fried rice with seafood and chicken
paella castellana [kastay-y**a**na] meat paella
paella de marisco shellfish paella
paella de pollo [p**o**-yo] chicken paella
paella especial [espeth-y**a**l] paella house speciality
paella mixta [m**ee**sta] shellfish and chicken paella
paella valenciana [balenth-y**a**na] paella with assorted shellfish and chicken
paleta de cordero lechal [kord**ai**ro] shoulder of lamb
paloma pigeon
pan bread
panaché de verduras [panach**ay** day baird**oo**rass] vegetable stew
pan blanco white bread
panceta [panth**ay**ta] bacon
pan de higos [**ee**goss] dried fig cake with cinnamon
pan integral wholemeal bread
parrilla: a la parrilla grilled
parrillada de caza [parree-y**a**da day k**a**tha] mixed grilled game
parrillada de mariscos mixed grilled shellfish
pasas raisins
pasta biscuit; pastry; pasta
pastel cake; pie
pastel de hígado de cerdo [**ee**gado day th**ai**rdo] pigs' liver pie
pastel de higos [**ee**goss] fig cake
pastel de ternera [tairn**ai**ra] veal pie

pastel de verduras con salsa de champiñones silvestres [bair**doo**rass –champeen-**yo**ness seelb**e**stress] vegetable pie with wild mushroom sauce
pasteles [past**ay**less] cakes
patas de cordero [kord**ai**ro] stewed leg of lamb
patata potato
patatas a la pescadora potatoes with fish
patatas asadas roast potatoes
patatas bravas [br**a**bass] potatoes in cayenne sauce
patatas con nâbos potatoes with turnips
patatas estofadas boiled potatoes
patatas fritas chips, French fries; crisps, potato chips
patitos rellenos [ray-y**ay**noss] stuffed duckling
pato duck
pato a la naranja [nar**a**n-Ha] duck à l'orange
pavipollo [pabeep**o**-yo] large chicken
pavo [p**a**bo] turkey
pavo a la Asturiana [astoor-y**a**na] turkey with red wine and paprika
pavo relleno a la catalana turkey stuffed with sausage, pork and plums
pavo trufado turkey stuffed with truffles
pecho de ternera [tairn**ai**ra] breast of veal
pechuga de pollo [p**o**-yo] breast of chicken
peixo-palo a la marinera [p**e**sho – mareen**ai**ra] stock-fish with potatoes and tomato
pepinillos [pepeen**ee**-yoss] gherkins
pepinillos en vinagreta [beenagr**ay**ta] gherkins in vinaigrette dressing
pepino cucumber
pera pear
percebes [pairth**ay**bess] barnacles (shellfish)
perdices [paird**ee**thess] partridges
perdices a la campesina partridges with vegetables
perdices a la manchega partridges cooked in red wine, garlic, herbs and pepper
perdiz encebollada [paird**ee**th enthebo-y**a**da] partridge with onion sauce
perejil [pairay-H**ee**l] parsley
pescaditos fritos fried sprats
pescado fish
pestiños [pest**ee**n-yoss] sugared pastries flavoured with aniseed
pestiños con miel [m-yel] fried sugared pastries flavoured with aniseed and honey
pez [payth] fish
pez espada ahumado [a-oom**a**do] smoked swordfish
picadillo [peekad**ee**-yo] salad of diced vegetables; OR stew

of pork, bacon, garlic and eggs

picadillo de ternera [tairn**ai**ra] minced veal

pichones estofados [peech**o**ness] stewed pigeon

pimentón paprika

pimienta (negra) [peem-y**e**nta] black pepper

pimienta blanca white pepper

pimienta de cayena [ka-y**ay**na] cayenne pepper

pimiento pepper

pimientos a la riojana [r-yoH**a**na] baked red peppers fried in oil and garlic

pimientos fritos fried peppers

pimientos morrones [morr**o**ness] strong peppers

pimientos rellenos [ray-y**ay**noss] stuffed peppers

pimientos verdes [b**ai**rdess] green peppers

pinchitos snacks/appetizers served in bars; kebabs

pinchos snacks served in bars

pinchos morunos kebabs

pintada guinea fowl

piña [p**ee**n-ya] pineapple

piña al gratén pineapple au gratin

piña fresca fresh pineapple

piñones [peen-y**o**ness] pine nuts

piparrada vasca [b**a**sca] pepper and tomato stew with ham and eggs

piriñaca [peereen-y**a**ka] tuna and vegetable salad

pisto fried peppers, onions, tomatoes and courgettes/zucchini

pisto manchego marrow, onion and tomato stew

plancha: a la plancha grilled

plátano banana

plátanos flameados [flamay-**a**doss] flambéed bananas

platos combinados meat and vegetables, hamburgers and eggs etc, mixture of various foods served as one dish; set menu

pochas con almejas [alm**ay**-Hass] white beans with clams

poco hecho [**e**cho] rare

pollo [p**o**-yo] chicken

pollo al ajillo [aH**ee**-yo] fried chicken with garlic

pollo a la parrilla [parr**ee**-ya] grilled chicken

pollo a la riojana [r-yoH**a**na] chicken with peppers and chillies

pollo asado roast chicken

pollo braseado [brasay-**a**do] braised chicken

pollo en cacerola [kathair**o**la] chicken casserole

pollo en chanfaina [chanf**a**-**ee**na] chicken with fried peppers, onions, tomatoes and courgettes/zucchini

pollo en pepitoria [pepeet**o**r-ya] chicken in wine with saffron, garlic and almonds

pollo reina clamart [**ray-ee**na]

roast chicken with vegetables
pollos tomateros con zanahorias [tomat**ai**ros kon thana-**o**r-yass] baby chickens with carrots
polvorones [polbor**o**ness] sugar-based dessert (eaten at Christmas)
pomelo grapefruit
postre [p**o**stray] dessert
postre sorpresa al DYC [sorpr**ay**sa al deek] whisky-flavoured dessert
potaje castellano [pot**a**Hay kastay-y**a**no] thick broth
potaje de garbanzos [garb**a**nthoss] chickpea stew
potaje de habichuelas [habeechw**ay**lass] white bean stew
potaje de lentejas [lent**ay**-Hass] lentil stew
primer plato starters
pucherete al estilo montañés [poochair**e**tay al est**ee**lo montan-y**e**ss] black pudding and spicy sausage stew
puchero canario [pooch**ai**ro kan**a**r-yo] casserole of meat, chickpeas and corn
puerro [pw**ai**rro] leek
pulpitos con cebolla [theb**o**-ya] baby octopuses with onions
pulpo octopus
puré de patata [poor**ay** day] potato purée, mashed potatoes
purrusalda cod soup with leeks and potatoes
PVP price

queso [k**ay**so] cheese
queso con membrillo [mem-br**ee**-yo] cheese with quince jelly
queso de bola Edam
queso de Burgos soft white cheese
queso de cabrales [kabr**a**less] Spanish Roquefort-type cheese
queso de cerdo [th**ai**rdo] similar to the pork in a pork pie, usually in slices
queso de Idiazábal [eed-yath**a**bal] strong sheeps' cheese from the Basque country
queso del país [pa-**ee**ss] local cheese
queso de oveja [ob**ay**-Ha] sheep's cheese
queso de Roncal strong sheep's cheese from Navarra
queso gallego [ga-y**ay**go] creamy cheese from Galicia
queso manchego hard, strong cheese from La Mancha
quisquillas [keesk**ee**-yass] shrimps

rábanos radishes
rabas squid rings fried in batter
rabo de buey [boo-**ay**] oxtail
ración [rath-y**o**n] portion

ración pequeña para niños [pek**ay**n-ya – n**ee**n-yoss] children's portion
ragout de ternera [rag**oo**t day tairn**ai**ra] veal ragoût
rape a la americana [r**a**pay] monkfish with brandy and herbs
rape a la cazuela [kathw**ay**la] monkfish casserole
rape a la plancha grilled monkfish
ravioles [rab-y**o**less] ravioli
raya [r**a**-ya] skate
raya con manteca negra skate in butter and vinegar sauce
redondo al horno [**o**rno] roast fillet of beef
redondo de ternera [tairn**ai**ra] fillet of veal
redondo en su jugo [H**oo**go] fillet of beef cooked in its own sauce
relleno [ray-y**ay**no] stuffed; stuffing
remolacha beetroot
repollo [rep**o**-yo] cabbage
repostería de la casa cakes and desserts made on the premises
requesón [rekay-s**o**n] cream cheese, curd cheese
revuelto de ajos [rebw**e**lto day **a**Hoss] scrambled eggs with garlic
revuelto de ajos tiernos [t-y**ai**rnoss] scrambled eggs with spring garlic
revuelto de espárragos trigueros [treeg**ai**ross] scrambled eggs with asparagus
revuelto de sesos scrambled eggs with brains
revuelto de setas scrambled eggs with mushrooms
revuelto mixto [m**ee**sto] scrambled eggs with mixed vegetables
riñones a la plancha [reen-y**o**ness] grilled kidneys
riñones al jerez [Hair**e**th] kidneys in a sherry sauce
rodaballo [rodab**a**-yo] turbot
rodaballo al cava [k**a**ba] turbot with champagne
romero [rom**ai**ro] rosemary
romesco de pescado mixed fish
roscas sweet pastries
rosquillas [rosk**ee**-yass] small sweet pastries
rovellons [robay-y**o**ns] mushrooms (Catalan)

sal salt
salchicha sausage
salchichas blancas fried sausages with onions
salchichas de Frankfurt frankfurters
salchichón cured white sausage with pepper
salmón [sal-m**o**n] salmon
salmón ahumado [a-oom**a**do] smoked salmon
salmonetes [sal-mon**ay**tess] red mullet
salmonetes en papillote [papee-y**o**tay] red mullet

cooked in foil
salmón frío [sal-m**o**n fr**ee**-o] cold salmon
salmorejo [salmor**ay**-Ho] thick sauce made from bread, tomatoes, olive oil, vinegar, green pepper and garlic, served cold with hard-boiled eggs and ham
salpicón de mariscos shellfish with vinaigrette dressing
salsa sauce
salsa ali oli/all-i-oli [alee-**o**lee] garlic mayonnaise
salsa bechamel béchamel sauce, white sauce
salsa de tomate [tom**a**tay] tomato sauce
salsa holandesa [oland**ay**sa] hollandaise sauce – hot sauce made with eggs and butter
salsa mayonesa [ma-yon**ay**sa] mayonnaise
salsa romesco sauce made from peppers, tomatoes and garlic
salsa tártara tartare sauce
salsa vinagreta [beenagr**ay**ta] vinaigrette dressing
salteado [saltay-**a**do] sautéed
sandía [sand**ee**-a] water melon
sandwich mixto [m**ee**sto] cheese and ham sandwich
sangre de cerdo [s**a**ngray day th**ai**rdo] pigs' blood
sardina sardine
sardinas a la asturiana [astoor-y**a**na] sardines in cider sauce
sardinas a la brasa barbecued sardines
sardinas a la parrilla [parr**ee**-ya] grilled sardines
sardinas fritas fried sardines
segundo plato main course
sesos brains
sesos a la romana brains in batter
sesos rebozados [reboth**a**doss] brains in batter
setas a la bordalesa [bordal**ay**sa] mushrooms cooked in red wine and onions
setas a la plancha grilled mushrooms
setas rellenas [ray-y**ay**nass] stuffed mushrooms
sobrasada soft red sausage with cayenne pepper
soldados de Pavia [pab**ee**-a] fillets of cod, marinaded and fried
solomillo al vino [solom**ee**-yo al b**ee**no] fillet steak with red wine
solomillo con guisantes [gees**a**ntess] fillet steak with peas
solomillo con patatas fritas fillet steak with chips/French fries
solomillo de cerdo [th**ai**rdo] fillet of pork
solomillo de ternera [tairn**ai**ra] fillet of veal
solomillo de vaca [b**a**ka] fillet of beef

solomillo frío [free-o] cold roast beef
solomillo Roquefort [rokayfor] fillet steak with Roquefort cheese
sopa soup
sopa al cuarto de hora [kwarto day ora] soup made from ham, veal, chicken, almonds, vegetables and eggs
sopa castellana [kastay-yana] vegetable soup
sopa de ajo [day aHo] bread and garlic soup
sopa de almendras almond-based pudding
sopa de calducho clear soup
sopa de cola de buey [boo-ay] oxtail soup
sopa de fideos [feeday-oss] noodle soup
sopa de frutos de mar shellfish soup
sopa de gallina [ga-yeena] chicken soup
sopa del día soup of the day
sopa de legumbres [legoombress] vegetable soup
sopa de lentejas [lentay-Hass] lentil soup
sopa de marisco fish and shellfish soup
sopa de pescado fish soup
sopa de rabo oxtail soup
sopa de rabo de buey [boo-ay] oxtail soup
sopa de tortuga [tortooga] turtle soup
sopa mallorquina [ma-yorkeena] soup with tomatoes, meat and eggs
sopa sevillana [sebee-yana] fish and mayonnaise soup
sorbete [sorbaytay] sorbet
soufflé de fresones [fresoness] strawberry soufflé
suplemento de verduras extra vegetables
supremas de rodaballo [soopraymass day rodaba-yo] fish slices

tallarines [ta-yareeness] noodles
tallarines a la italiana [eetal-yana] tagliatelle
tapa de ternera rellena [tairnaira ray-yayna] stuffed veal hock
tapas appetizers
tarta cake
tarta Alaska baked alaska
tarta de almendra almond tart or gâteau
tarta de arroz [arroth] cake or tart containing rice
tarta de la casa tart or gâteau baked on the premises
tarta helada [elada] ice cream gâteau
tarta moca mocha tart
tartar crudo raw minced steak, steak tartare
tejos de queso [tay-Hoss day kayso] cheese pastries
tencas tench
tencas con jamón [Hamon] tench with ham
ternera [tairnaira] veal

ternera asada roast veal
tigres [t**ee**gress] mussels in cayenne sauce
tocinillo de cielo [totheen**ee**-yo day th-y**ay**lo] rich, thick crème caramel
todo incluido all inclusive
tomate [tom**a**tay] tomato
tomates rellenos [tom**a**tess ray-y**ay**noss] stuffed tomatoes
tomatics a es forn baked tomatoes
tomillo [tom**ee**-yo] thyme
tordo thrush
tordos braseados [brassay-**a**doss] grilled thrushes
tordos estofados braised thrushes
torrijas [torr**ee**-Hass] sweet pastries
torta de chicharrones [cheecharr**o**ness] pie filled with assorted cooked and cured meats
torta de sardinas sardine pie
tortilla [tort**ee**-ya] omelette
tortilla a la paisana [pa-ees**a**na] omelette containing a variety of vegetables
tortilla aliada [al-y**a**da] omelette with mixed vegetables
tortilla al ron omlette with rum
tortilla a su gusto omlette made as the customer wishes
tortilla de bonito tuna fish omlette
tortilla de champiñones [champeen-y**o**ness] mushroom omelette
tortilla de chorizo [chor**ee**tho] spicy sausage omelette
tortilla de escabeche [eskab**e**chay] fish omelette
tortilla de espárragos asparagus omelette
tortilla de gambas prawn omelette
tortilla de jamón [Ham**o**n] ham omelette
tortilla de morcilla [morth**ee**-ya] black pudding omelette
tortilla de patata potato omelette
tortilla de sesos brains omelette
tortilla de setas mushroom omelette
tortilla española [espan-y**o**la] (cold slice of) Spanish omelette with potato, onion and garlic
tortilla francesa [franth**ay**sa] plain omelette
tortilla granadina omelette with artichokes, asparagus, brains and peppers
tortilla sacromonte [sakrom**o**ntay] vegetable, brains and sausage omelette
tortillas variadas [bar-y**a**dass] assorted omelettes
tostada toast
tostón sucking pig
tostón asado roast sucking pig
tournedó fillet steak
tournedó a la salsa foie [fwa] fillet steak in pâté sauce
trucha [tr**oo**cha] trout

trucha ahumada [a-oom**a**da] smoked trout
trucha con jamón [Ham**o**n] trout with ham
trucha escabechada marinated trout
truchas a la marinera [mareen**ai**ra] trout in white wine sauce
truchas molinera [moleen**ai**ra] trout meunière – trout coated in flour, fried and served with butter, lemon juice and parsley
trufas truffles (edible fungus)
trufas al jerez [Hair**e**th] truffles in sherry
turbante de arroz [toorb**a**ntay day arr**o**th] rice served with steak, sausage, peppers and bacon
turrón [toorr**o**n] nougat
turrón de coco coconut nougat
turrón de Alicante [aleek**a**ntay] hard nougat
turrón de yema [**ya**yma] nougat with egg yolk
turrón de Jijona [HeeH**o**na] soft nougat
txangurro [chang**oo**rro] spider crab cooked in its shell

uvas [**oo**bass] grapes
vaca estofada [b**a**ka] stewed beef
verduras [baird**oo**rass] vegetables
vieiras [bee-**ay-ee**rass] scallops
vinagre [been**a**gray] vinegar

xoric amb patates [soreek am pat**a**tess] tern with potatoes (type of swallow)

yogur [yo-g**oo**r] yoghurt

zanahoria [thana-**or**-ya] carrot
zanahorias a la crema [kr**ay**ma] carrots à la crème
zarzuela de mariscos [tharthw**ay**la day mar**ee**skoss] shellfish stew
zarzuela de pescados y mariscos fish and shellfish stew

Menu Reader:

Drink

agua [**a**g-wa] water
agua mineral [meenair**a**l] mineral water
agua mineral con gas fizzy mineral water
agua mineral sin gas [seen] still mineral water
agua potable [pot**a**blay] drinking water
Alella [al**ay**-ya] region near Barcelona producing red, white and rosé wines
Alicante [aleek**a**ntay] region in the south producing red and rosé wines matured in oak casks
Ampurdán region at the foot of the Pyrenees which produces rosé wine
anís [an**ee**ss] aniseed-flavoured alcoholic drink
año vintage
aperitivo aperitif

batido milkshake
batido de chocolate [day chokol**a**tay] chocolate milkshake
batido de fresa [fr**ay**sa] strawberry milkshake
batido de frutas fruit milkshake
batido de plátano banana milkshake
batido de vainilla [ba-een**ee**-ya] vanilla milkshake
bebida drink
bebidas alcohólicas alcoholic drinks
bebidas refrescantes soft drinks
cacao [kak**ow**] cocoa
café con leche [l**e**chay] coffee with milk (large cup)
café cortado coffee with milk (small cup)
café descafeinado [deskafay-een**a**do] decaffeinated coffee
café escocés [eskoth**ay**ss] black coffee, whisky and vanilla ice cream
café instantáneo [eenstant**a**nay-o] instant coffee
café irlandés [eerland**ay**ss] black coffee, whisky, vanilla ice cream and whipped cream
café solo black coffee
café vienés [b-yen**ay**ss] black coffee and whipped cream
caña (cerveza) [k**a**n-ya thairb**ay**-tha] 250cc of draught beer
carajillo [karaH**ee**-yo] black coffee with brandy
carajillo de ron black coffee with rum
carajillo de vodka black coffee with vodka
Cariñena [kareen-y**ay**na] region in the north producing red and rosé wines
carta de vinos [day b**ee**noss] wine list
Cava [k**a**ba] Spanish champagne
cerveza [thairb**ay**-tha] beer, lager
cerveza de barril draught beer
Chacolí fruity white wine produced in the Basque Country

champán [champ**a**n] champagne
champaña [champ**a**n-ya] champagne
chato glass of red wine
Cheste [ch**e**stay] region to the west of Valencia producing dry and sweet white wines
chiquito [cheek**ee**to] glass of red wine
chocolate caliente [chokol**a**tay kal-y**e**ntay] hot chocolate
Cigales [theeg**a**less] region in Valladolid producing light rosé wines
clara shandy
cóctel cocktail
Conca de Barbera [barb**ai**ra] region in Catalonia producing red and white wines
Condado de Huelva [w**e**lba] region in the south producing dry, mellow and sweet white wines
con gas fizzy, sparkling
coñac [kon-y**a**k] brandy
corto (de cerveza) [thairb**ay**-tha] 125cc of draught beer (1/2 caña)
cosecha vintage
cosechero [kosech**ai**ro] red wine of the last vintage
cubalibre [koobal**ee**bray] rum and cola
cubata a spirit with a soft drink of lemon or cola
cubito de hielo [y**ay**lo] ice cube
cucaracha [kookar**a**cha] tequila and coffee-flavoured strong alcoholic drink

destornillador [destornee-yad**o**r] vodka and orange juice

espumoso sparkling

gaseosa [gasay-**o**sa] lemonade
ginebra [Heen**ay**-bra] gin
granizada/granizado [graneeth**a**da] crushed ice drink

hielo [y**ay**lo] ice
horchata (de chufas) [orch**a**ta day] cold almond-flavoured milk drink

infusión [eenfooss-y**o**n] herb tea

jarra de vino [H**a**rra day b**ee**no] jug of wine
jerez [Hair**e**th] sherry
jerez amontillado [amontee-y**a**do] pale dry sherry
jerez fino pale light sherry
jerez oloroso sweet sherry
jugo [H**oo**go] juice
jugo de albaricoque [day albareek**o**kay] apricot juice
jugo de lima [l**ee**ma] lime juice
jugo de limón lemon juice
jugo de melocotón peach juice
jugo de naranja [nar**a**n-Ha] orange juice
jugo de piña [p**ee**n-ya] pineapple juice
jugo de tomate [tom**a**tay] tomato juice
Jumilla [Hoom**ee**-ya] region in the south producing dry,

light red wines and sweet white wines

kirsch strong alcoholic drink made from cherries

leche [**le**chay] milk
licor liqueur
licor de avellana [day abay-y**a**na] hazelnut-flavoured liqueur
licor de manzana [manth**a**na] apple-flavoured liqueur
licor de melocotón peach-flavoured liqueur
licor de melón melon-flavoured liqueur
licor de naranja [nar**a**n-Ha] orange-flavoured liqueur
limonada lemonade
lista de precios [pr**ay**th-yoss] price list

Málaga region on the south coast producing sweet and dry white wines
Mancha region of the interior producing mainly white, but also red wines
manzanilla [manthan**ee**-ya] dry sherry-type wine; camomile tea
media de agua [m**ay**d-ya day **a**g-wa] half-bottle of mineral water
menta poleo [pol**ay**-o] mint tea
Mentrida central region producing dark-coloured red wines
Montilla-Moriles [mont**ee**-ya-mor**ee**less] region in Andalusia producing sherry-like white wines
mosto grape juice

Oporto port
orujo [or**oo**Ho] colourless, strong alcoholic drink made from wine
orujo de miel [m-yayl] orujo with honey

pacharán strong alcoholic drink made from sloes
Penedés [pened**ay**ss] region in Catalonia producing in particular sparkling white wines
Priorato [pree-or**a**to] wine-growing region near Tarragona

refresco soft drink
reserva especial quality wine matured in casks
Ribeiro [reeb**ay-ee**ro] region in Galicia producing slightly sparkling red and white wines; type of white wine
Rioja [r-y**o**Ha] region in the north producing some of the finest red and white wines
romeral wine
ron rum

sangría [sangr**ee**-a] mixture of red wine, lemonade, spirits and fruit
seco dry
semidulce [say-mee-d**oo**lthay] medium-sweet

sidra cider
sin gas [seen] still
sol y sombra [ee] brandy and anís

Tarragona region on the Mediterranean coast producing red and white wines
té [tay] tea
Tierra Alta [t-y**ai**rra] region in the province of Tarragona producing red and white wines
tila [t**ee**la] lime tea
tinto de Toro [t**ee**nto] dry, red wine from Zamora
tónica tonic
tónica con ginebra [Heen**e**bra] gin and tonic

Utiel-Requena [oot-yeel-rek**ay**na] region in Valencia producing mild red and rosé wines

Valdeorras [balday-**o**rrass] region in Galicia producing red and white wines
Valdepeñas [balday-p**ay**n-yass] central region producing pale and dark, fruity red wines; type of fruity red wine
Valencia [bal**e**nth-ya] region on the Mediterranean producing red and white wines
Valle de Monterrey [b**a**-yay day mont**ai**rray] region in Galicia producing full-bodied red and white wines
vino [b**ee**no] wine
vino blanco white wine
vino de aguja [day ag**oo**Ha] slightly sparkling rosé and white wines
vino de jerez [Hair**e**th] sherry
vino del país [pa-**ee**ss] local wine
vino de mesa [m**ay**sa] table wine
vino rosado rosé wine
vino tinto red wine
viñedo vineyard

Yecla region in the south producing smooth red and light rosé wines

zumo [th**oo**mo] fruit juice
zumo de albaricoque [day albareek**o**kay] apricot juice
zumo de lima [l**ee**ma] lime juice
zumo de limón lemon juice
zumo de melocotón peach juice
zumo de naranja [nar**a**nHa] orange juice
zumo de piña [p**ee**n-ya] pineapple juice
zumo de tomate [tom**a**tay] tomato juice
zurito [thoor**ee**to] 125 cc of draught beer (1/2 caña)
zurracapote [thoorrakap**o**tay] wine with sugar and cinnamon